Data Analysis Using
SAS Enterprise Guide

This book presents the basic procedures for utilizing *SAS Enterprise Guide* to analyze statistical data. *SAS Enterprise Guide* is a graphical user (point-and-click) interface to the main SAS application. Each chapter contains a brief conceptual overview and then guides the reader through concrete step-by-step examples to complete the analyses.

The 11 sections of the book cover a wide range of statistical procedures, including descriptive statistics, correlation and simple regression, *t* tests, one-way chi-squares, data transformations, multiple regression, analysis of variance, analysis of covariance, multivariate analysis of variance, factor analysis, and canonical correlation analysis.

Designed to be used as either a stand-alone resource or an accompaniment to a statistics course, the book offers a detailed path to statistical analysis with *SAS Enterprise Guide* for advanced undergraduate and beginning graduate students, as well as professionals in psychology, education, business, health, social work, sociology, and many other fields.

Lawrence S. Meyers is Professor of Psychology at California State University, Sacramento. He teaches undergraduate and graduate courses in research design, data analysis, data interpretation, testing and measurement, and the history and systems of psychology. He was the coauthor of a textbook on research methods in the 1970s, has recently coauthored books on multivariate research design and analysis of variance, and has more than three dozen publications; some of his relatively recent work has been in areas such as measurement and testing and positive psychology. He received his doctorate from Adelphi University and worked on a National Science Foundation Postdoctoral Fellowship at the University of Texas, Austin and Purdue University.

Glenn Gamst is Professor and Chair of the Psychology Department at the University of La Verne, where he teaches the doctoral advanced statistics sequence. He received his doctorate from the University of Arkansas in experimental psychology. His research interests include the effects of multicultural variables, such as client–therapist ethnic match, client acculturation status and ethnic identity, and therapist cultural competence, on clinical outcomes. Additional research interests focus on conversation memory and discourse processing.

A. J. Guarino is on the faculty at Alabama State University, where he teaches graduate statistics courses in the Psychology Department. He received his bachelor's degree from the University of California, Berkeley, and he earned a doctorate in statistics and research methodologies from the University of Southern California through the Department of Educational Psychology.

Data Analysis Using *SAS* *Enterprise Guide*

Lawrence S. Meyers
California State University, Sacramento

Glenn Gamst
University of La Verne

A. J. Guarino
Alabama State University

CAMBRIDGE
UNIVERSITY PRESS

CAMBRIDGE UNIVERSITY PRESS
Cambridge, New York, Melbourne, Madrid, Cape Town, Singapore,
São Paulo, Delhi, Dubai, Tokyo

Cambridge University Press
32 Avenue of the Americas, New York, NY 10013-2473, USA

www.cambridge.org
Information on this title: www.cambridge.org/9780521130073

First published 2009

Printed in the United States of America

A catalog record for this publication is available from the British Library

Library of Congress Cataloging in Publication data

Meyers, Lawrence S.
Data analysis using *SAS Enterprise Guide* / Lawrence S. Meyers, Glenn
Gamst, A. J. Guarino.
    p.   cm.
Includes bibliographical references and index.
ISBN 978-0-521-11268-0 (hbk.) – ISBN 978-0-521-13007-3 (pbk.)
1. SAS (Computer file)   2. Enterprise guide.   3. Social sciences – Statistical methods – Data processing.
4. Mathematical statistics – Data processing.   I. Gamst, Glenn.   II. Guarino, A. J.   III. Title.
HA32.M499   2009
330.0285′555–dc22   2009012822

ISBN   978-0-521-11268-0 Hardback
ISBN   978-0-521-13007-3 Paperback

Contents

IV Describing Data

V Score Distribution Assumptions

Preface

The present book, *Data Analysis Using SAS Enterprise Guide*, provides readers with an overview of *Enterprise Guide*, the newest point-and-click interface from SAS. *SAS Enterprise Guide* is a graphical user (point-and-click) interface to the main SAS application, having relatively recently replaced the Analyst interface, which itself had replaced the original Assist interface. *Enterprise Guide* makes it easier than ever to access many SAS statistical analyses without learning to write the SAS code underlying its procedures.

We have written this book for readers who have little or no knowledge of *SAS Enterprise Guide* but who may wish to employ it for statistical analysis. Some of these readers will be students in an introductory statistics or data-analysis course; other readers will have taken an introductory statistics course and possibly a research methods course at some time in their past; and still other readers may have had several statistics and research design courses as a part of their background. We have therefore included in this book a relatively wide range of statistical procedures to meet the needs of various readers. There are chapters devoted to the more basic procedures such as descriptive statistics, correlation and simple linear regression, *t* tests, and one-way chi-square analysis. In addition, we have also included statistical procedures at a somewhat higher level; these include data transformations and other types of computations, multiple linear regression, logistic regression, and some analysis of variance designs. Finally, we have incorporated topics that are more advanced for those readers who might have the need to use such techniques as analysis of covariance, multivariate analysis of variance, factor analysis, and canonical correlation analysis.

Given the wide range and level of topics that we cover, it may not be surprising that the present book is intended to be neither a stand-alone statistics text nor a SAS "cookbook." Rather, our intent is to instruct readers on how to use *SAS*

Enterprise Guide to perform the statistical data analyses covered in the book as well as to understand the concepts underlying those procedures. That is, it is our belief that an exclusive and isolated "select this, then select that" robotic or cookbook synopsis of the steps involved in a given statistical analysis does not serve the needs of most readers. For this reason, we supply for each chapter some analytic and methodological context for the particular statistical procedure that we are describing, enabling readers to gain a sense of the research and statistical framework within which the particular procedure can be used. We also provide interpretations of the statistical results rather than just discussing how to read the output tables that were obtained from *SAS Enterprise Guide*.

There are 33 chapters in this book. They are organized into the following 11 sections.

Section I, "Introducing *SAS Enterprise Guide*," consists of two chapters presenting the basics of *SAS Enterprise Guide*. The software is designed to work on "projects." Chapter 1 describes what projects are and focuses on creating projects and navigating within them. Chapter 2 describes how to import data into projects, how to enter data directly into projects, and how to save projects.

Section II, "Performing Analyses and Viewing Output," consists of two chapters describing how to use *SAS Enterprise Guide*. Chapter 3 informs readers about how to select the statistical procedure they intend to use and how to interact with the dialog screens presented by *SAS Enterprise Guide* in the process of structuring the analysis. Chapter 4 addresses the management and viewing of output.

Section III, "Manipulating Data," contains three chapters focusing on some ways to organize existing data and generate new variables. Chapter 5 deals with sorting data and selecting a subset of the cases in the data set. Chapter 6 discusses how to recode variables into new or existing variables. Chapter 7 shows how to compute new variables.

Section IV, "Describing Data," consists of four chapters focused on descriptive statistical and graphical summary procedures. Chapter 8 focuses on computing measures of central tendency and variability. Chapter 9 shows how to graph data in different ways. Chapters 10 and 11 demonstrate how to generate standardized scores based on the sample mean and standard deviation (Chapter 10) and based on existing norms (Chapter 11).

Section V, "Score Distribution Assumptions," contains three chapters concerning some of the assumptions underlying most of the statistical procedures covered in this book. Chapter 12 explains what statistical outliers are and how to detect them. Chapter 13 focuses on the assessment of normality. Chapter 14 demonstrates how to perform data transformations in order to drive skewed distributions toward normality.

Section VI, "Correlation and Prediction," contains five chapters dealing with correlation as well as linear and nonlinear regression. Chapter 15 demonstrates how to perform a bivariate correlation analysis by using the Pearson product–moment correlation (r) and Spearman rho. Chapters 16 and 17 cover simple and multiple linear (ordinary least squares) regression, respectively. Chapters 18 and 19 describe the procedures involved in performing simple and multiple logistic regression, respectively.

Section VII, "Comparing Means: The t Test," contains three chapters encompassing different types of t tests. Chapters 20, 21, and 22 demonstrate how to conduct independent-groups t tests, correlated-samples t tests, and single-sample t tests, respectively.

Section VIII, "Comparing Means: ANOVA," contains four chapters. Chapters 23, 24, 25, and 26 describe the steps involved in computing analysis of variance (ANOVA) designs for a one-way between-subjects design, a two-way between-subjects design, a one-way within-subjects design, and a two-way mixed design ANOVA, respectively.

Section IX, "Nonparametric Procedures," consists of three chapters presenting some ways of analyzing frequency and rank-ordered data. Chapters 27 and 28 cover one-way and two-way contingency (chi-square) tables, respectively. Chapter 29 examines nonparametric one-way comparisons of means based on ranked data.

Section X, "Advanced ANOVA Techniques," is the first section focusing on advanced topics. It contains two chapters extending our treatment of ANOVA to more complex designs. Chapter 30 describes how to perform an analysis of covariance (ANCOVA). Chapter 31 demonstrates how to conduct a one-way multivariate analysis of variance (MANOVA).

Section XI, "Analysis of Structure," completes our book with two additional chapters on advanced topics, this time covering structural analysis. Chapter 32 describes how to perform and interpret an exploratory factor analysis. Chapter 33 focuses on canonical correlation analysis.

With the exception of those chapters in the first section in which we introduce the software and its interface, the chapters are generally structured in the following manner. We begin with an overview of the topic.

We then present some historical information on the statistical procedure where it is appropriate. We follow this by a numerical example – a data set that we subject to the statistical procedure that is the topic of the chapter. Most of the examples are based on data sets that we have created for this book, but a few draw on real data sets that we or our students have collected in the past; we make clear which is which when we present the data. We also very briefly describe the research design elements involved in the data collection to provide the context for the data sets. For each numerical example, we also include a description of the *SAS Enterprise Guide* data set structure and a screen shot showing at least a portion of the data set.

We follow the numerical example by presenting step-by-step guidelines for setting up the analysis in *SAS Enterprise Guide*. Our presentation includes a narration of what has to be done and why it has to be done. This is accompanied by screen shots of the various dialog windows. Finally, we offer step-by-step guidelines for reading and interpreting the output (the printed results) of the analysis. These, too, are accompanied by screen shots of the output.

Acknowledgments

We wish to acknowledge and thank the following individuals for their efforts in maximizing the quality of this book. Lauren Cowles, our editor, has been most helpful and supportive to us during the entire writing process, and her assistant, David Jou, has been very responsive to our inquiries and requests. Peter Katsirubas, our Project Manager at Aptara, kept the production process moving and helped us through that stage of preparing the book. Finally, we are extremely grateful to Susan Zinninger for her marvellous copyediting skills; her time and effort have made the narrative smoother, more readable, and more consistent than what it was when we mailed it to Lauren.

Section I

Introducing *SAS Enterprise Guide*

1 *SAS Enterprise Guide* Projects

1.1 A brief history of SAS

The SAS Web site provides a comprehensive history of the software and the company. Here is a synopsis of that information. SAS, an acronym for Statistical Analysis Software, is a set of statistical analysis procedures housed together within a large application. The idea for it was conceived by Anthony J. Barr, a graduate student at North Carolina State University, between 1962 and 1964. Barr collaborated with Jim Goodnight in 1968 to integrate regression and analysis of variance (ANOVA) procedures into the software. The project received a major boost in 1973 from the contribution of John P. Sall. Other participants in the early years of SAS development included Caroll G. Perkins, Jolayne W. Service, and Jane T. Helwig. The SAS Institute was established in Raleigh, NC in 1976 when the first base SAS material was released. The company moved to its present location of Cary, NC in 1980.

SAS began being used on mainframe computers several decades ago. At that time, the only way to instruct the software to perform the statistical analyses was by punching holes on computer cards via a card-reader machine. Later this instruction occurred by typing in this code on an otherwise blank screen. The majority of SAS users still prefer this latter process.

SAS released its first Windows version in 1993. Windows uses a graphical user interface (abbreviated GUI but thought of by most people as a point-and-click interface) to make selections from menus and enter some limited text into dialog screens. These selections are translated "behind the scenes" to SAS code but the code can be viewed by a click of the mouse. *SAS Enterprise Guide* succeeded the Analyst interface and is the third iteration of SAS' GUI. It runs only in the Windows operating environment. Because *SAS Enterprise Guide* writes code and submits it

3

to SAS as you make selections with the mouse or type text into dialog screens, you also need to be using a computer on which SAS is installed, either a stand-alone personal computer or one that is connected to an organization's network.

This book was written by us based on SAS version 9.1 together with *SAS Enterprise Guide* version 4.0. This configuration is currently available under an organizational license, such as that purchased by a university or government agency. Therefore, certain users may have the software installed on computers owned by the organization, such as computers in a statistics laboratory. This same configuration under the title *SAS Publishing SAS Learning Edition 4.1* was also available from JourneyEd.com at the time we were writing this at a considerably discounted price (compared with the organizational license fees) to students and faculty members to load on their own personal computers with the Windows XP operating system.

1.2   Opening a project

We will assume that the shortcut to *SAS Enterprise Guide* 4.0 is visible on your desktop (if it is not then you can navigate to it in the **Program Files** folder on your internal drive). Open *Enterprise Guide* by double-clicking on its icon. This brings you to the window shown in Figure 1.1.

Everything in *SAS Enterprise Guide* is done within the context of a *project*. A project contains the data set and a history of its use, including the output of any statistical analyses that were performed. This will become quite familiar to you as we work through the chapters of this book; for now, treat this as information that you can read again as necessary. The initial screen for *SAS Enterprise Guide* therefore provides choices of which project or type of project we would like to open. Here are three of the more frequently used options:

- The top portion of our opening screen under **Open a project** lists some of the projects that we have recently opened. If we wished to open one of those, we would simply click on its name.
- If we wished to start a new project, we would select **New Project** in the **New** portion of the screen.
- If we wished to open an existent project whose name is not displayed on the initial screen, we would select **More projects** and then use the menu system to navigate to and open the desired project. Alternatively, we could select **New Project** and then select our project as described in the following section.

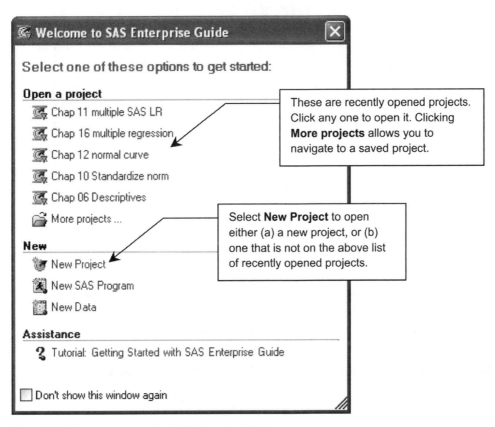

Figure 1.1. The startup screen for *SAS Enterprise Guide*.

1.3 The contents of projects

Selecting **New Project** brings us to the screen shown in Figure 1.2. We are presented with the **Process Flow** screen of the **Project Designer**. It is empty now but at various stages of our work it will contain a data set, the specifications of our analysis, and the results of the data analysis. The screen shows a grid that looks like graph paper – this is the background used by **Process Flow**. Because there is nothing in the project at this time, an empty **Process Flow** window is displayed.

We will open a project in order to show you what a typical project might contain. From the main menu, select **File → Open → Project** (see Figure 1.3). *SAS Enterprise Guide* will require you to indicate where your projects are located (see Figure 1.4); as ours are on the internal drive of our personal computer, we choose **Local Computer**,

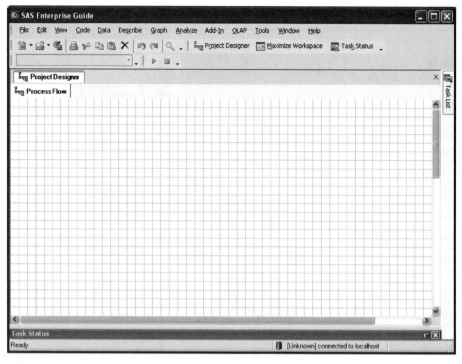

Figure 1.2. The **Project Designer** tab with an empty **Process Flow** window.

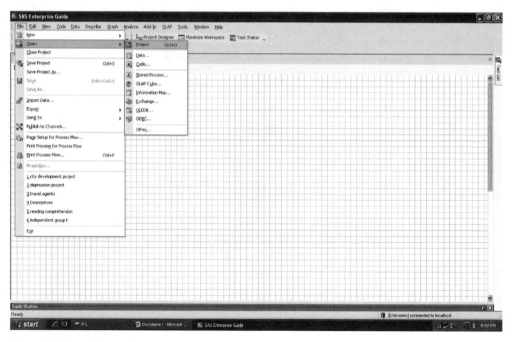

Figure 1.3. Opening a project.

6

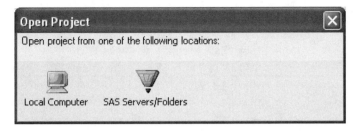

Figure 1.4. Select the system on which your projects are located.

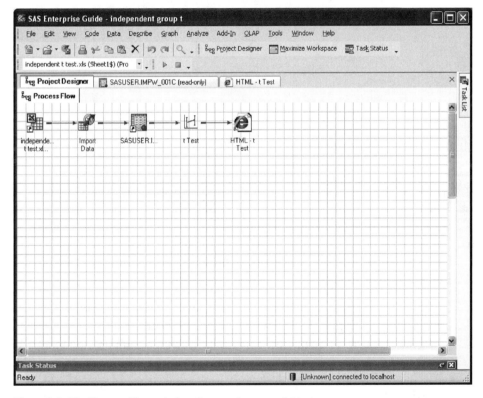

Figure 1.5. The **Process Flow** window for a project named **t test**.

navigate to the folder on our desktop containing our projects, and select **independent group *t***.

We have opened a project whose **Process Flow** screen is displayed in Figure 1.5. It is named **independent group t**, as can be seen in the Windows title bar at the top

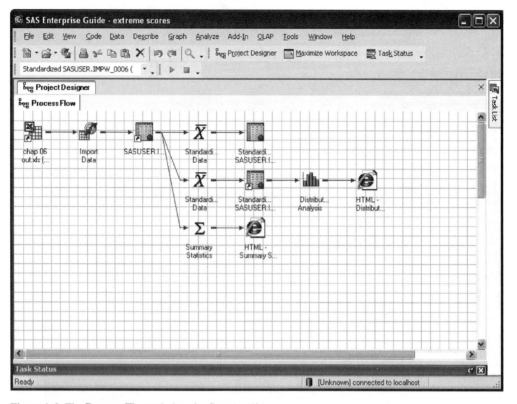

Figure 1.6. The **Process Flow** window for **Standardize**.

of the screen. **Process Flow** is a pictorial representation of the history of the project. Reading the icons from left to right unfolds the following story:

- The first icon represents an Excel file. At the time we began this project, the data were imported from an Excel file named **independent t test**.
- The second icon shows that the data in the Excel file were imported into *SAS Enterprise Guide*.
- The third icon stands for the *SAS Enterprise Guide* data set. The name **SASUSER** is read as "SAS user."
- The fourth icon represents the statistical analysis procedure **t test**.
- The fifth icon represents the output file. Results of a statistical procedure are placed in output files, which can have different formats. This output file is in HTML format, and this is how we display output in this book. We will talk more about this and other output formats in Chapter 4.

Multiple analyses can be performed and preserved in projects. Figure 1.6 displays the **Process Flow** screen for another project. The large X-bar symbol represents

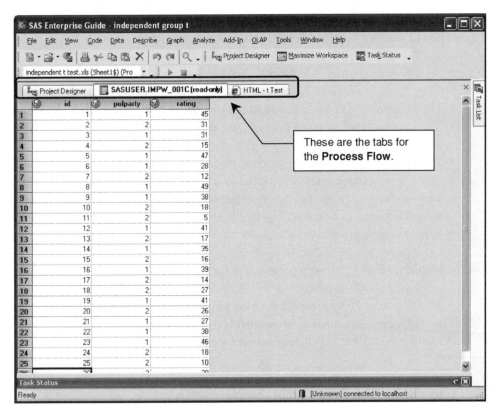

Figure 1.7. A view of the data set with the **Process Flow** tabs just above it.

standardization of a variable. As we can see, two standardizations and one **Summary Statistics** procedure (uppercase Greek sigma) have been performed; to picture this, a set of different arrows emerge from the data set on the first row.

1.4   Navigating tabs in the Process Flow screen

We return to **Process Flow** for the project named **independent group t** as shown before in Figure 1.5. By clicking on the icon for the data set, we can display it. This is shown in Figure 1.7. Each column is a variable.

Our interest for the moment is in the tabs just above the data set. The **Project Designer** tab is the one furthest to the left and is dimmed on the screen, indicating that it is not currently active. The **Project Designer** tab contains the pictorial representation of the project in the form of the **Process Flow** screen.

The active tab is labeled **SASUSER.IMPW_001C** (**read-only**). It refers to the displayed data set. Here is what the parts of the label mean:

- As before, the name **SASUSER** is read as "SAS user."
- The expression **IMPW** indicates that the file was imported (**IMP**) from someplace unspecified in the label and that it is in the Working Library of SAS (**W**).
- The number **001C** is just a count of the work we have done during the current session.
- The expression **read-only** reminds us that to protect data sets from unintentionally being changed, they are opened in a protected or read-only mode. When we wish to modify the data set in some way, such as computing a new variable from the existent ones, it will be necessary to actively (and easily) turn off the read-only protection.

The tab furthest to the right is the output file named the **HTML t test**. By clicking on it we would open the output file.

Note that these tabs mirror the **Process Flow** screen and can be used to navigate between its elements directly. If the number of tabs exceeds the horizontal space allowed on the tab bar, scroll arrows will appear at the far right of the tab bar.

1.5   The main *SAS Enterprise Guide* menu

Figure 1.8 shows a portion of an existent *SAS Enterprise Guide* process flow. At the top of the window the main *SAS Enterprise Guide* menu (**File**, **Edit**, and so on) appears. You will make use of some of these menus much more frequently than others. When you click on one of these menu items, you will open a secondary menu from which you select what you would like to do. Very briefly, these menu items contain the following:

- **File:** Contains a variety of functions including **Open**, **Import Data**, **Print Preview** (the data set name will appear here), and **Exit**.
- **Edit:** Allows you to **Cut**, **Copy**, **Paste**, **Select All**, and so on.
- **View:** Controls **Toolbars**, **Task Status**, and so on.
- **Code:** Allows you to run the analysis that has been set up, stop the processing, and deal with macros.
- **Data:** Allows you to deal with the data set; among other things, you can select options to **sort** (reorder) the cases, **Transpose** the rows and columns, and **standardize** the data.

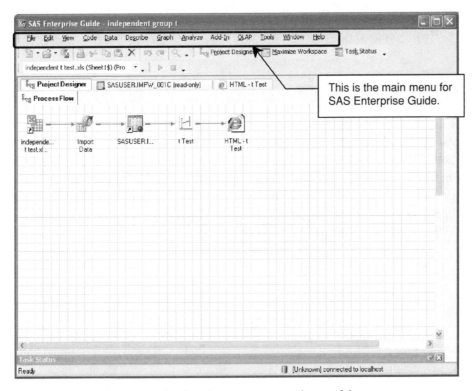

Figure 1.8. The *SAS Enterprise Guide* main menu appears at the top of the screen.

- **Describe:** Allows you to **List Data** (e.g., identify each case by variables that you designate), acquire **Summary Statistics**, and produce a **Frequency** table on a specified variable.
- **Graph:** Contains a variety of preformatted ways to plot your data.
- **Analyze:** Contains the statistical procedures you use to analyze your data.
- **Add-In:** Gets you to the **Add-In Manager**, which allows you to add, remove, and update commonly used procedures, such as **Standardize Data** and **Summary Statistics**.
- **OLAP:** This acronym stands for online analytical processing. According to the SAS Web site, the OLAP Server is a multidimensional data store designed to provide quick access to presummarized data generated from vast amounts of detailed data.
- **Tools:** Allows you to access sample data sets through **SAS Enterprise Guide Explorer**, place your project in a particular library through **Assign Library**, and produce your statistical output in HTML, PDF, RTF, and other formats through **Options**.

- **Window:** Allows you to reach particular screens.
- **Help:** Contains documentation explaining how to work with SAS.

1.6 Additional resources

Readers are encouraged to consult additional resources describing *SAS Enterprise Guide*. Such resources include Constable (2007), Davis (2007), Der and Everitt (2007), Gamst, Meyers, and Guarino (2008), McDaniel and Hemedinger (2007), Slaughter and Delwiche (2006), and SAS Institute (2002). Additional resources describing SAS include Cody and Smith (2006), Hatcher (2003), Hatcher and Stepanski (1994), Marasinghe and Kennedy (2008), Peng (2009), SAS Institute (1990), and Schlotzhauer and Littell (1997).

2 Placing Data into *SAS Enterprise Guide* Projects

2.1 Overview

There are many ways to place data into a *SAS Enterprise Guide* project. Two of them may be more frequently used than the others. The first is entering data directly into the project. The second is importing data to a project from a spreadsheet such as Excel. We describe, in order, each of these in this chapter.

2.2 Entering data directly into *SAS Enterprise Guide*

We will begin the process of entering data directly into *SAS Enterprise Guide* by opening a new project. Open *SAS Enterprise Guide* and select **New Project** from the initial screen. You will then be presented with an empty **Process Flow** grid.

From the main menu select **File → New → Data**. This selection brings you to the initial **New Data** screen seen in Figure 2.1.

The initial **New Data** screen in Figure 2.1 provides places for you to supply two pieces of information:

- *Name*: This field is used to name the project that you are about to build. File names can be no longer than 32 characters, must contain only alphanumeric characters or underscores, and must begin with either a letter or an underscore; no spaces are allowed in the name. Select a name that meaningfully relates to your research project. We will name our file **Reading_Comprehension_Study**.
- *Location*: *SAS Enterprise Guide* will use one of its **Libraries** as the start location. By default, it has selected the **Work Library**. This is acceptable because once we have entered the data we will save the project in a location of our choice.

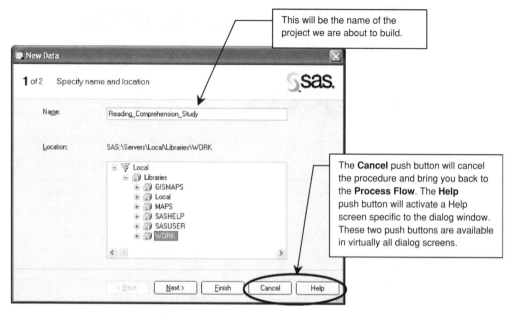

Figure 2.1. The initial **New Data** screen.

It is also worthwhile to note that most of the dialog screens we discuss in this book also have two additional push buttons (these can be seen in Figure 2.1) that can be especially useful:

- The **Cancel** push button cancels the procedure and brings you back to the **Process Flow** screen.
- The **Help** push button activates a window specific to the dialog screen you are using. Most or all of the options you have available in the dialog screen are explained.

When you have finished with the first **New Data** window, click **Next**. This brings you to the second **New Data** screen shown in Figure 2.2. It is in this window that you identify the variables and their properties in advance of typing the data. In the left panel are the generic variable names supplied by *SAS Enterprise Guide* (**A**, **B**, **C**, and so on) listed vertically; in the right panel are the properties that will be associated with each variable. In the data set, **A** will be the first variable and will occupy the first column, **B** will be the second variable and occupy the second column, and so on.

When a variable is highlighted in the **New Data** window, you may specify its properties. For example, consider variable **A**. The icon next to it (a "tent" surrounding

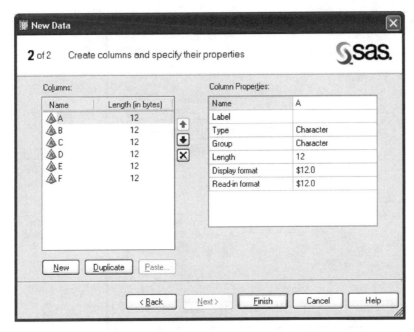

Figure 2.2. The **New Data** screen in which we specify the variable properties.

an "A") represents the default of a **Character** (an alphanumeric string of characters with the "A" in the tent standing for *alphanumeric*) variable. Such a variable is treated as a string of letter and number characters, and it is a naming or nominal variable. SAS will not perform arithmetic operations (e.g., calculating a mean) on such variables. Note that in the right panel for **Properties**, the **Type** of variable is listed as **Character**.

The first variable we will specify is our case-identification variable. Our specifications are shown in Figure 2.3. Assume that in the data set each participant has been assigned an arbitrary identification code, and that we named this variable **id**. To accomplish this naming, in the **Properties** panel we have highlighted the letter **A** in the **Name** row and typed in **id**. In the **Label** area, we have indicated that the variable is an **identification code**; although the fact that **id** represents an identification code may be obvious here, it is a good habit to label all variables whose meaning may not be immediately clear by its name.

In the **Type** panel, we have clicked **Character** to obtain a drop-down menu with the choices **Character** and **Numeric** and have chosen **Numeric**. That selection caused the **Group** choice to switch to **Numeric** as well (the choices are **Numeric**, **Date**, **Time**, and **Currency**), which is what we wish. It also caused the icon next

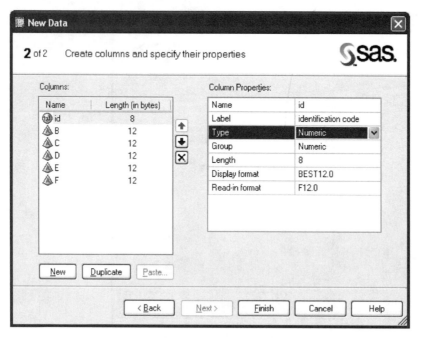

Figure 2.3. The variable we have named **id** is now specified.

to **A** in the left panel to change to a circle containing the numerals 1, 2, and 3 to represent the fact that **id** has been specified as a numeric variable.

The remaining two variables in our illustration data set are both numeric, and we will specify them as well (see Figures 2.4 and 2.5). These other variables are as follows:

- **gender** is a variable containing codes to indicate whether the participant was male or female. We use a code of 1 for the female gender and a code of 2 for the male gender.
- **readscore** is the value that the participant registered on the dependent variable, which would be a reading comprehension score in the present example.

When you have specified these other variables, click **Finish**. This brings you to the empty data grid shown in Figure 2.6.

The data may be entered as we would do for any type of spreadsheet. Type the value in each cell and use the **Tab** or **Arrow** keys to move from one cell to another. We have entered a small data set, shown in Figure 2.7, to illustrate the process.

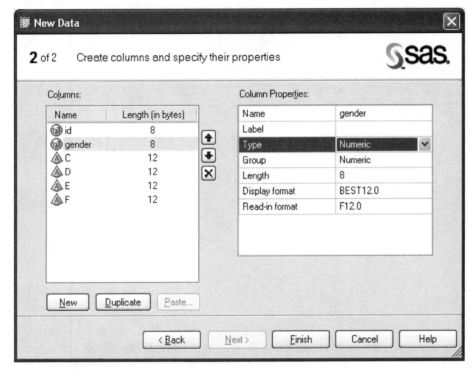

Figure 2.4. The variable we have named **gender** is now specified.

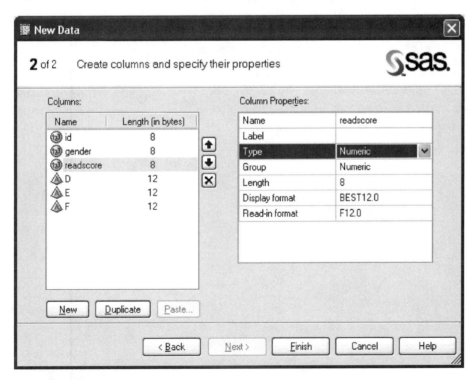

Figure 2.5. The variable we have named **readscore** is now specified.

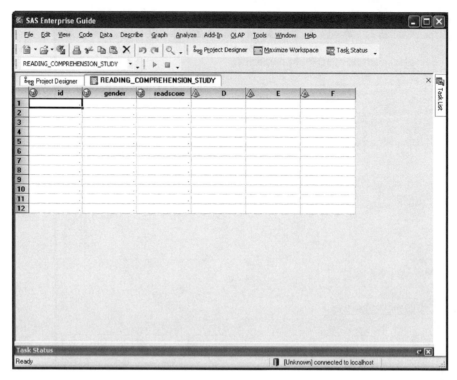

Figure 2.6. The data grid is now ready for us to input our data.

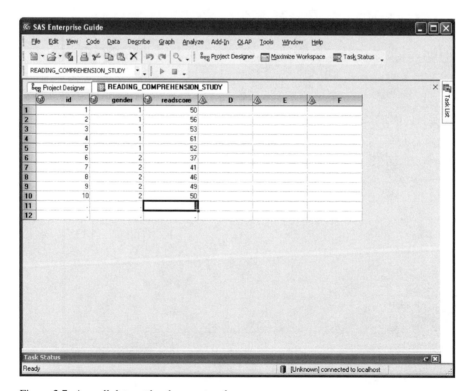

Figure 2.7. A small data set has been entered.

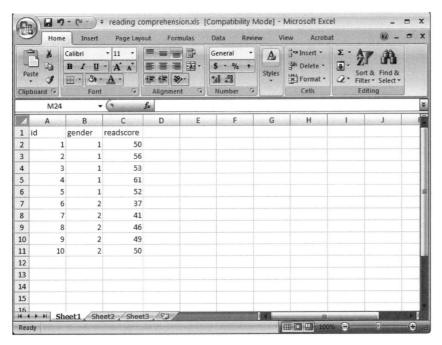

Figure 2.8. An Excel spreadsheet is to be imported into SAS.

2.3 Saving a project

To save the project that is currently open, from the main *SAS Enterprise Guide* menu select **File → Save Reading_Comprehension_Study Project**. This allows us to choose between **Local Computer** and **SAS Servers/Folders**. Select **Local Computer** and navigate to any place on your internal drive or to external media such as a USB flash drive where you want to save the project. Give it a reasonable name to replace the default name of **Project** and **Save**. The data set is now saved within that project. If you wish to change the name of the project (or save a variation of the project) under a different name, select **File → Save Reading_Comprehension_Study Project As**.

2.4 Importing data from Excel

We could have constructed the data set in Excel and then imported it into *SAS Enterprise Guide*. We illustrate this process here. The Excel spreadsheet is shown in Figure 2.8, which must be saved in Microsoft Excel 1997–2003 (.xls) format. Note that we have placed the variable names in the first row of the grid.

Figure 2.9. We have saved the Excel file to our local computer and will therefore select **Local Computer**.

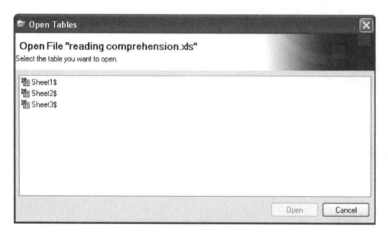

Figure 2.10. Our data set is on Sheet 1 of the Excel file.

From the main *SAS Enterprise Guide* menu, select **File → Import Data**. This brings you to the screen shown in Figure 2.9, which gives you a choice of opening a project from either **Local Computer** or **SAS Servers/Folder**. We will assume that you are working on a stand-alone computer and that your file is located on your computer or some media (e.g., USB flash drive, CD) that is acknowledged by your computer. Thus, select **Local Computer**.

When you have selected **Local Computer**, you will see the standard Windows **Open File** screen. Navigate to the Excel file containing the data that you have saved. Make sure **Files of type** show either **All Files** or those with the .xls (Microsoft Excel 1997–2003) extension.

Selecting the Excel file results in an **Open Tables** window that asks for the Excel sheet number (see Figure 2.10). We used Sheet 1 in the Excel file so we have selected that and then clicked the **Open** push button.

Clicking the **Open** push button presents us with an **Import Data** window as shown in Figure 2.11. Note that in the far left panel are tabs indicating the information about

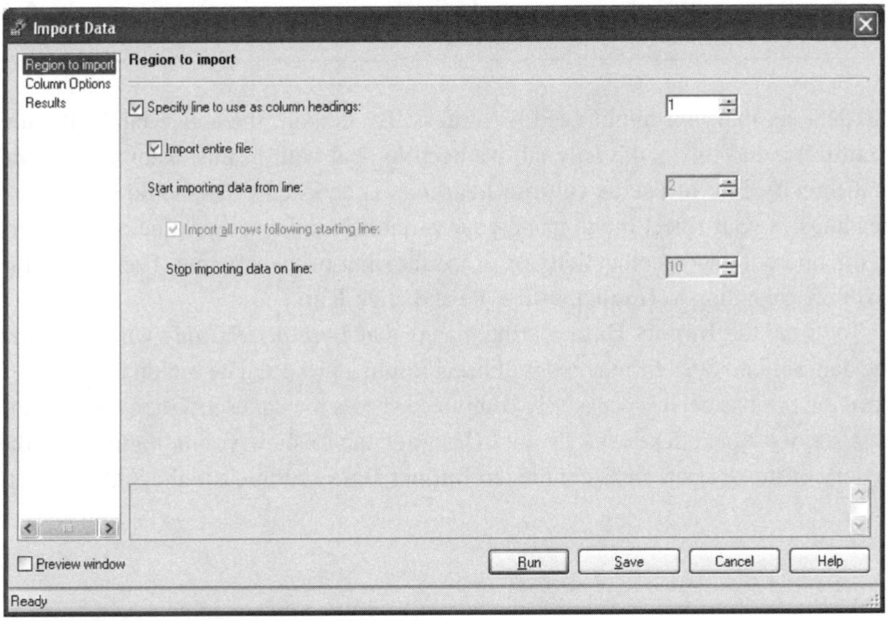

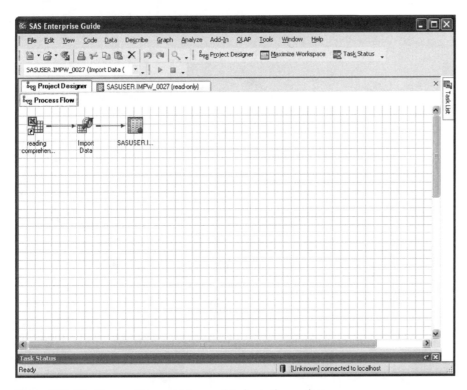

Figure 2.11. The **Import Data** screen.

Figure 2.12. The **Process Flow** grid for our data-importing project.

the data set that you might need to address. By default, the active tab is **Region to import**, and this is the only tab we need to deal with in this example. Be sure that **Specify line to use as column headings** is checked (you should always use headings in your Excel file to name your variables) and that the value of **1** appears in the line number specification box at the far right of the window. Then check the box corresponding to **Import entire file** and click **Run**.

To "run" the **Import Data** routine means that *Enterprise Guide* will transform the data set into SAS format and will bring it into a project. The screen that appears once the run has been successfully completed shows the data set. When viewing the data set, we have clicked the **Project Designer** tab to show you in Figure 2.12 the history of the project: an Excel file, an **Import Data** routine, and the SAS data set.

Section II

Performing Analyses and Viewing Output

3 Performing Statistical Analyses in *SAS Enterprise Guide*

3.1 Overview

Although there are many statistical analyses available in *SAS Enterprise Guide*, the screens within each procedure have been structured to be similar to each other as much as possible. Thus, users can develop generalized skills in working with the software to the point where they can perform an analysis they have not yet tried because they have learned how to set up any analysis. In this chapter, we take advantage of this structural similarity to briefly present generic information on how to perform statistical analyses in general.

3.2 Numerical example

A portion of the data set we will use to illustrate how to perform statistical analyses is shown in Figure 3.1. In addition to an identification code (**id** in the data set), we have the demographic variables of **sex**, **age**, and marital status (**marital**). The final variable is a measure of depression (**depress**). Because we are concerned here only with the structure of the dialog windows and not with implications of the results, we will not bother to indicate the coding of the demographic variables.

3.3 Selecting the procedure

The main menu of *SAS Enterprise Guide* can be used to access statistical procedures. Most of the procedures we use in this book are found on the **Analyze** menu, but some will be drawn from the **Describe** menu and a few will be drawn from the

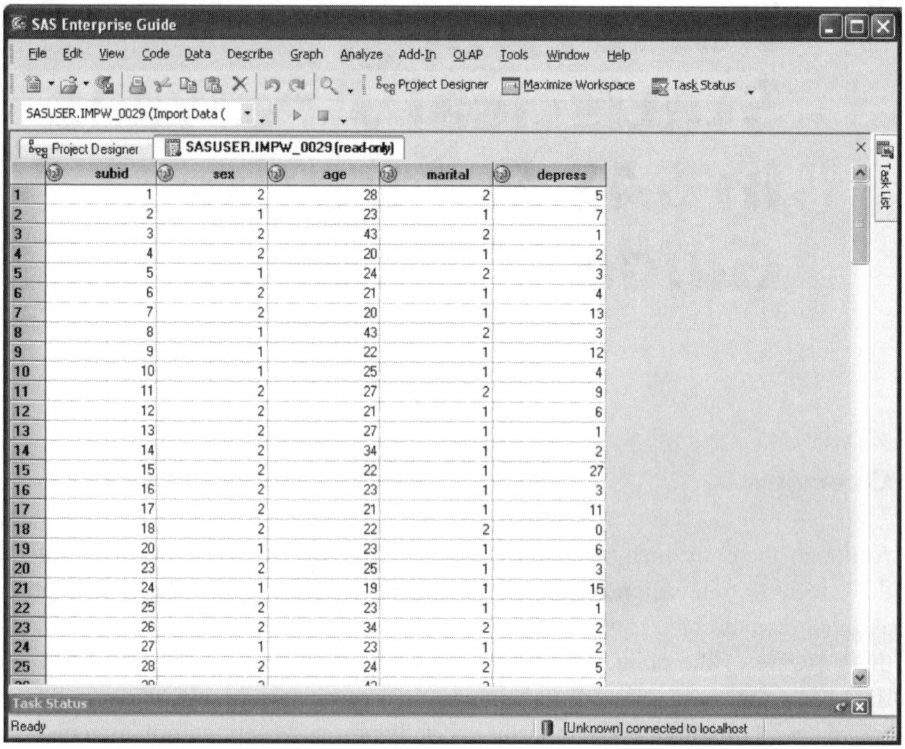

Figure 3.1. A portion of the data set.

Data menu. We use the **Linear Regression** procedure to illustrate how to work with *SAS Enterprise Guide* windows. Specifically, we will regress **depress** on **age** (we will predict the depression variable based on age). The statistical features of this procedure are described in Chapter 16.

From the main menu, select **Analyze → Regression → Linear** as shown in Figure 3.2. It is not uncommon to be presented with a secondary menu after making a choice under the main menu.

3.4 Assigning Task roles

Selecting the **Linear Regression** procedure brings us to the main dialog window for the procedure as shown in Figure 3.3. The navigation panel at the very left of the window will appear in every procedure and allows us to reach different parts of the specifications for the analysis. Typically, we begin our navigation in the

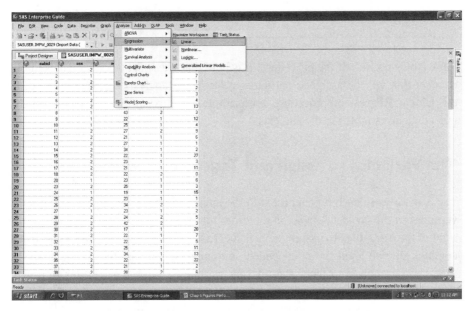

Figure 3.2. We have selected the **Linear Regression** procedure from the **Analyze** menu.

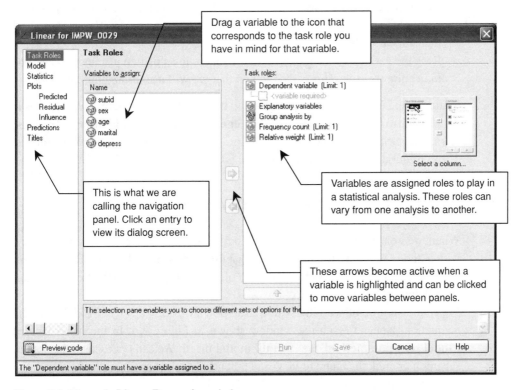

Figure 3.3. The main **Linear Regression** window.

Task Roles portion of the procedure. It is here that we select those variables in our data set that will be assigned particular roles in the analysis we have invoked. In this **Linear Regression** procedure, for example, we must specify the dependent and independent variables in the analysis.

3.5   The Variables to assign and Task roles panels

The **Variables to assign** panel (next to the navigation panel) in Figure 3.3 lists the variables in the project data set in the order that they appear in the data set. To the right of the **Variables to assign** panel is the **Task roles** panel. The **Task roles** panel contains slots to identify the dependent and independent variables in the analysis. The user is required to place the relevant variables from the **Variables to assign** panel into the **Task roles** panel.

There are two ways to place variables into the **Task roles** panel:

- Highlight the variable, click the directional arrow between the **Variables to assign** panel and the **Task roles** panel (which become active once a variable is highlighted), and select the role to be assigned the variable. The variable will then appear under that role.
- Drag the variable to the icon next to the role or to a position just under the words indicating the role. This is the method that we will use throughout this book.

In the present example, we drag **depress** to the icon for **Dependent variable**; this is the variable to be predicted. We then drag **age** to the icon for **Explanatory variables**; this is the variable serving as the predictor or independent variable in the analysis. The configuration we have just described is shown in Figure 3.4.

3.6   Other choices in the navigation panel

When we select another choice in the navigation panel, we are often presented with a dialog window structured somewhat differently from the **Task Roles** screen. In some of these other windows, we are often asked to either select choices from drop-down menus or mark checkboxes.

As an example of working with a drop-down menu, we select **Model** from the navigation panel to reach the window shown in Figure 3.5. In the panel labeled **Model selection method**, we see **Full model fitted**. We can opt to keep the default selection or click the menu to view and potentially select an alternative method. We can see a portion of the alternatives in Figure 3.6.

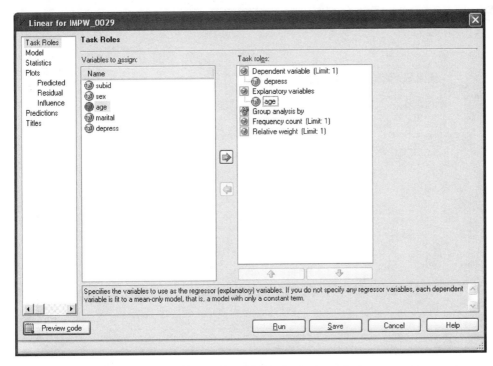

Figure 3.4. The variables have now been assigned their roles in the analysis.

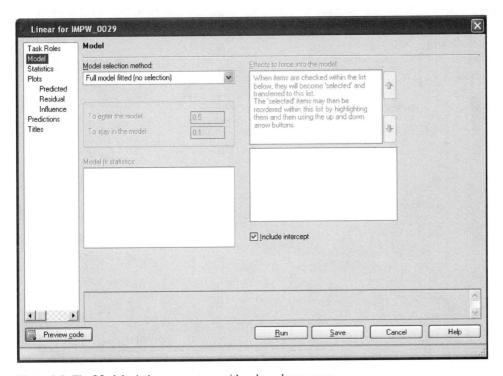

Figure 3.5. The **Model** window presents us with a drop-down menu.

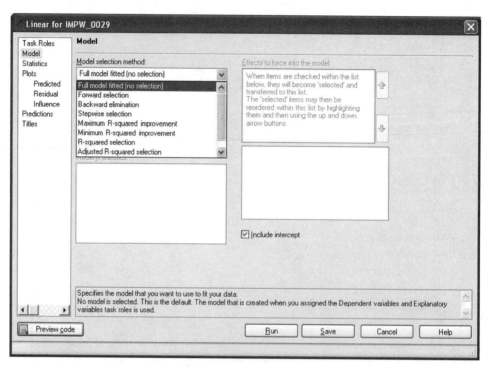

Figure 3.6. Other methods are available under **Model selection method** on the drop-down menu.

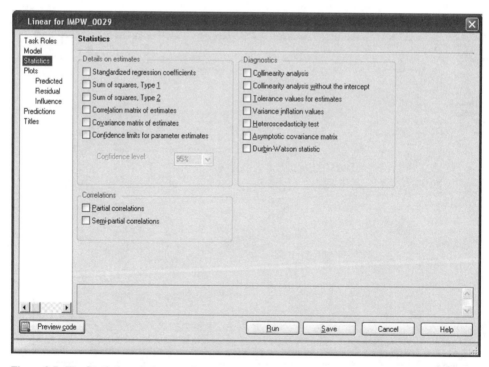

Figure 3.7. The **Statistics** window requires us to check the boxes corresponding to the information that we wish to obtain.

We can see an example of working with checkboxes when we select **Statistics** from the navigation panel. This brings us to the window shown in Figure 3.7. In this type of dialog window, we click the checkboxes corresponding to the information that we wish to obtain in the output.

3.7 Performing the analysis

Virtually every dialog window contains a **Run** push button. This button will become active once enough information has been specified to perform an analysis. After we have configured the analysis to our satisfaction, we can click this push button to have *SAS Enterprise Guide* perform the analysis.

4 Managing and Viewing Output

4.1 Overview

When you instruct SAS to perform a statistical analysis, it displays the results as output in a window in the form that you have specified on the **Tools** menu as described in Section 4.3. An icon for the output will also appear in the **Process Flow** screen. If you have specified that one output format is to be PDF, then you can save that file to view on a computer not containing or not having access to *SAS Enterprise Guide*. We treat these topics in turn.

4.2 Numerical example

We will use the regression example from Chapter 3 to illustrate these output issues. You may recall that we intended to predict the level of depression (**depress**) based on our age variable.

4.3 Specifying the output format

We specify the output format(s) we prefer by selecting **Tools → Options**. The window opens on the **General** screen (see Figure 4.1). Clicking on **Results** in the navigation window brings you to the **Results > Results General** screen shown in Figure 4.2.

The different formats available in *SAS Enterprise Guide* are listed under the **Result Formats** panel. Each format has a checkbox and it is possible to check more

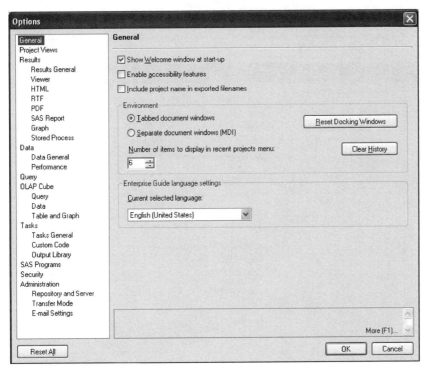

Figure 4.1. Selecting **Tools → Options** brings us to the **General** screen.

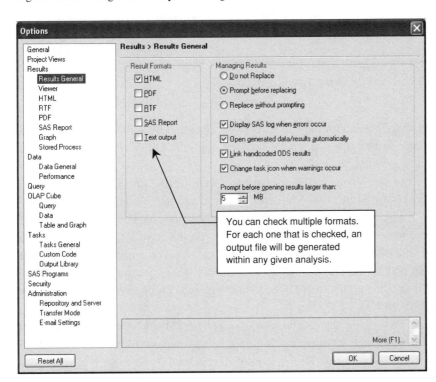

Figure 4.2. The **General Results** screen.

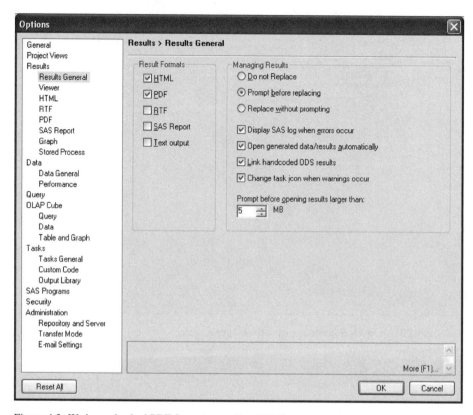

Figure 4.3. We have checked PDF format as well as HTML.

than one box. For each format that is checked, an output file will be generated. Thus, with many formats checked, each statistical analysis will cause that many output files to be generated.

As we can see, on our system we have only one format checked, namely **HTML**, which stands for HyperText Markup Language and was designed for use on the Internet. If you intend to work with SAS output on personal computers that are not connected to an organizational network or that do not have *SAS Enterprise Guide* loaded on them, then the only way to view the statistical results is by opening a PDF document containing the output. We will discuss this in Section 4.5; for now, it is sufficient to indicate that the PDF box should now be checked here as well. This is done in Figure 4.3.

Click **HTML** in the navigation panel to reach the **HTML** screen. There are quite a few styles available to display this output. We show a small portion of the drop-down menu in Figure 4.4. The style used in this book is Seaside, but we suggest

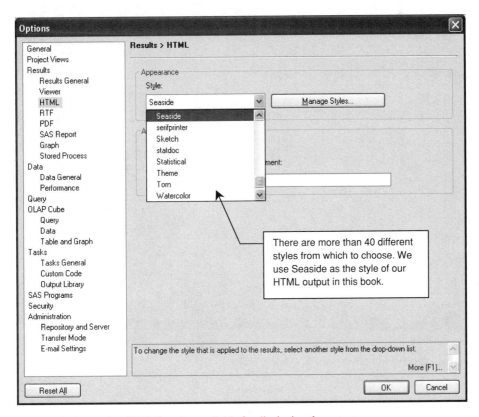

Figure 4.4. A sample of HTML styles available for displaying the output.

you try out several or all of them and select the one you prefer. Click **OK** to register your menu choices with *SAS Enterprise Guide*.

4.4 Examining the statistical results

We have performed a linear regression analysis in order to show you a sample of the output. The **Process Flow** screen for our project is displayed in Figure 4.5. Linear regression is pictured as a scatterplot icon with a regression line through it. There are two output files for the analysis, identical in content but differing in format: the HTML file and the PDF file.

To view the HTML file, double-click its icon. We present a portion of the file in Figure 4.6. The title of the output gives useful information about the analysis. **REG Procedure** is the name of the procedure in SAS code; because *SAS Enterprise*

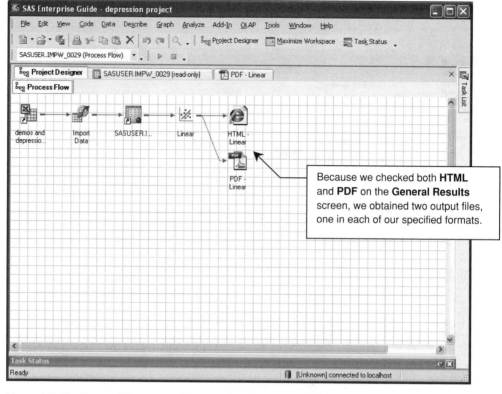

Because we checked both **HTML** and **PDF** on the **General Results** screen, we obtained two output files, one in each of our specified formats.

Figure 4.5. The **Process Flow** screen for our example project.

The REG Procedure
Model: Linear_Regression_Model
Dependent Variable: depress depress

Number of Observations Read	147
Number of Observations Used	147

Analysis of Variance					
Source	DF	Sum of Squares	Mean Square	F Value	Pr > F
Model	1	52.59617	52.59617	1.14	0.2879
Error	145	6702.62832	46.22502		
Corrected Total	146	6755.22449			

Root MSE	6.79890	R-Square	0.0078
Dependent Mean	7.30612	Adj R-Sq	0.0009
Coeff Var	93.05755		

Parameter Estimates													
Variable	Label	DF	Parameter Estimate	Standard Error	t Value	Pr > |t|	Standardized Estimate	Squared Semi-partial Corr Type I	Squared Partial Corr Type I	Squared Semi-partial Corr Type II	Squared Partial Corr Type II	Variance Inflation	95% Confidence Limits	
Intercept	intercept	1	9.37112	2.01548	4.65	<.0001	0	.	.	.	.	0	5.38762	13.35463
age	age	1	-0.08710	0.08166	-1.07	0.2879	-0.08824	0.00779	0.00779	0.00779	0.00779	1.00000	-0.24850	0.07429

Figure 4.6. A portion of the linear regression output in HTML format with Seaside style.

The REG Procedure
Model: Linear_Regression_Model
Dependent Variable: depress depress

Number of Observations Read	147
Number of Observations Used	147

Analysis of Variance					
Source	DF	Sum of Squares	Mean Square	F Value	Pr > F
Model	1	52.59617	52.59617	1.14	0.2879
Error	145	6702.62832	46.22502		
Corrected Total	146	6755.22449			

Root MSE	6.79890	R-Square	0.0078
Dependent Mean	7.30612	Adj R-Sq	0.0009
Coeff Var	93.05755		

Parameter Estimates

Figure 4.7. A portion of the linear regression output in PDF format.

Guide is simply a point-and-click façade to the main SAS application, it is this latter software that is actually performing the data analysis. The dependent variable is also listed in the title.

SAS output in both HTML and PDF format provides for portions of the analysis to be presented in tables. Each table focuses on a particular aspect of the results. In the Seaside style of HTML output, table titles, as well as row and column labels, are displayed on a tinted (beige or tan) background so that they may be quickly distinguished from the numerical results.

We can view the PDF file at this point in one of two ways:

- We can single-click on the **PDF** tab just above the results window.
- We can click on the **Project Designer** tab just above the results window and then double-click the **PDF** icon in the **Process Flow** screen.

A portion of the output file in PDF format is presented in Figure 4.7. It is the same information but the font is different and somewhat larger; in addition, the tinting is a relatively darker grey.

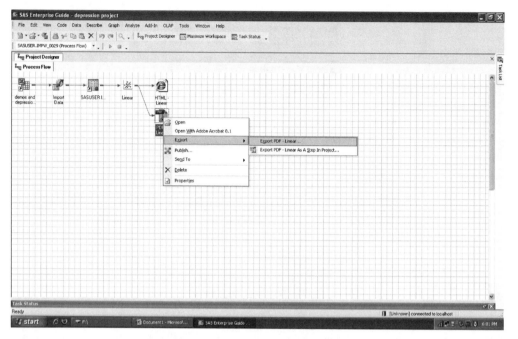

Figure 4.8. Right-clicking the icon for the PDF output displays a menu system that allows us to select **Export PDF – Linear** to save the PDF file.

4.5   Saving the output as a PDF document

4.5.1   PDF format

A PDF document is a type of file that is in Portable Document Format. It is a faithful copy of the original but it is not editable unless you have the full version of Adobe Acrobat or some comparable application.

When PDF documents are viewed on the computer screen or are printed, they mirror what you saw on the screen when viewing the original document. This transferability works even though your computer may not have the fonts that are used in the document and even if you are using a different computer platform (e.g., PDF documents created on a PC can be opened, viewed, and printed on a Mac) – that is what makes them portable. The Portable Document Format contains within it all the information necessary for the document to be displayed on the screen or to be printed.

Saving the output as a PDF document is extremely valuable for students and also for those who may not have SAS loaded on the computer that they will be using away from the organizational setting (perhaps their home computer or their personal laptop). Thus, they can view the results of their analysis in order to study their results or to prepare a report at a location and on a computer of their convenience.

To view or print a PDF document, you must have the appropriate software. Adobe Acrobat Reader is a free application for both PCs and Macs that can be downloaded from the Adobe Web site; with it, you can open and view PDF files. If you use a Mac, the Preview application (equivalent to Adobe Acrobat Reader) is packaged into the OS X operating system, bypassing the need to download Acrobat Reader.

4.5.2 Saving PDF files

The existence of the PDF file inside of the project is not sufficient for you to access it outside of the project. You must save the PDF file to either the internal drive or to an external USB flash drive so that you can e-mail it or transfer it to another computer.

To save the file, have the **Process Flow** screen displayed. Then right-click the icon for the PDF file. The results of the right-click action are shown in Figure 4.8. Select **Export → Export PDF → Linear** (this is the name assigned to the file because we performed a linear regression analysis; if we had performed a different procedure, the file would have the name of that procedure). As an alternative, we could have selected **File → Export** from the main menu (so long as the icon for the PDF file is highlighted). After making either of these selections, select **Local Computer** from the choices and navigate to the location where you intend to save the file. Then click **Save**.

Section III

Manipulating Data

5 Sorting Data and Selecting Cases

5.1 Overview

Once a data set is available within a project, it may be convenient to perform some operations on the values of one or more of the variables to either facilitate viewing the data or to prepare the data for later analysis. *SAS Enterprise Guide* classifies a variety of operations or manipulations of the data set as *queries*. Examples of queries include sorting data and selecting cases (covered in this chapter), recoding a variable in the data set (covered in Chapter 6), and computing a new variable (covered in Chapter 7).

5.2 Numerical example

We have constructed a simplified numerical example to illustrate sorting and selection. The data set is shown in Figure 5.1. Twenty-one experienced travel agents assigned identification codes of 1 to 21 (**id** in the data set) visited one of three comparably priced resorts managed by a particular resort company (coded under **location** in the data set). The travel agents rated the resorts on a variety of dimensions, with their composite evaluation shown under **rating** in the data set; higher values denote more positive evaluations.

5.3 Sorting data

At times it might be useful to sort the data in some systematic way. This helps us view the data and perhaps helps to anticipate what the data analysis will show in

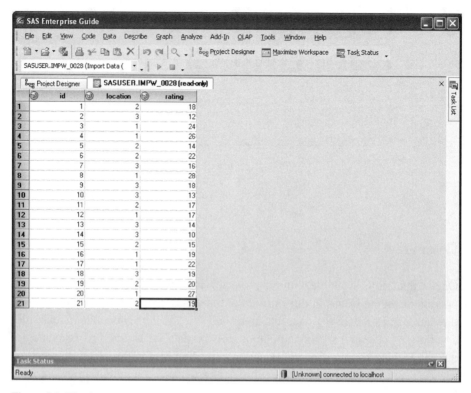

Figure 5.1. The data set.

more detail. Currently, the data set is ordered by the identification codes of the travel agents primarily because this is the way the data were originally entered. In viewing the data set it might be useful to see the data set sorted (grouped) by the location variable.

To perform the sorting, select **Data → Sort Data**. This brings you to the **Task Roles** window for **Sort Data** as shown in Figure 5.2. Drag **location** to the slot under **Sort by** in the rightmost panel. Click the **Run** push button to accomplish the sort.

The result of the sort is shown in Figure 5.3. All of the locations coded as 1 are in the first seven rows, followed by the locations coded as 2, followed by the locations coded as 3. Now we can more easily scan across to see the ratings corresponding to each location.

We show the **Process Flow** screen for the project in Figure 5.4. The icon with a downward arrow against a grid represents a sorting operation, which resulted in a newly sorted data set.

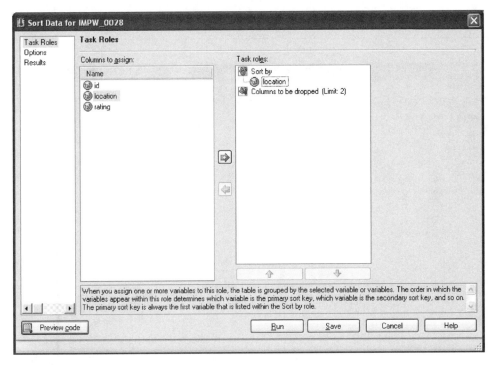

Figure 5.2. The **Task Roles** screen for **Sort Data**.

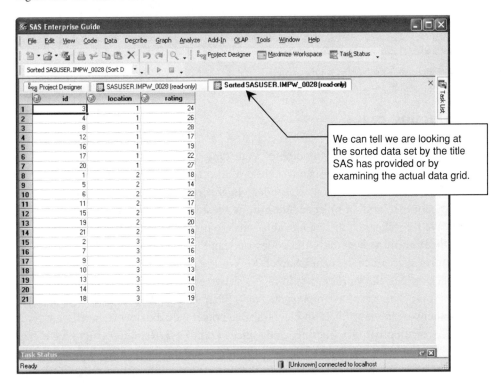

Figure 5.3. The data set has been sorted by **location**.

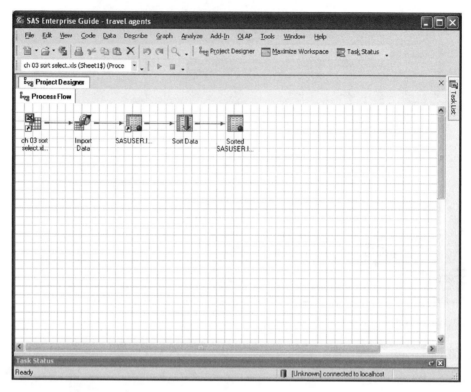

Figure 5.4. The **Process Flow** screen for the project.

5.3   Selecting cases

There may be occasions in some of your data analyses when you might wish to perform a statistical analysis on a subset of the cases in the data set. *SAS Enterprise Guide* labels this selection as a *filter*. In the present example, assume that we wished to perform an independent-groups *t* test to determine if Locations 1 and 3 received significantly different evaluations. To perform the *t* test, the variable coded as **location** must have only the codes of 1 and 3 in it. We will show you how to perform such an analysis in Chapter 20. For the present purposes, we just want to isolate (select) the scores representing these two groups. Thus, our goal is to filter the data set such that we have represented only the travel agents from Locations 1 and 3; another way to view this is to select travel agents if they did not evaluate Location 2.

To accomplish this filtering goal, select **Data → Filter and Query** (see Figure 5.5). This brings you to the main **Query** screen as shown in Figure 5.6. The variables in the data set are listed in the panel on the left of the screen. Over the panel to its right are three tabs with the **Select Data** tab currently active.

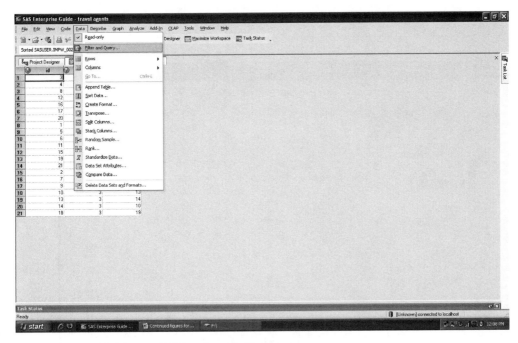

Figure 5.5. Selecting **Filter and Query** from the **Data** menu.

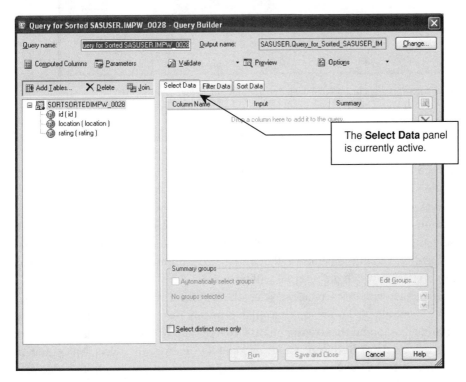

Figure 5.6. The **Query** screen.

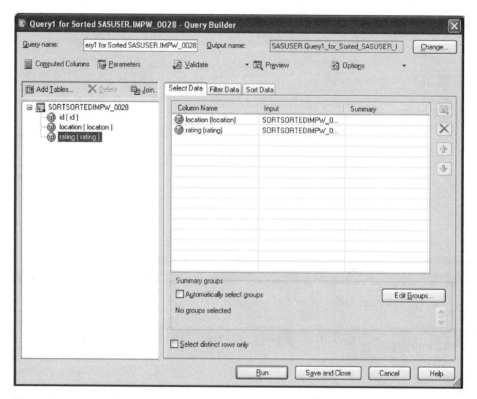

Figure 5.7. Both **location** and **rating** have been dragged into the **Select Data** panel.

Because our ultimate goal is to perform a *t* test by using location (Location 1 vs. Location 3) as our independent variable and rating as our dependent variable, we need to have both variables appear in the filtered data set. Thus, we drag both **location** and **rating** into the **Select Data** panel. This is shown in Figure 5.7.

Clicking the **Filter Data** tab brings us to the screen shown in Figure 5.8. We drag **location**, the variable which we wish to filter, to the **Filter Data** panel. This action automatically opens the **Edit Filter** dialog screen as seen in Figure 5.9. Note that our **location** variable is named in the row labeled **Column**; this reminds us that it is this variable on which the filtering will take place.

To interact with this screen, we select the **Operator** row. Figures 5.10A through 5.10C show all of the operators available in this menu; these operators include **Equal to, Not equal to, Greater than, Greater than or equal to, Less than, Less than or equal to, Between, Contains**, and so on. We will select **Not equal to** and type in the value **2** in the **Value** panel (we could have selected the value of **2** from the **Value** drop-down menu instead). Our selections are shown in Figure 5.11.

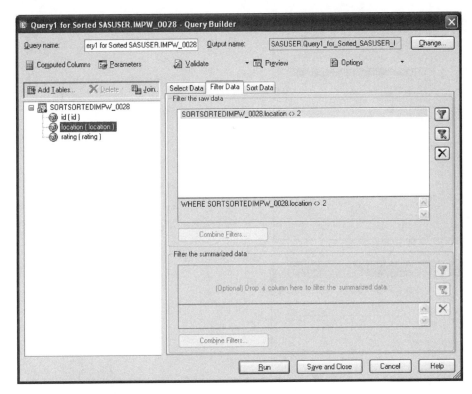

Figure 5.8. The **Filter Data** tab of the **Query** screen.

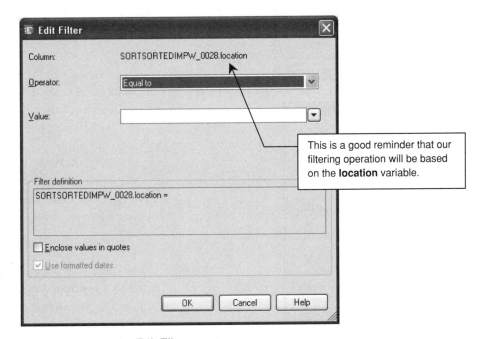

This is a good reminder that our filtering operation will be based on the **location** variable.

Figure 5.9. The opening **Edit Filter** screen.

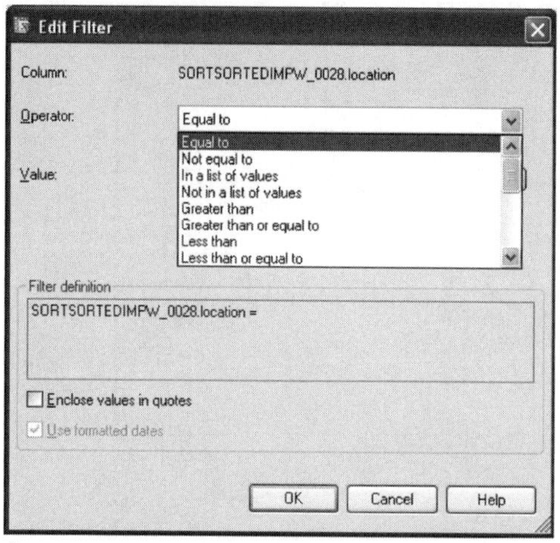

A

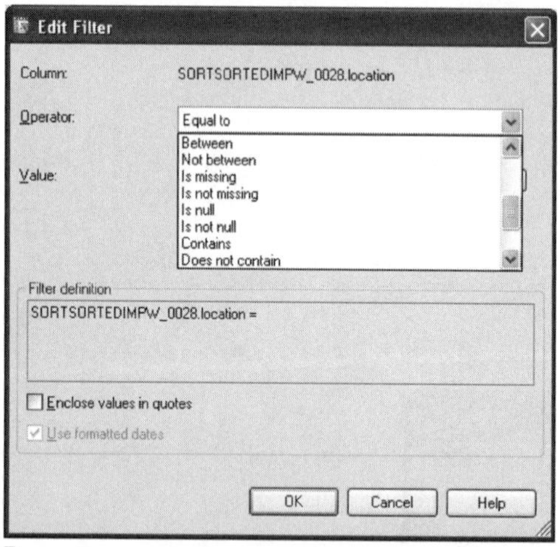

B

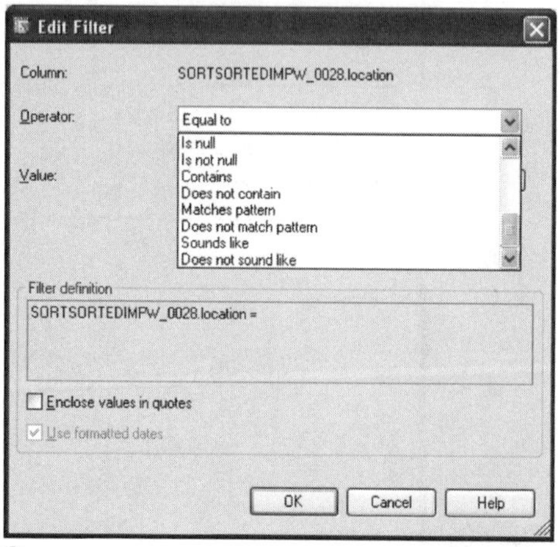

C

Figure 5.10. The **Operator** drop-down menu in the **Edit Filter** screen: A, top portion; B, middle portion; and C, bottom portion.

Figure 5.11. We have opted to select the **Not equal to** operator with a value of **2** (i.e., the location is not equal to 2).

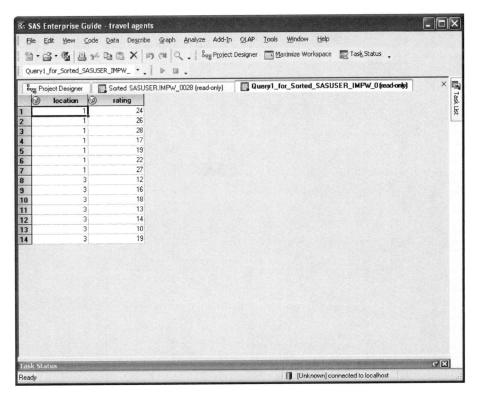

Figure 5.12. The filtered data set is now ready for further analysis.

Click **OK** to return to the main **Query** window and click **Run** to execute the procedure.

The result of this process is shown in Figure 5.12 together with the ratings of each travel agent in each group. We can now perform whatever data analysis we might wish, such as a t test, on this data set.

6 Recoding Existing Variables

6.1 Overview

To recode a variable is to change the values of a variable. In the process of doing this, we create another variable to represent these changes. Recoding is typically performed to achieve one of two goals:

- We may wish to modify or exchange the values of the variable. For example, items that are reverse worded in a survey must be realigned. Assume our inventory assesses self-esteem, with items rated on a 7-point scale with the anchor of 1 indicating *not very true for me* and the anchor of 7 indicating *very true for me*. Higher scores on the inventory reflect greater levels of self-esteem. Further assume that one of the several items on the inventory that is reverse worded reads, "I don't like myself." Respondents with high levels of self-esteem should rate this item quite low, perhaps a 1 or 2, whereas those with low levels of self-esteem should rate this item relatively high, perhaps with a 5 or 6. Before combining this item with the other items (which are positively worded), it must be reverse scored such that 1s must be converted to 7s, 2s converted to 6s, and so on prior to combining items together. In this sense, the values of the item (a variable in the data set) must be *recoded*.
- We may wish to consolidate codes or information. For example, each different ethnicity originally might be assigned a different code during data entry but we may need to combine individuals into ethnic groups for certain analyses. Thus, the ethnicity variable would have to be *recoded*.

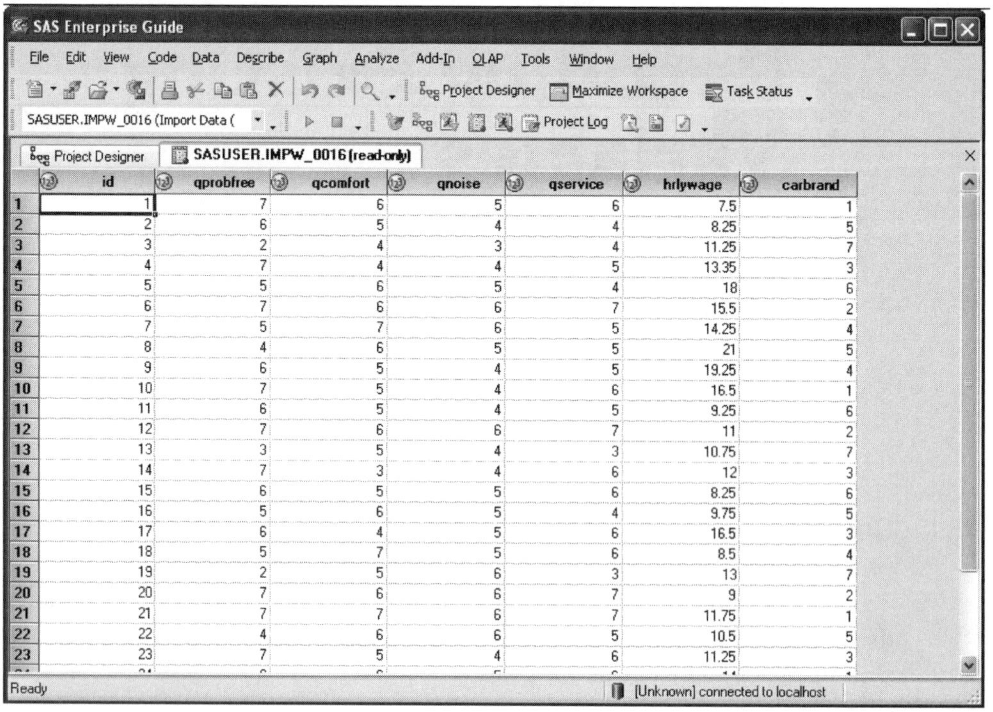

	id	qprobfree	qcomfort	qnoise	qservice	hrlywage	carbrand
1	1	7	6	5	6	7.5	1
2	2	6	5	4	4	8.25	5
3	3	2	4	3	4	11.25	7
4	4	7	4	4	5	13.35	3
5	5	5	6	5	4	18	6
6	6	7	6	6	7	15.5	2
7	7	5	7	6	5	14.25	4
8	8	4	6	5	5	21	5
9	9	6	5	4	5	19.25	4
10	10	7	5	4	6	16.5	1
11	11	6	5	4	5	9.25	6
12	12	7	6	6	7	11	2
13	13	3	5	4	3	10.75	7
14	14	7	3	4	6	12	3
15	15	6	5	5	6	8.25	6
16	16	5	6	5	4	9.75	5
17	17	6	4	5	6	16.5	3
18	18	5	7	5	6	8.5	4
19	19	2	5	6	3	13	7
20	20	7	6	6	7	9	2
21	21	7	7	6	7	11.75	1
22	22	4	6	6	5	10.5	5
23	23	7	5	4	6	11.25	3

Figure 6.1. A portion of the data set.

6.2 Numerical example

Our example is a hypothetical study of how satisfied recent car buyers were with their recently purchased automobile. They were asked to rate on a 7-point scale, in which 7 was the highest evaluation, how free the car was of problems (**qprobfree** in the data set), how comfortable the car was (**qcomfort** in the data set), the noise level while driving (**qnoise** in the data set), and the quality of the service by the dealership (**qservice** in the data set). The income of the buyers was recorded in terms of hourly wage (**hrlywage** in the data set). Finally, the brand of car (**carbrand** in the data set) was coded as follows: 1 = Honda, 2 = Toyota, 3 = Subaru, 4 = Nissan, 5 = GM, 6 = Ford, and 7 = Chrysler. A portion of the data set is shown in Figure 6.1.

6.3 Performing the recoding

In the present example, we wish to recode the four Japanese auto brands into the code of 1 and the American brands into a code of 2. Recoding of an existent variable

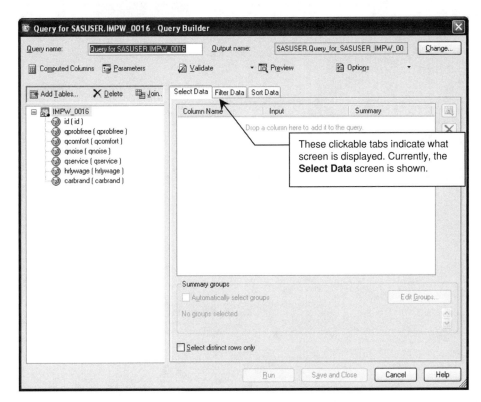

Figure 6.2. The main **Query** screen.

is defined by *SAS Enterprise Guide* as a *query* (see Chapter 5). To accomplish this recoding, select **Data → Filter and Query**. This brings you to the main **Query** screen as shown in Figure 6.2. The variables in the data set are listed in the panel on the left of the screen. Over the blank panel to its right are three tabs with the **Select Data** tab currently active. Because we want the full set of variables in the new data set containing the variable we intend to recode, we drag all of the variables over to the **Select Data** panel as shown in Figure 6.3.

We will be adding our recoded variable as a new column to the end of the data set. Thus, we click the **Computed Columns** push button toward the top left portion of the screen. This opens the **Computed Columns** dialog window (see Figure 6.4).

Click the **New** push button and select **Recode a Column** from the two-choice drop-down menu. This opens the **Select Item** screen as seen in Figure 6.5. Select the variable intended to be recoded – in this example it is **carbrand** – and click **Continue**.

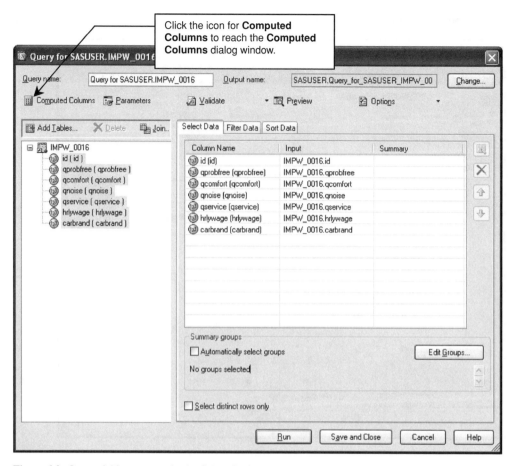

Figure 6.3. Our variables are now in the **Select Data** panel.

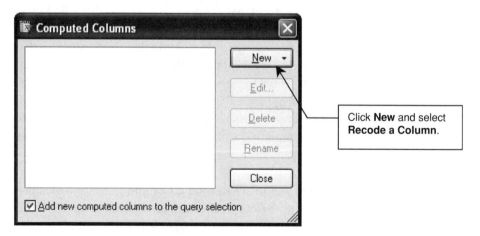

Figure 6.4. The opening **Computed Columns** window.

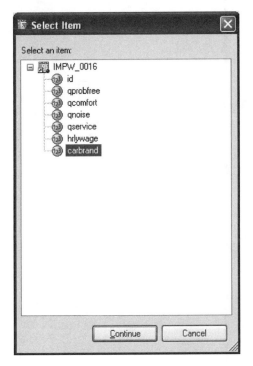

Figure 6.5. We have selected **carbrand** as the variable we intend to recode.

We have finally reached the **Recode Column** screen as shown in Figure 6.6. The new column name by default is given as **Recode_carbrand**; we will keep it but we could highlight it and type in a new name if we wished.

Clicking the **Add** push button activates the **Specify a Replacement** window (see Figure 6.7). It begins on the **Replace Values** tab, but not coincidentally, our values are already in ranges. Thus, we click the **Replace a Range** tab, which presents us with the screen shown in Figure 6.8.

The four Japanese cars are coded 1 through 4 in the original **carbrand** variable. We perform the following steps, the results of which are shown in Figure 6.9:

- Click the checkbox for **Set a lower limit** and type the value of **1** in the panel below it.
- Click the checkbox for **Set an upper limit** and type the value of **4** in the panel below it.
- In the panel below **With the value**, type the numeral 1.
- Click **OK** to return to the main **Recode Columns** screen.

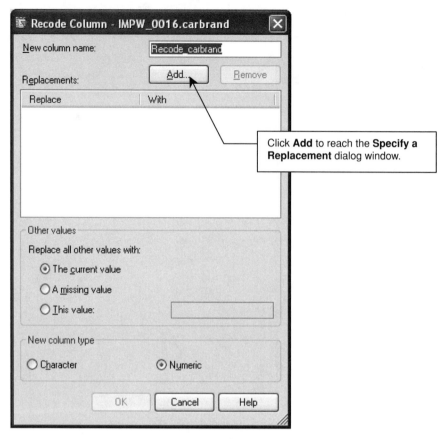

Click **Add** to reach the **Specify a Replacement** dialog window.

Figure 6.6. The main **Recode Column** screen.

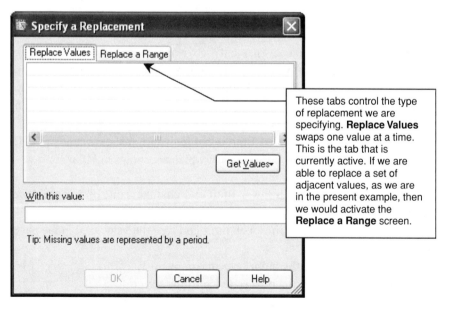

These tabs control the type of replacement we are specifying. **Replace Values** swaps one value at a time. This is the tab that is currently active. If we are able to replace a set of adjacent values, as we are in the present example, then we would activate the **Replace a Range** screen.

Figure 6.7. Here we specify the values we want to replace and the value to use instead.

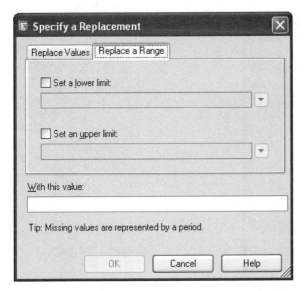

Figure 6.8. We will be replacing the range of Japanese cars with the value of 1.

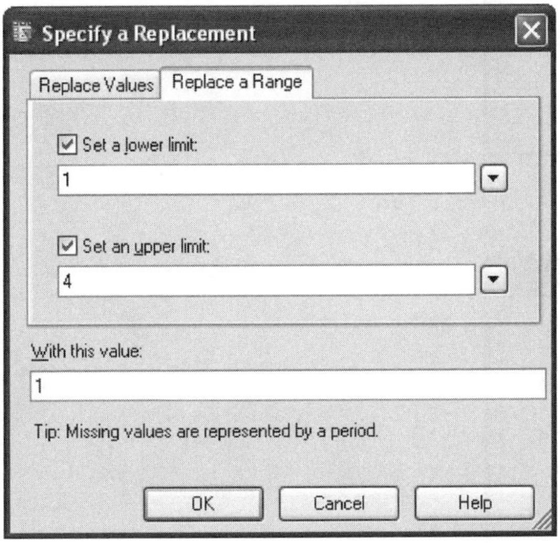

Figure 6.9. We have now recoded the range of values from 1 to 4 into the code of 1.

Figure 6.10 shows the results of this first half of our recoding work. The second half is accomplished in the same fashion. The American cars are coded 5 through 7 in the original **carbrand** variable. We click the **Add** push button and perform the same steps as in the previous list, but we use the appropriate numerical codes (see Figures 6.11 and 6.12).

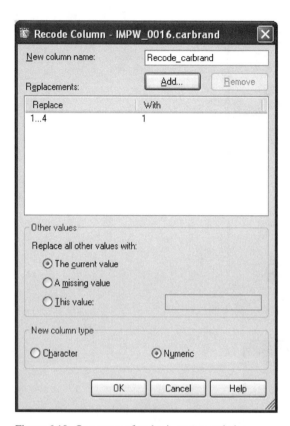

Figure 6.10. One range of codes is now recoded.

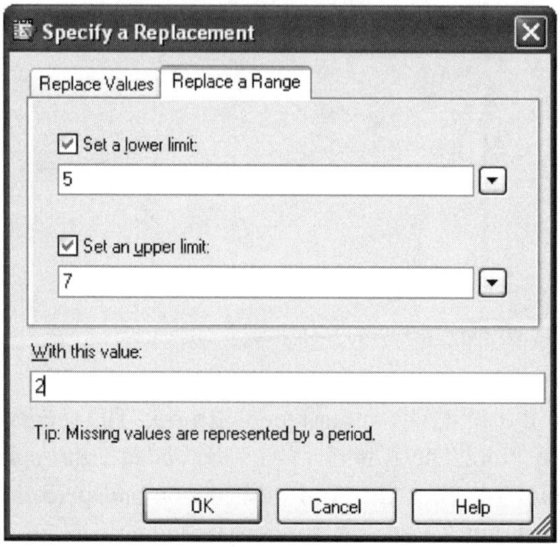

Figure 6.11. The second set and the last set of codes are now recoded.

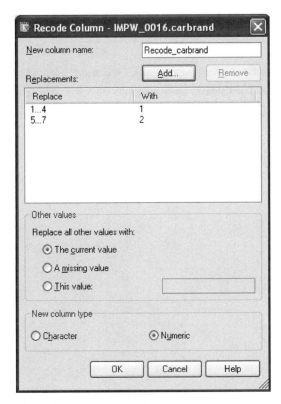

Figure 6.12. The full recoding is now set.

	id	qprobfree	qcomfort	qnoise	qservice	hrlywage	carbrand	Recode_carbrand
1	1	7	6	5	6	7.5	1	1
2	2	6	5	4	4	8.25	5	2
3	3	2	4	3	4	11.25	7	2
4	4	7	4	4	5	13.35	3	1
5	5	5	6	5	4	18	6	2
6	6	7	6	6	7	15.5	2	1
7	7	5	7	6	5	14.25	4	1
8	8	4	6	5	5	21	5	2
9	9	6	5	4	5	19.25	4	1
10	10	7	5	4	6	16.5	1	1
11	11	6	5	4	5	9.25	6	2
12	12	7	6	6	7	11	2	1
13	13	3	5	4	3	10.75	7	2
14	14	7	3	4	6	12	3	1
15	15	6	5	5	6	8.25	6	2
16	16	5	6	5	4	9.75	5	2
17	17	6	4	5	6	16.5	3	1
18	18	5	7	5	6	8.5	4	1
19	19	2	5	6	3	13	7	2
20	20	7	6	6	7	9	2	1
21	21	7	7	6	7	11.75	1	1
22	22	4	6	6	5	10.5	5	2
23	23	7	5	4	6	11.25	3	1

Figure 6.13. The data set now has the recoded variable as the last column.

The full recoding is now ready to be implemented. Click **OK** in the **Specify a Replacement** window to return to the **Computed Columns** screen. Click **Close** to return to the main **Query** screen. Click **Run** to perform the recode. The result of the recoding is shown in Figure 6.13. Our new variable, **Recode_carbrand**, appears at the end of the new data set.

7 Computing New Variables

7.1 Overview

To compute a new variable is to apply some type of mathematical or logical operation on the values of one or more variables. The results of the operation are placed in a separate column or variable with each case in the data set receiving the computed value. We illustrate in this chapter how to accomplish the following:

- We compute a new variable from an existing variable in Section 7.3.
- We compute a new variable by combining several variables in Section 7.4.

Chapter 14 addresses the issue of data transformations as a means of modifying the shape of a distribution. The process to accomplish a transformation is a variant on computing a new variable from an existent variable.

7.2 Numerical example

We continue with our example of automobile purchasers from Chapter 6. The data set, shown at the end of the chapter (see Figure 6.13), contains responses to the four survey questions (**qprobfree**, **qcomfort**, **qnoise**, and **qservice**), the hourly wage of the car buyers (**hrlywage**), the brand of car that was purchased (**carbrand**), and the recoded variable indicating whether the purchased car was produced by a Japanese or American company (**Recode_carbrand**).

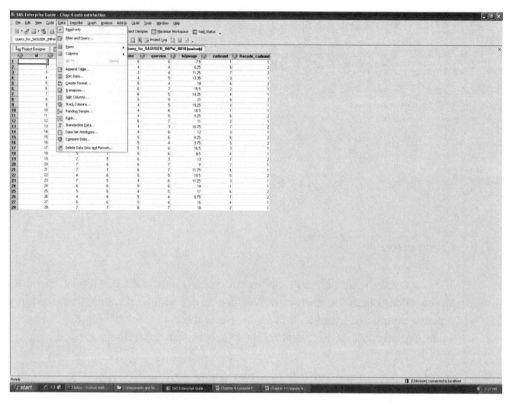

Figure 7.1. The data set is in the **Read-only** mode and has to be changed by selecting the checked box.

7.3 Computing a new variable from an existent variable

To demonstrate how to compute a new variable from an existent one, we will create a yearly wage variable by multiplying the hourly wage variable by 40 to obtain a weekly salary and by 52 to obtain a yearly salary. With the project open and the data set visible in the active window, select **Data → Read-only** from the main *SAS Enterprise Guide* menu as shown in Figure 7.1. Note that **Read-only** is currently checked as a way for SAS to protect the data set. Because we are going to have *SAS Enterprise Guide* compute a new variable (add a new variable to the data set), we must first lift the **Read-only** restriction.

Select the **Read-only** box. This will remove the **Read-only** restriction by switching to the **Update** mode, allowing the data set to be modified by users. A dialog box (see Figure 7.2) will ask you to confirm your choice; click the **Yes** push button. The data set is now in the **Update** mode (you can confirm this by clicking **Data** from the main menu and noting that the check next to **Read-only** is now gone).

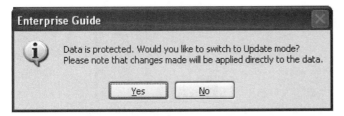

Figure 7.2. Confirmation that we wish to switch to the **Update** mode.

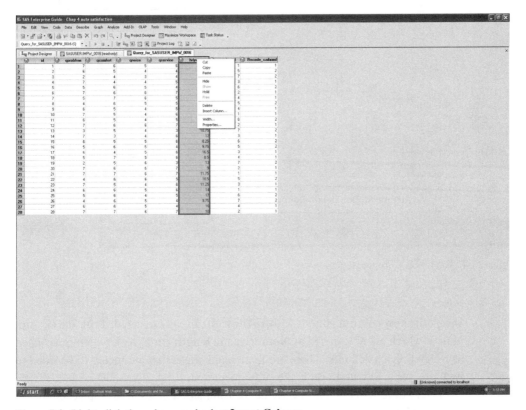

Figure 7.3. Right-click the column and select **Insert Column**.

Right-click the name of the hourly wage variable (**hrlywage**) at the top of its data column. This action will highlight the column and will cause a menu to appear as shown in Figure 7.3. Choose **Insert Column** from the drop-down menu to reach the **Column Properties** dialog window.

The **Insert Column** window opens on the **General** screen and is shown in Figure 7.4. There are four areas already filled in with *SAS Enterprise Guide* defaults:

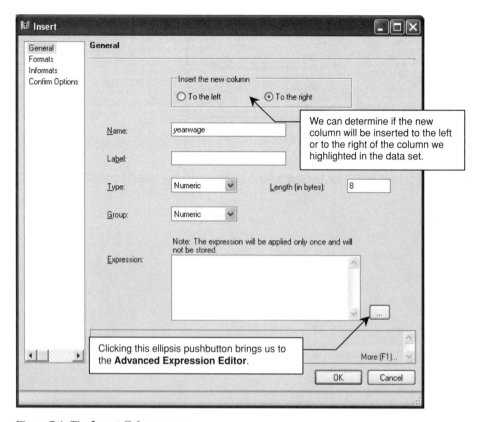

Figure 7.4. The **Insert Column** screen.

Insert the new column buttons with **To the right** already selected, **Type** and **Group**, both of which are designated as **Numeric**, and **length (in bytes)**, which is assigned as **8**. Keep these defaults. There are three blank areas that are meant to be filled in by users; we deal with these in the subsequent text.

By choosing **Insert Column**, we are causing a new column to be placed into the data set. Columns are variables in a spreadsheet and they must be assigned certain properties. Here, we are required to provide a **Name** for the variable and we have the opportunity to supply a more complete **Label** for it if we choose. We have created the name **yearwage** but forgo the label as the name is sufficiently descriptive of the variable for our purposes.

The **Expression** panel is where users type in the algebraic transformation that is to be performed. As an option, we can go to the more complete **Advanced Expression Editor** screen, which is what we do here. Click the little ellipsis (three-dot) push

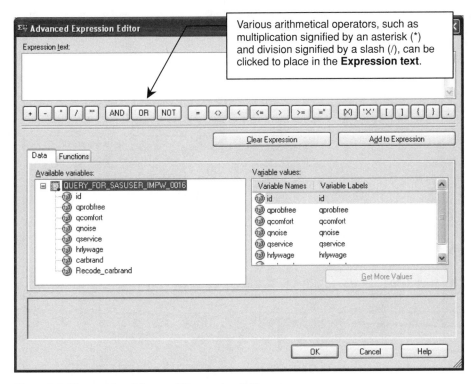

Figure 7.5. The opening **Advanced Expression Editor** screen.

button to reach the **Advanced Expression Editor** screen shown in Figure 7.5. We enter the dialog window on the **Data** tab and will remain here. Follow these steps, the result of which is shown in Figure 7.6:

- Highlight hrlywage in the **Available variables** panel.
- Click **Add to Expression**. This will place the variable into the top panel labeled **Expression text**.
- Click the asterisk in the row just below the **Expression text** panel. This is the multiplication operator.
- Type in the numeral **40**.
- Click the asterisk in the row just below the **Expression text** panel. This is the multiplication operator.
- Type in the numeral **52**.

Clicking **OK** brings us back to the **Insert Column** screen. Click **OK**. We are then presented with one last opportunity to take back our work (see Figure 7.7).

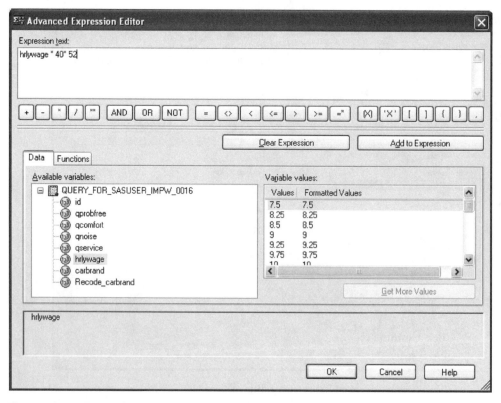

Figure 7.6. The **Expression text** panel is now complete.

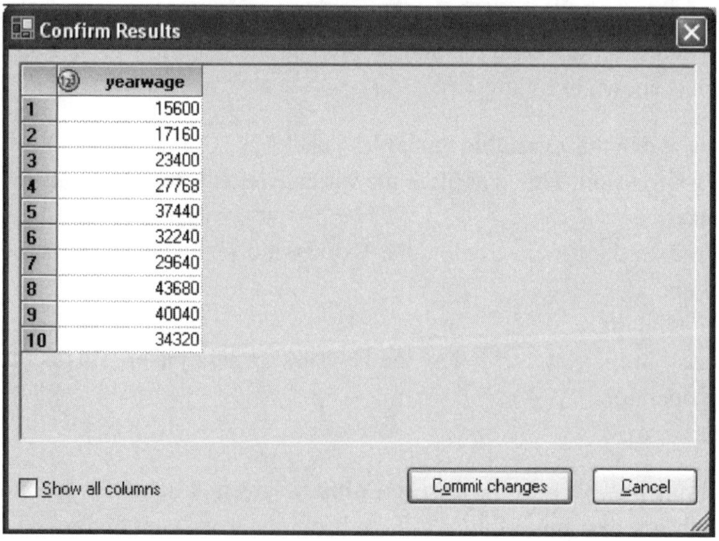

Figure 7.7. Click **Commit changes** to accept the computation.

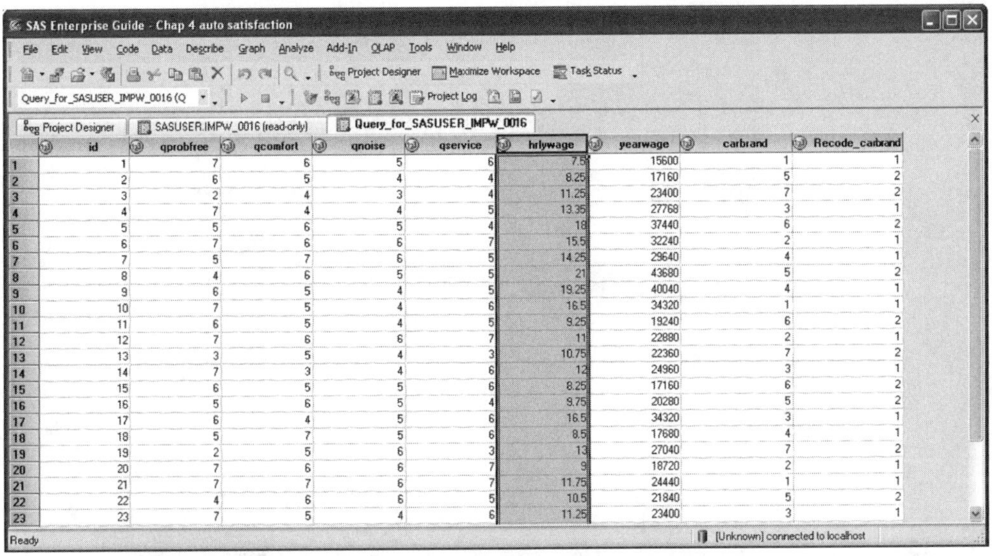

	id	qprobfree	qcomfort	qnoise	qservice	hrlywage	yearwage	carbrand	Recode_carbrand
1	1	7	6	5	6	7.5	15600	1	1
2	2	6	5	4	4	8.25	17160	5	2
3	3	2	4	3	4	11.25	23400	7	2
4	4	7	4	4	5	13.35	27768	3	1
5	5	5	6	5	4	18	37440	6	2
6	6	7	6	6	7	15.5	32240	2	1
7	7	5	7	6	5	14.25	29640	4	1
8	8	4	6	5	5	21	43680	5	2
9	9	6	5	4	5	19.25	40040	4	1
10	10	7	5	4	6	16.5	34320	1	1
11	11	6	5	4	5	9.25	19240	6	2
12	12	7	6	6	7	11	22880	2	1
13	13	3	5	4	3	10.75	22360	7	2
14	14	7	3	4	6	12	24960	3	1
15	15	6	5	5	6	8.25	17160	6	2
16	16	5	6	5	4	9.75	20280	5	2
17	17	6	4	5	6	16.5	34320	3	1
18	18	5	7	5	6	8.5	17680	4	1
19	19	2	5	6	3	13	27040	7	2
20	20	7	6	6	7	9	18720	2	1
21	21	7	7	6	7	11.75	24440	1	1
22	22	4	6	6	5	10.5	21840	5	2
23	23	7	5	4	6	11.25	23400	3	1

Figure 7.8. The newly computed variable is in the column to the right of **hrlywage**.

Click **Commit changes**, and the new variable is placed in the column to the right of **hrlywage** as shown in Figure 7.8.

7.4 Computing a new variable by combining several variables

Our goal here is to compute an overall satisfaction rating based on the four survey questions. We will compute the mean of the four responses for each buyer, which can be interpreted on the same 7-point scale used by the respondents to answer the individual survey.

Place the data set in the **Update** mode if it is not already in that state. Right-click the **qservice** column (see Figure 7.9) to insert a new column to the right of it as described in Section 7.3. In Figure 7.10 we have named the new variable that we will compute as **mean_satisfaction**. Click the little ellipsis (three-dot) push button to reach the **Advanced Expression Editor** screen. We enter the dialog window on the **Data** tab.

Select the **Functions** tab. This brings you to the screen shown in Figure 7.11. There are quite a few functions available in *SAS Enterprise Guide*, including absolute value, natural log, square root, and mean. In general, we select the function we intend to use, place the variable(s) in the expression, and then carry out that function. In this present example, we will compute the mean of the four satisfaction survey

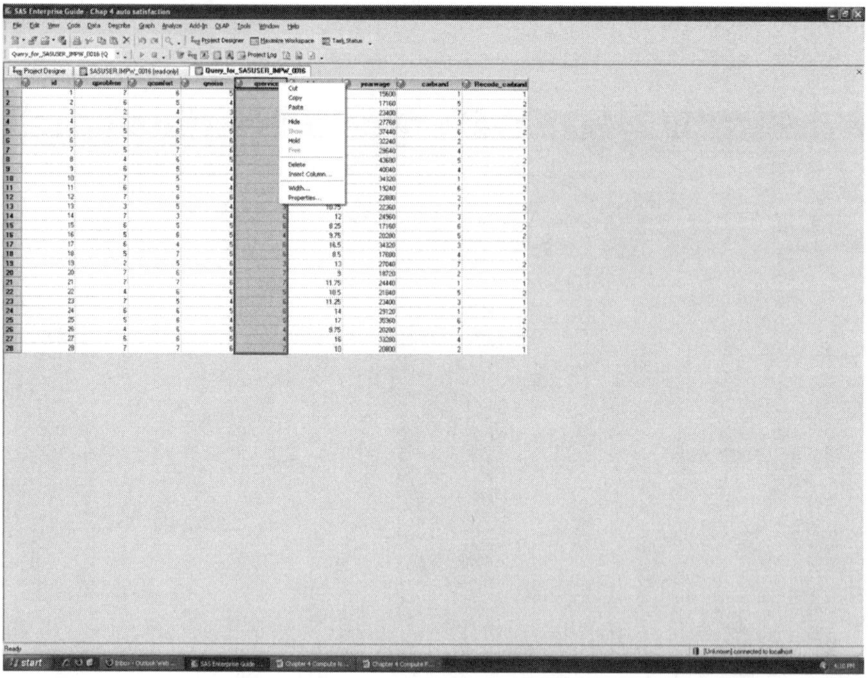

Figure 7.9. Right-click **qservice** to insert a column to its right.

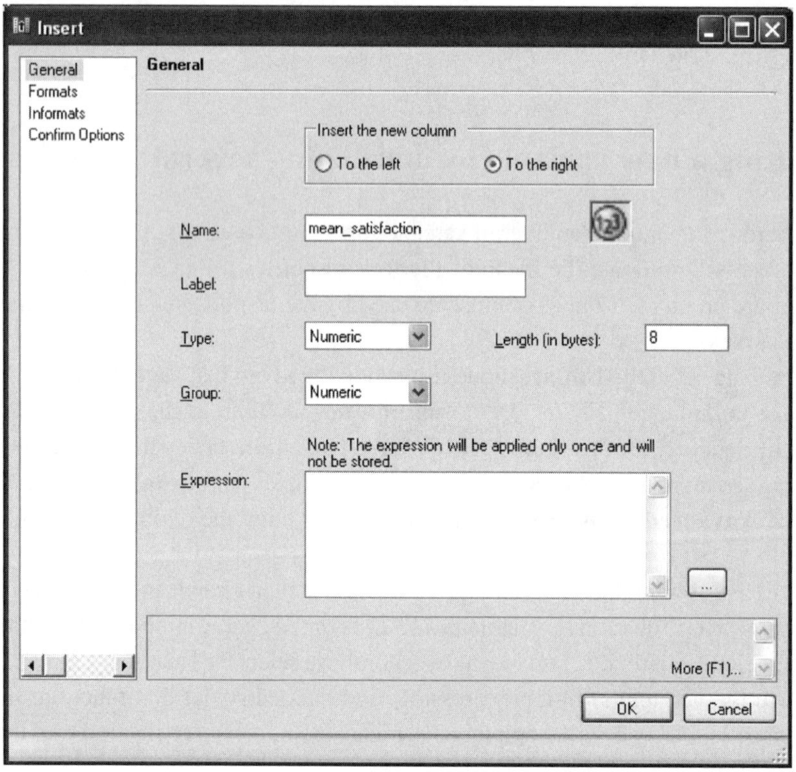

Figure 7.10. The new variable will be named **mean_satisfaction**.

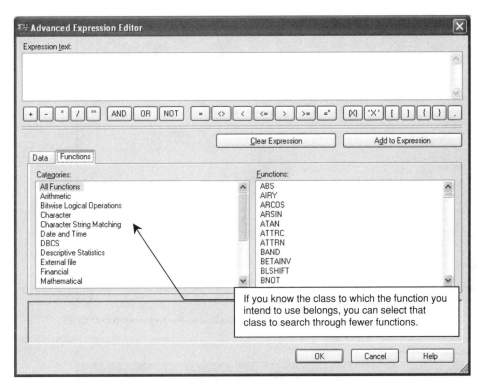

Figure 7.11. The **Functions** tab of the **Advanced Expression Editor**.

questions. As a result of performing this function, we will have a mean score on the four questions for each buyer in the data set.

Scroll down the alphabetically ordered functions panel to the Mean function (**MEAN**). The Mean function (**MEAN**) has to be placed in the **Expression text** panel by clicking the **Add to Expression** push button. This has been done in Figure 7.12. Now follow these steps:

- Select the **Data** tab.
- The expression <**numValue**>, <**numValue**> appears in the **Expression text** panel following the word **MEAN**. Delete <**numValue**>, <**numValue**> but retain the parentheses (see Figure 7.13).
- Keep the cursor inside the parentheses.
- Highlight **qprobfree** in the **Available variables** panel.
- Click the **Add to Expression** push button.
- Type a comma and a space.
- Repeat this for the next three survey question variables so that your screen matches what is shown in Figure 7.14. Do not place a comma following the last variable.

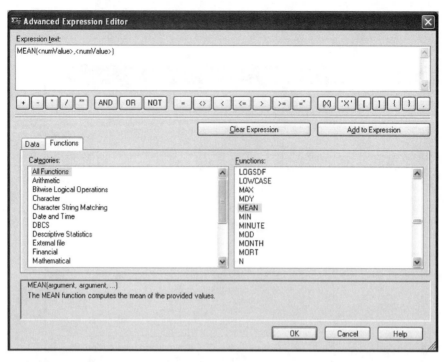

Figure 7.12. The function for computing the mean has been added to the **Expression text** panel.

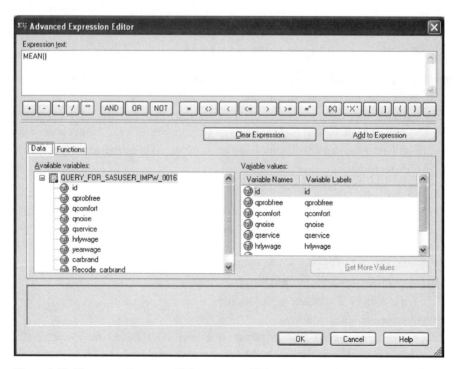

Figure 7.13. The expression <**numValue**>, <**numValue**> has been deleted from the parentheses.

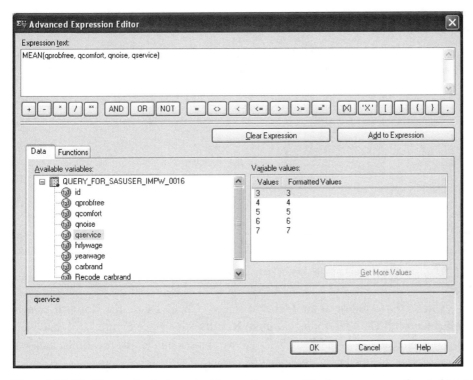

Figure 7.14. The **Expression text** panel will cause the mean of the four survey questions to be computed.

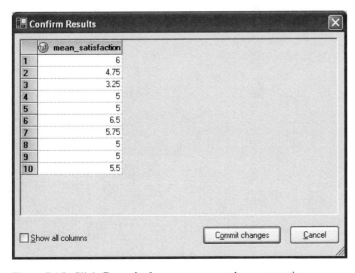

Figure 7.15. Click **Commit changes** to accept the computation.

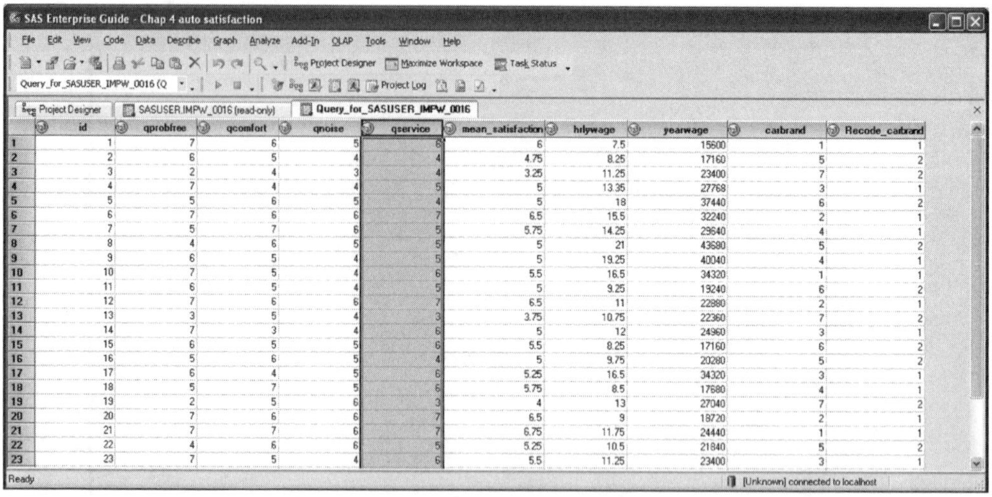

Figure 7.16. The data set now contains the **mean_satisfaction** variable.

Click **OK** to return to the **General** screen. Click **OK** on the **General** screen, click **Commit changes** on the **Confirm Results** screen (see Figure 7.15), and view the outcome as shown in Figure 7.16. As we can see on the first row of the data set, for example, the mean of 7, 6, 5, and 6 is 6.

Section IV

Describing Data

8 Descriptive Statistics

8.1 Overview

As an initial step in the statistical analysis process, it is useful to describe some of the characteristics of the variables in your data set. The statistics that are used to accomplish this are often referred to as *descriptive statistics*. Descriptive statistics focus on individual variables; they serve to characterize the distribution (set of scores) for each variable in the data set that researchers opt to examine.

8.2 Categories of descriptive statistics

Researchers may differ on which statistics they include in their particular or personalized set of descriptive statistics, but the set used by most researchers typically includes measures of both *central tendency* and *dispersion (variability)*.

8.2.1 Measures of central tendency

The following are commonly used measures of central tendency.

- *Mean*: This is the arithmetic average; it is sum of scores divided by N, the total number of cases with valid data entries for the variable.
- *Median*: This is the middle value of the distribution when the scores are ordered from lowest to highest.
- *Mode*: This is the score that occurs most frequently in the distribution.

8.2.2   Measures of dispersion

The following are commonly used measures of dispersion.

- *Minimum and maximum*: These are the lowest and highest values, respectively, in the distribution.
- *Variance*: This is the sum of squared deviations (the mean is subtracted from each score, each difference value is squared, and the squared values are summed) divided by $N - 1$. The variance represents the dispersion of scores around the mean.
- *Standard deviation*: This is computed as the square root of the variance. In a normal distribution, (a) the standard deviation is the distance between the mean and the inflexion point of the curve, and (b) a bit over 68% of the scores fall between 1.00 and -1.00 standard deviation unit, or ± 1.00 *SD*.
- *Standard Error of the Mean*: This is computed as the standard deviation divided by the square root of N. The standard error of the mean is used to generate a confidence interval around the mean. For example, a 95% confidence interval can be computed around the sample mean by multiplying the standard error of the mean by the value corresponding to appropriate degrees of freedom in the Student t distribution (for large sample sizes, one can use the normal curve value of ± 1.96 as a satisfactory approximation) and adding those values to the sample mean. We often use this 95% band or interval to assert with the given level of confidence that the true mean of the population lies within that value range (see Guilford & Fruchter, 1978 and Hays, 1981 for a traditional treatment of this topic; see Estes, 1997 and Rosenthal & Rosnow, 2008 for a discussion of the history and complexity of standard error and confidence intervals).
- *Skewness*: Skewness is the degree to which the distribution is symmetrical. Values between 0 and ± 0.5 represent a good approximation to symmetry, with the normal curve having a skewness of 0. Negatively skewed distributions have their "tails" pointing toward the left; positively skewed distributions have their tails pointing toward the right. Classically, values between ± 0.5 and ± 1.00 have been taken to suggest some asymmetry, and values in excess of ± 1.00 have been taken to represent more substantial departures from symmetry (see Meyers, Gamst, & Guarino, 2006). Recently, some authors have suggested additional or alternative criteria. For example, Curran, West, and Finch (1997) and Kline (2005) have proposed that values in excess of ± 3.00 can be considered extreme. In a similar vein, Warner (2008) has endorsed a proposal by SPSS that the statistical significance of skewness can be tested by using a z-score criterion of 1.96 (skewness divided by the standard error or skewness).
- *Kurtosis*: Kurtosis is the degree to which the distribution is peaked or flattened relative to the normal curve; values between 0 and ± 0.5 represent a degree of

kurtosis comparable with the normal curve whose value is 0. Negative kurtosis indicates that the distribution is relatively flatter than the normal curve (such distributions are *platykurtic*); positive kurtosis indicates that the distribution is relatively more peaked than the normal curve (such distributions are *leptokurtic*). Values between ± 0.5 and ± 1.00 suggest some kurtosis, and values in excess of ± 1.00 represent substantial kurtosis. Kline (2005) and DeCarlo (1997) have suggested that values in excess of ± 10.00 may be excessive and therefore of concern to researchers.

8.3 Numerical example

The data set we will use for our numerical example is based on a hypothetical random sample of 60 workers at a local factory. It is composed of four variables, two of which are quantitative and two of which are categorical. A portion of the data set is displayed in Figure 8.1.

8.3.1 Quantitative variables

The quantitative variables are motivation and beginning salary.

- *Motivation*: Scores can range from 0 to 25; higher values indicate greater motivation toward doing the job.
- *Beginning salary*: This is the yearly salary at which the individuals were hired.

8.3.2 Categorical variables

The categorical variables are school type and job type.

- *School type*: Individuals had attended either public schools (coded as 0) or private schools funded by a religious organization (coded as 1).
- *Job type*: Individuals were classified as unskilled (coded as 1), semiskilled (coded as 2), or skilled (coded as 3).

8.4 Obtaining basic descriptive statistics for the quantitative variables

From the main *SAS Enterprise Guide* menu, select **Describe → Summary Statistics**. This brings you to the **Task Roles** window. Drag **Motivation** to the slot under

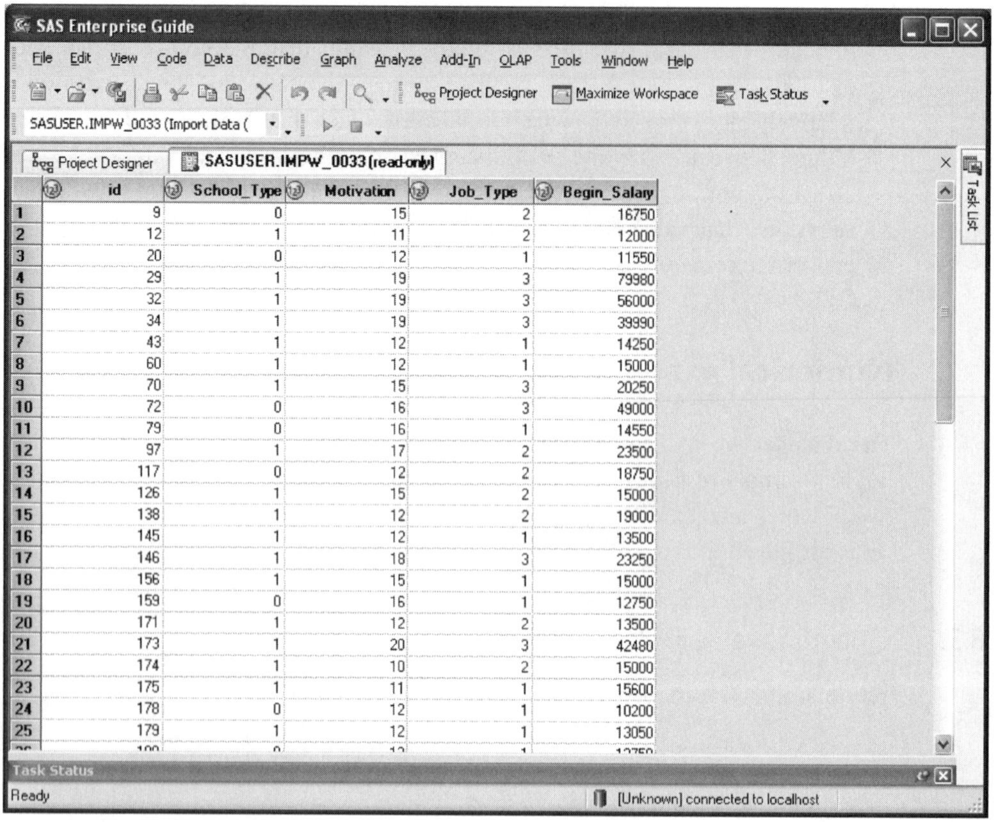

	id	School_Type	Motivation	Job_Type	Begin_Salary
1	9	0	15	2	16750
2	12	1	11	2	12000
3	20	0	12	1	11550
4	29	1	19	3	79980
5	32	1	19	3	56000
6	34	1	19	3	39990
7	43	1	12	1	14250
8	60	1	12	1	15000
9	70	1	15	3	20250
10	72	0	16	3	49000
11	79	0	16	1	14550
12	97	1	17	2	23500
13	117	0	12	2	18750
14	126	1	15	2	15000
15	138	1	12	2	19000
16	145	1	12	1	13500
17	146	1	18	3	23250
18	156	1	15	1	15000
19	159	0	16	1	12750
20	171	1	12	2	13500
21	173	1	20	3	42480
22	174	1	10	2	15000
23	175	1	11	1	15600
24	178	0	12	1	10200
25	179	1	12	1	13050

Figure 8.1. A portion of the data set.

Analysis variables in the rightmost panel. Repeat this for **Begin_Salary**. This is shown in Figure 8.2.

From the navigation panel on the far left select **Statistics**. This will bring you to the **Statistics > Basic** window. Some statistics are the defaults for *SAS Enterprise Guide* and their checkboxes are already selected: **Mean**, **Standard deviation**, **Minimum**, **Maximum**, and **Number of observations**. As seen in Figure 8.3, we have also selected **Standard error**.

From the navigation panel on the far left select **Percentiles**. As shown in Figure 8.4, select **Lower quartile**, **Median**, and **Upper quartile**. Keep **Order statistics** (this is the default) under **Quartile method**.

From the navigation panel on the far left select **Additional**. As we can see in Figure 8.5, select **Confidence limits of the mean**. When you select this choice, the

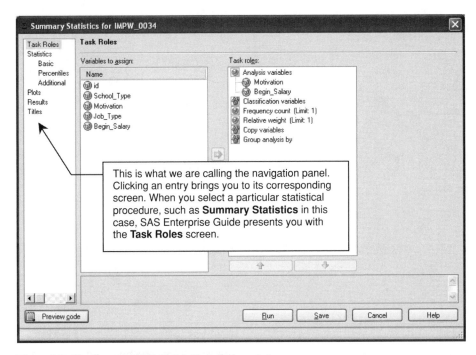

Figure 8.2. The **Summary Statistics Task Roles** window.

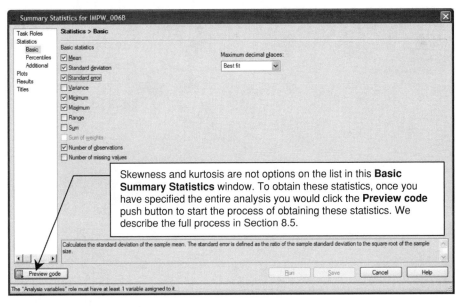

Figure 8.3. The **Summary Statistics > Basic** window.

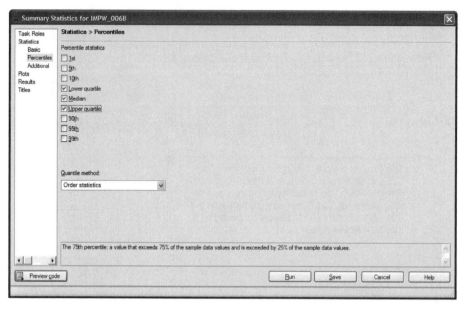

Figure 8.4. The **Summary Statistics > Percentiles** window.

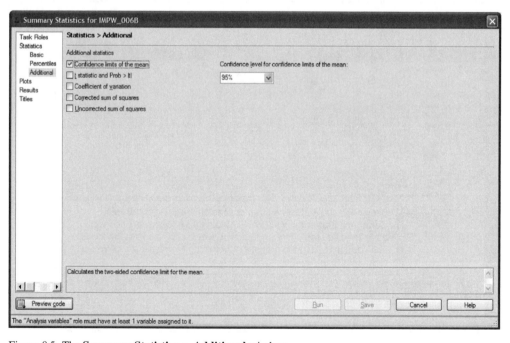

Figure 8.5. The **Summary Statistics > Additional** window.

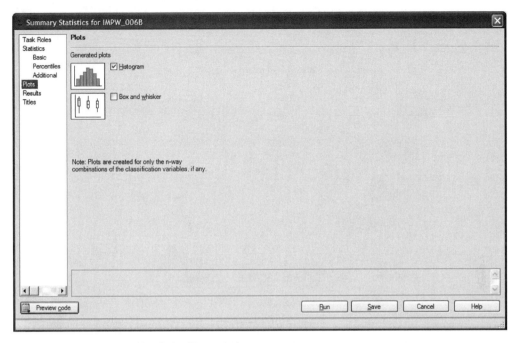

Figure 8.6. The **Summary Statistics Plots** window.

Summary Statistics

Results

The MEANS Procedure

Variable	Label	Mean	Std Dev	Std Error	Minimum	Maximum	N	Lower Quartile	Median	Upper Quartile	Lower 95% CL for Mean	Upper 95% CL for Mean
Motivation	Motivation	13.4333333	2.9421926	0.3798354	8.0000000	20.0000000	60	12.0000000	12.0000000	15.5000000	12.6732844	14.1933823
Begin_Salary	Begin_Salary	20844.67	13772.50	1778.02	10200.00	79980.00	60	12750.00	15300.00	23125.00	17286.85	24402.48

Figure 8.7. The summary statistics.

Confidence level for confidence limits of the mean panel will be activated. We suggest keeping the **95%** value.

From the navigation panel on the far left select **Plots**. As shown in Figure 8.6, you have available both a histogram and box and whisker plots. For illustration purposes here, select **Histogram**. With the analysis now configured, select the **Run** push button to perform the analysis.

The output table presenting the summary statistics is presented in Figure 8.7. Note that the statistics that we requested are presented in the table. Each variable occupies a row in the table; columns represent the requested information regarding

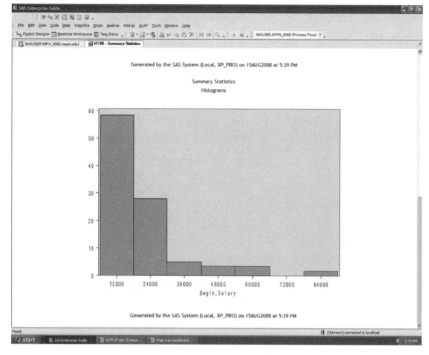

Figure 8.8. The histogram for **Begin_Salary**.

the variables. For example, the **Motivation** mean is approximately 13.43; its 95% confidence limit (**CL** in the output) is approximately 12.67 to 14.19. We can therefore assert, with a confidence of 95%, that the true mean of the population falls within the range between 12.67 and 14.19.

The histograms appear under the output table. We show in Figure 8.8 the distribution for **Begin_Salary**. Note through visual inspection that the distribution appears to be positively skewed. Unfortunately, *SAS Enterprise Guide* does not provide menu choices for obtaining the skewness and kurtosis values. To acquire these, we must write a couple of words in SAS code.

8.5 Obtaining skewness and kurtosis statistics

Skewness and kurtosis are sufficiently important that it is worth supplementing our point-and-click treatment by entering a few words of SAS code to obtain these statistics. Set up the analysis as described in Section 8.4. After specifying your plot, click the **Preview code** push button located in the lower left corner of the screen (pointed

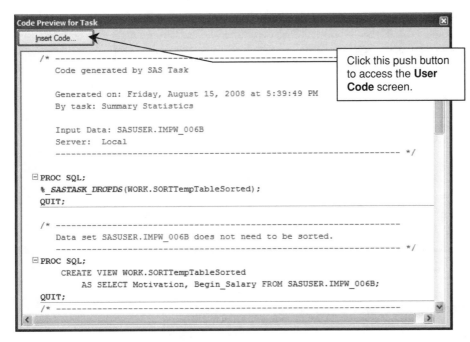

Figure 8.9. The **Code Preview for Task** window.

out in Figure 8.3). That brings you to the **Code Preview for Task** window shown in Figure 8.9. Click the **Insert Code** push button to open the **User Code** screen.

The **User Code** window is shown in Figure 8.10. Scroll down to the area just below the listing of the descriptive statistics as shown in Figure 8.11. Just below the letters **CLM** (these stand for "confidence limits of the mean") you will see a tinted line with the expression <**double-click to insert code**>. Double-click any place in the tinted area.

Double-clicking in the tinted area will open the **Enter User Code** window with the cursor at the start of the first line. Type the word **skewness** followed by ↵ **Enter** (uppercase or lowercase lettering is okay as *SAS Enterprise Guide* is not case sensitive in this window). Then type the word **kurtosis**. This is shown in Figure 8.12. Once you have completed the typing, click the **OK** push button. This will return you to the **User Code** window, where you will now see the code that you have just entered (see Figure 8.13). Click the **OK** push button in the bottom of the **User Code** window to confirm your typed code. Close the **Code Preview for Task** window (click the **X** in the upper right corner of the window) and click the **Run** push button in the **Summary Statistics** window (which is active once you close the **Code Preview for Task** window) to obtain the output.

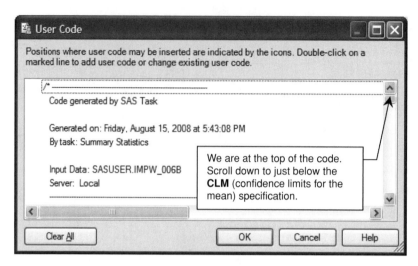

Figure 8.10. The initial **User Code** window.

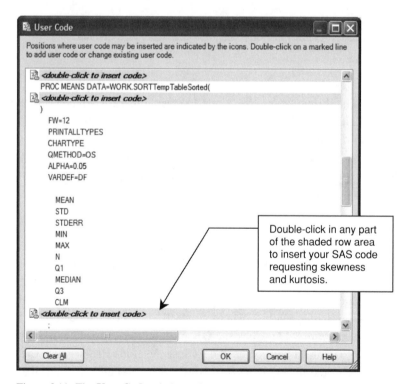

Figure 8.11. The **User Code** window where you will be inserting SAS code.

Figure 8.12. The **Enter User Code** window with the necessary code typed in.

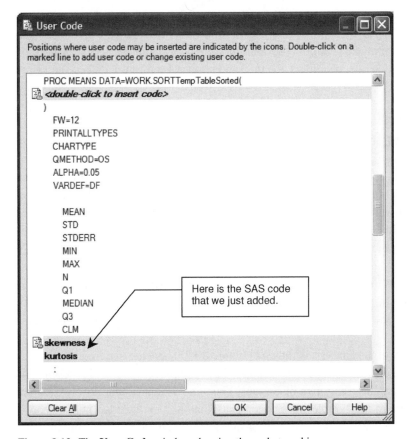

Figure 8.13. The **User Code** window showing the code typed in.

The statistics results, complete with the skewness and kurtosis values, are shown in Figure 8.14. For example, the mean beginning salary was $20,844.67. However, viewing its histogram (see Figure 8.8) and noting that it has a skewness value of approximately 2.46, we can determine that the distribution is fairly positively

Summary Statistics
Results

The MEANS Procedure

Variable	Label	Mean	Std Dev	Std Error	Minimum	Maximum	N	Lower Quartile	Median	Upper Quartile	Lower 95% CL for Mean	Upper 95% CL for Mean	Skewness	Kurtosis
Motivation	Motivation	13.4333333	2.9421926	0.3798354	8.0000000	20.0000000	60	12.0000000	12.0000000	15.5000000	12.6732844	14.1933823	0.2844336	-0.2149721
Begin_Salary	Begin_Salary	20844.67	13772.50	1778.02	10200.00	79980.00	60	12750.00	15300.00	23125.00	17286.85	24402.48	2.4626404	6.6673282

Figure 8.14. Output with skewness and kurtosis.

skewed. In this case, the median (which is the middle value) of $15,300.00 may be a somewhat better representation of the central tendency of the distribution. The kurtosis value of approximately 6.67 informs us that the distribution is considerably more peaked than the normal curve is; as we can see in the histogram, this compression seems evident for the scores toward the lower end of the salary range.

8.6 Obtaining frequency counts for the categorical variables

Because type of school and job type are categorical, the only type of description that is appropriate for these variables is a frequency count. From the main *SAS Enterprise Guide* menu, select **Describe → One-Way Frequencies**. This brings you to the **Task Roles** window. Drag **School_Type** to the slot under **Analysis variables** in the rightmost panel. Repeat this for **Job_Type**. This is shown in Figure 8.15.

From the navigation panel on the far left, select **Statistics**. This will bring you to the **Statistics** window. The default used by *SAS Enterprise Guide* is sufficient for our purposes and is shown in Figure 8.16. Click the **Run** push button to perform the analysis.

The output of the analysis is shown in Figure 8.17. There are two frequency tables in the output, one for each of our variables. For example, the first table presents the frequencies for the categories of **School_Type** and indicates that 26 (43.33%) of the 60 people in the sample were coded as 0; that is, they attended public school. Note that the lower row of the **Cumulative Frequency** column presents the total sample size in that it shows the sum of the first row (the 26 people who attended public school) and the second row (the 34 people who attended private religious school).

This **Frequencies** procedure in SAS is one way in which we would obtain the mode of the distribution, which can be used to describe both categorical and quantitative variables. In the output for **Job_Type** for example, we note that

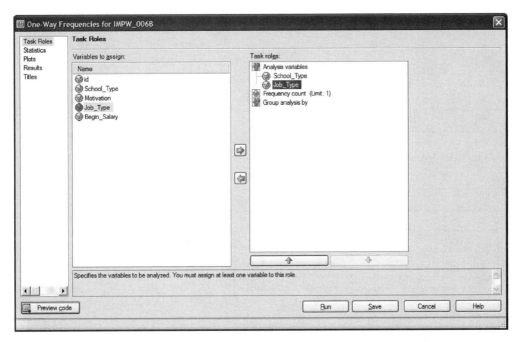

Figure 8.15. The **One-Way Frequencies Task Roles** window.

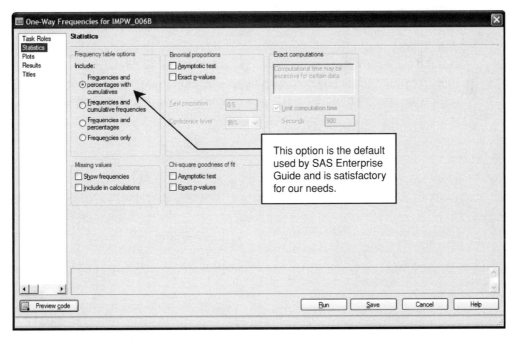

Figure 8.16. The **One-Way Frequencies Statistics** window.

One-way Frequencies

Results

The FREQ Procedure

School_Type				
School_Type	Frequency	Percent	Cumulative Frequency	Cumulative Percent
0	26	43.33	26	43.33
1	34	56.67	60	100.00

> **Cumulative Frequency** provides a running total count down the rows of the table.

Job Type				
Job_Type	Frequency	Percent	Cumulative Frequency	Cumulative Percent
1	23	38.33	23	38.33
2	17	28.33	40	66.67
3	20	33.33	60	100.00

Figure 8.17. The output of the analysis.

Job_Type 1 (unskilled workers) was most represented in the sample. Although it is technically correct, it is somewhat "awkward" to talk about the mode for a set of three possible values; however, with larger ranges of possible values for a variable it becomes more "comfortable" to identify one of the values as the mode.

9 Graphing Data

9.1 Overview

Pictures are one of the oldest and most effective ways to communicate, and they are marvelous devices to make numerical information come alive. Graphs of data summaries can be seen regularly in the professional literature, and most statistical software packages can produce various types of displays. *SAS Enterprise Guide* has a variety of pictorial representations available in its **Graph** menu. We present two of them in this chapter: bar charts and line plots. Knowing the basics of structuring these will allow you to work with others types of graphic displays as your needs dictate.

9.2 Numerical example

The data set for this example is shown in Figure 9.1. Twenty-four medium-sized cities (with their identity represented in the data set by **id** codes) from one of two different eastern regions in the United States (northeast or southeast **region** in the data set) were tracked by the amount of money that was invested in development projects (e.g., building offices and shopping space) within their jurisdictions during the spring of a recent year. This development took place in either downtown or suburban areas (**city part** in the data set). The dollar figure (shown under the variable named **development**) is the number of dollars in millions. Knowing that we are going to focus on graphing summaries of the results in which the levels of the variables will appear in the graphs, we have defined **region** and **city part** as character variables and have used words rather than numeric codes to identify the levels of these variables.

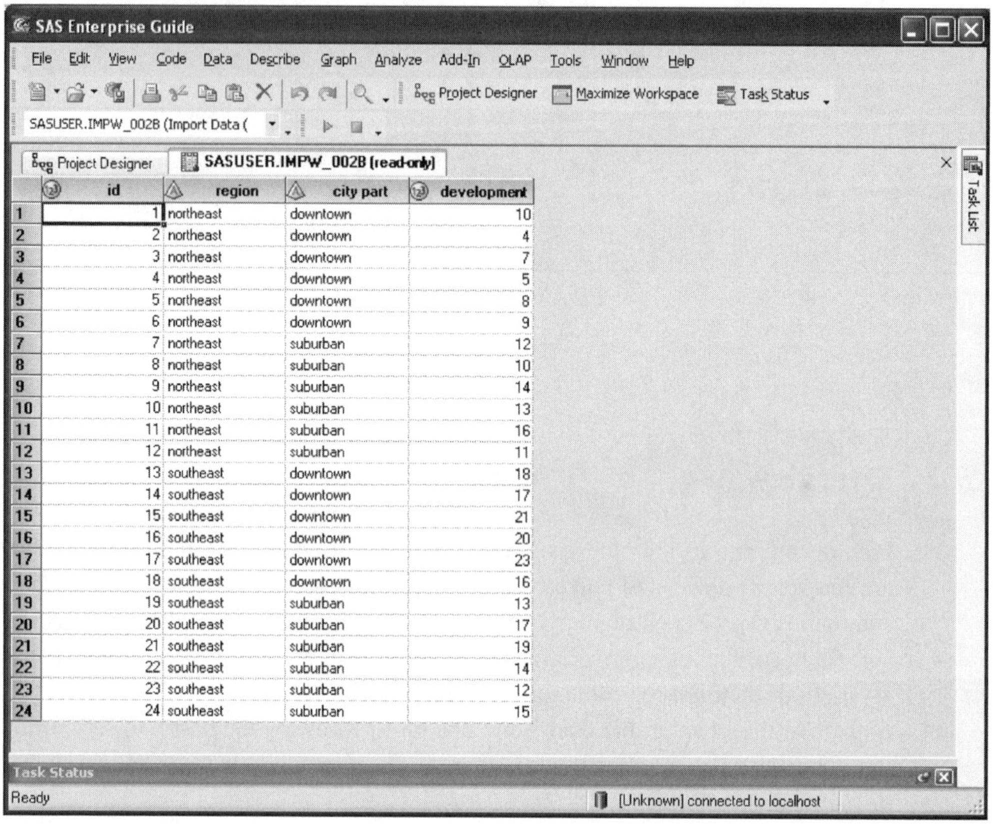

	id	region	city part	development
1	1	northeast	downtown	10
2	2	northeast	downtown	4
3	3	northeast	downtown	7
4	4	northeast	downtown	5
5	5	northeast	downtown	8
6	6	northeast	downtown	9
7	7	northeast	suburban	12
8	8	northeast	suburban	10
9	9	northeast	suburban	14
10	10	northeast	suburban	13
11	11	northeast	suburban	16
12	12	northeast	suburban	11
13	13	southeast	downtown	18
14	14	southeast	downtown	17
15	15	southeast	downtown	21
16	16	southeast	downtown	20
17	17	southeast	downtown	23
18	18	southeast	downtown	16
19	19	southeast	suburban	13
20	20	southeast	suburban	17
21	21	southeast	suburban	19
22	22	southeast	suburban	14
23	23	southeast	suburban	12
24	24	southeast	suburban	15

Figure 9.1. The data set for our numerical example.

9.3 Constructing bar charts

From the main *SAS Enterprise Guide* menu select **Graph → Bar Chart**. The window that opens is shown in Figure 9.2. We need to select the type of display we will use from an array of different types of bar charts. The icons provide a generic preview of what each will look like. Given that we have two classification variables, the geographic region of the country and the part of the city in which the development occurred, we need to select a bar chart that allows us to view their systematic combination. There is a certain element of user preference that enters into this decision, as many of the available choices meet this criterion, so our choice may not precisely coincide with yours. We have selected the structure labeled **3D Grouped Vertical Colored Groups** as shown in Figure 9.3.

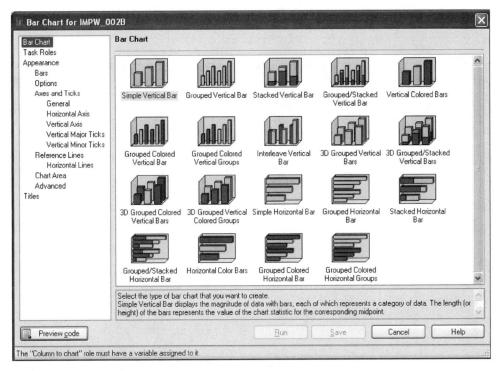

Figure 9.2. The initial **Bar Chart** window in which we choose the type of chart.

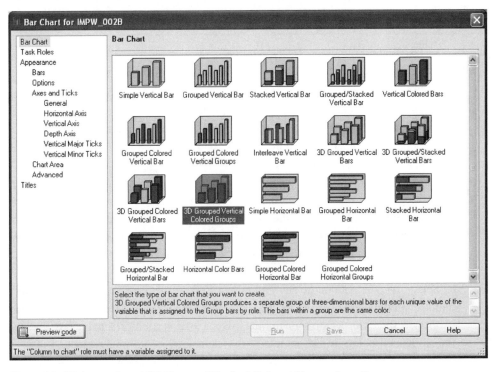

Figure 9.3. We have selected **3D Grouped Vertical Colored Groups** from the array.

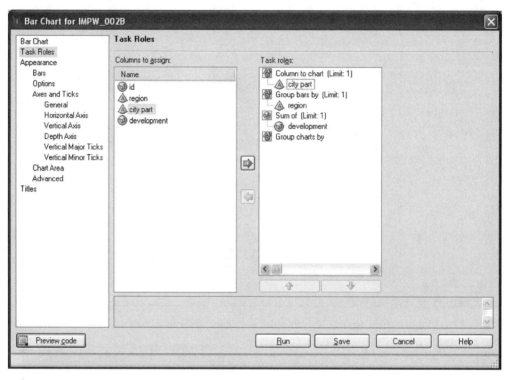

Figure 9.4. The **Task Roles** screen of **Bar Chart**.

Double-clicking the icon of **3D Grouped Vertical Colored Groups** brings us to the **Task Roles** screen as seen in Figure 9.4. The easiest role to assign is the **Sum of** role, because that is the quantitative variable on which we are focused. In our example, that is the **development** variable, and we drag it over first. It will be the vertical axis of the bar chart.

The more difficult decision is how to group the bars. We opt here to have the part of the city (downtown and suburban) on the horizontal axis. For each city area we want to see two bars, one for the northeast region and the other for the southeast region. These bars will be lined up one behind the other. To accomplish such a configuration we drag **city part** to the icon for **Column to chart** and we drag **region** to the icon for **Group bars by**.

Select **Appearance** in the navigation panel. This opens the **Appearance > Bars** dialog window shown in Figure 9.5. The drop-down menu under **Scheme** allows us to vary the color scheme of the bars. By selecting a color scheme, we can see the associated colors in the sample bars. The selection will not be locked in until we navigate to another window or click the **Run** push button; users can thus try

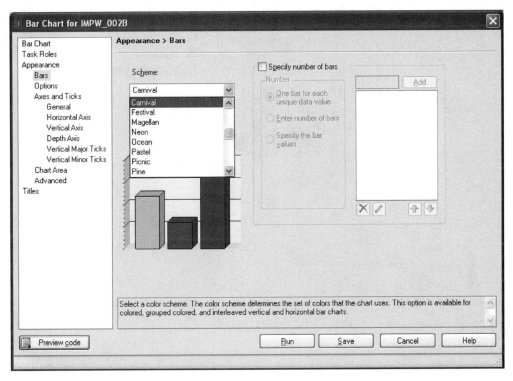

Figure 9.5. We have selected **Carnival** as our color scheme.

out several different schemes until settling on the one they prefer. We have chosen **Carnival** as our color scheme because it provides a good contrast between the light and dark colors.

Selecting **Options** under **Appearance** in the navigation panel brings us to the **Appearance > Options** dialog window shown in Figure 9.6. The drop-down menu under **Shape** allows us to vary the shape of the bars. We have chosen **Cylinder** as our shape.

Click **Vertical axis** in the navigation panel. Under the **Label** tab we are invited to provide a label for the axis and have done so in Figure 9.7. The other axes are labeled as a default by taking the words from the data set, and we need not change them. Click **Run** to generate the graph.

The completed bar chart is shown in Figure 9.8. Note that **downtown** is located on the left because it was the first level of **city part** recorded in the data set. Similarly, the **northeast** bar is in front of the **southeast** bar because it was the first level of **region** recorded in the data set. The graph makes it very clear that downtown areas

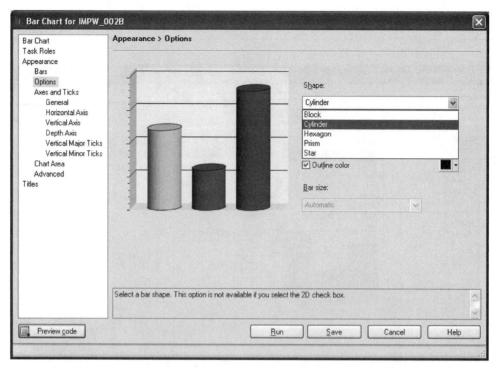

Figure 9.6. We have selected **Cylinder** as the shape of our bars.

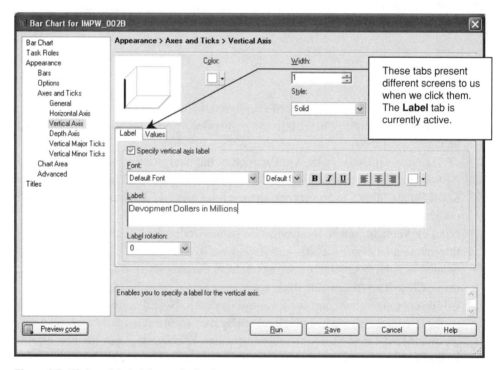

Figure 9.7. We have labeled the vertical axis.

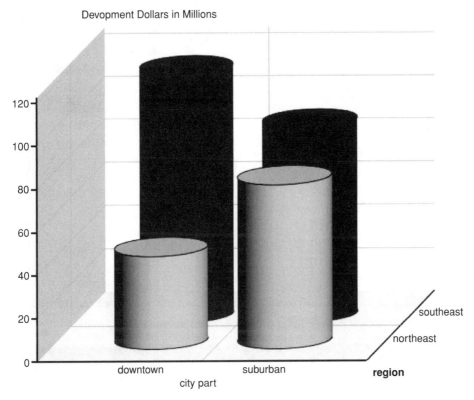

Figure 9.8. The finished bar chart.

were developed more heavily in southeastern rather than northeastern cities, whereas there was a closer alignment between the regions in suburban development.

9.4 Constructing line plots

From the main *SAS Enterprise Guide* menu, select **Graph → Line Plot**. The window that opens is shown in Figure 9.9. As was true in constructing a bar chart, once again we need to select from an array of different types of displays. This time there is only one that is appropriate for our needs; we select **Multiple line plots by group column**.

Double-clicking the icon for **Multiple line plots by group column** brings us to the **Task Roles** screen shown in Figure 9.10. The easiest role to assign is the **Vertical** role, because that is the quantitative variable on which we are

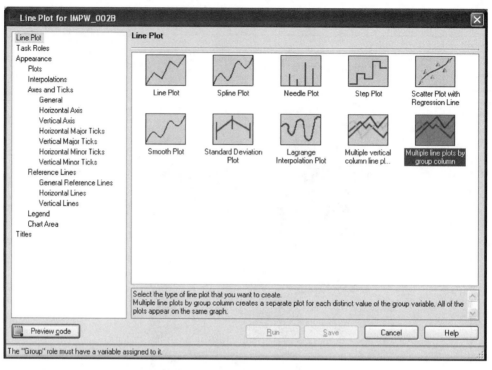

Figure 9.9. We select the line plot named **Multiple line plots by group column**.

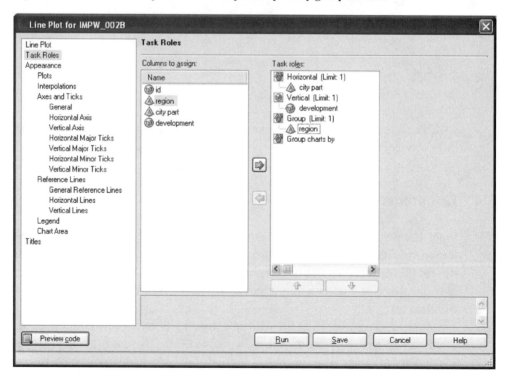

Figure 9.10. The **Task Roles** screen for **Line Plot**.

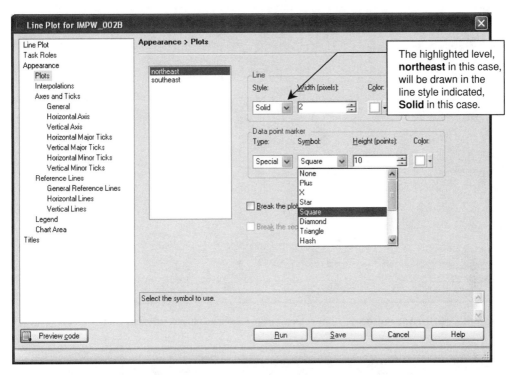

Figure 9.11. In the **Appearance > Plots** screen we see that **northeast** will be drawn in a solid line.

focused. In our example, that is the **development** variable, and we drag it over first.

The other two variables are both categorical and it is arbitrary as to which is placed on the horizontal axis and which has its levels represented by separate lines. We opt to place **city part** on the **Horizontal** axis of the plot. Under **Group** we place our **region** variable, which will give us separate lines for each of the two regions in the data set.

Clicking **Appearance** in the navigation panel brings us to the **Appearance > Plots** dialog screen (see Figure 9.11). We note that **northeast** is highlighted on the opening screen and that it will be drawn in a solid line (**Solid** is the default for all lines). We accept that. For its **Symbol**, we have selected **Square** from the drop-down menu. Now highlight **southeast**.

When we highlight **southeast** we note that it, too, is set to be drawn in the default solid line. Using the drop-down menu, we select **Dashed** instead as shown in Figure 9.12. For its **Symbol**, we have selected **Star** from the drop-down menu.

Click **Horizontal axis** in the navigation panel. Under the **Label** tab we are invited to provide a label for the axis and have done so in Figure 9.13.

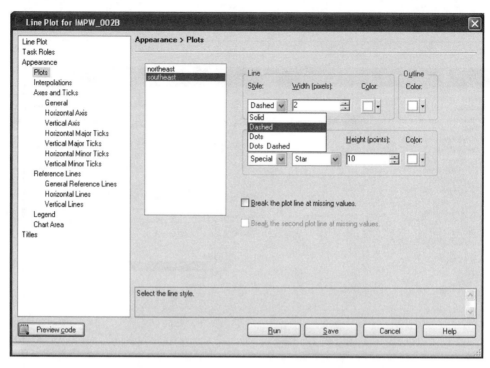

Figure 9.12. In the **Appearance > Plots** screen we have indicated that **southeast** will be drawn in a dashed line.

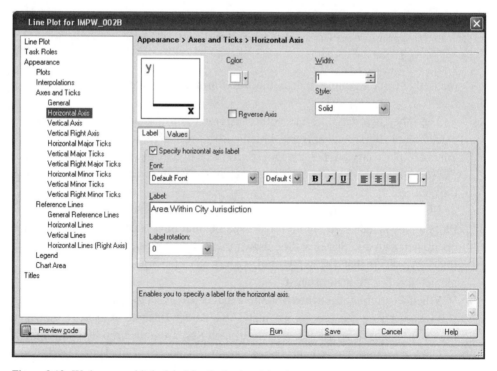

Figure 9.13. We have provided a label for the horizontal axis.

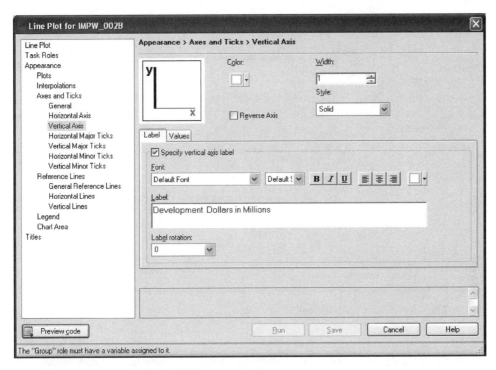

Figure 9.14. We have provided a label for the vertical axis.

Click **Vertical axis** in the navigation panel. Under the **Label** tab we are invited to provide a label for the axis and have done so in Figure 9.14.

Clicking **Legend** in the navigation panel opens the **Appearance > Legend** dialog screen (see Figure 9.15). The checkbox for **Outside** is checked, but we find placing the legend outside the plot is less desirable than placing it in the figure itself. We therefore make the following modifications as shown in Figure 9.16:

- We remove the check for the legend to be located **Outside**.
- We select **Northeast** (this is in the upper right corner) as the **Position** for the legend.
- We check **Block** style under **Style**.
- Use the drop-down color menu under **Frame** to set it to black.
- Use the drop-down color menu under **Block** to set it to 40% grey.

We then click **Run** to produce the line plot.

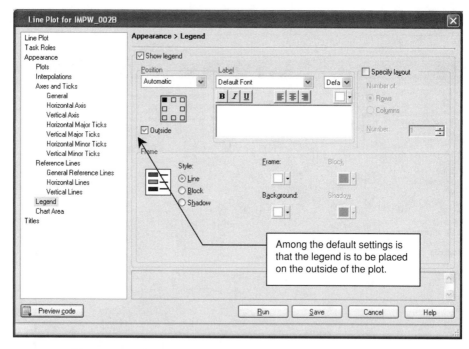

Figure 9.15. The screen setting up the default for the legend.

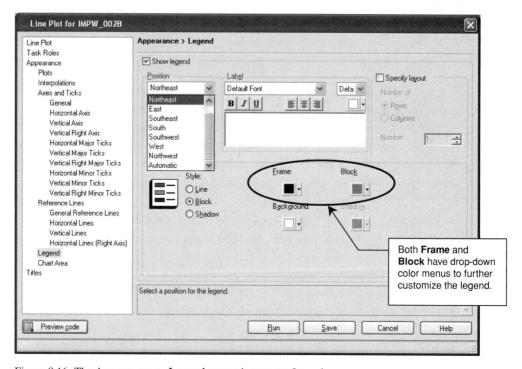

Figure 9.16. The **Appearance** > **Legend** screen is now configured.

Development Dollars in Millions

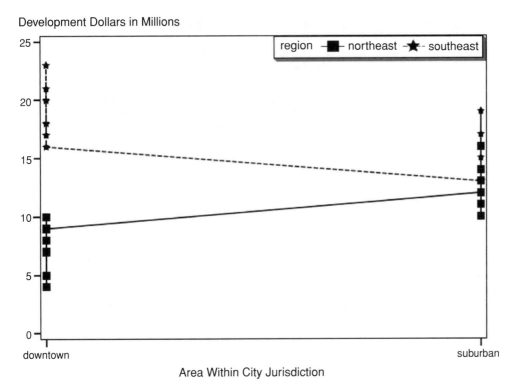

Area Within City Jurisdiction

Figure 9.17. The output of the **Line Plot**.

The line plot is shown in Figure 9.17. The northeast region is drawn in a solid line and the southeast region is drawn in a dashed line. It is much less "journal ready" than the bar graph we had generated earlier, but it does present a visual representation of the data that would be of great use to researchers.

10 Standardizing Variables Based on the Sample Data

10.1 Overview

10.1.1 General meaning of standardizing

To standardize a variable is to transform the obtained values of a variable in such a way that we can immediately determine the following two features of any score: first, its position with respect to the mean, which is whether the score is below or above the mean of the distribution; second, the magnitude of its distance from the mean, which is how far from the mean the score falls in terms of standard deviation units (i.e., how many standard deviation units separate the score from the mean of the distribution). We do this because it is often the case that such information is not always apparent from a raw score.

10.1.2 Conveying direction

Direction is signified by standard scores because the value of the mean is set (transformed) to a known, fixed, arbitrary value. Three examples of commonly used standardized scores and their known or fixed means are as follows:

- z scores have a mean of 0. Negative z scores are below the mean and positive ones are above the mean.
- Linear T scores have a mean of 50. Linear T scores lower than 50 are below the mean and linear T scores higher than 50 are above the mean.
- Intelligence test scores – the Wechsler Intelligence Test for Children (WISC) is a good example – commonly have a mean of 100. Scores lower than 100 are below the mean and those higher than 100 are above the mean.

10.1.3 Conveying magnitude

Magnitude is conveyed in terms of standard deviation units. As was true for the mean, the value of the standard deviation is set (transformed) to a known, fixed, arbitrary value. Here are some examples:

- Note that z scores have a standard deviation of 1 (or 1 *SD*). Given the fixed mean of 0, a z score of 1.00 falls exactly 1 *SD* above the mean and a z score of –0.5 falls exactly 0.5 *SD* below the mean.
- Linear *T* scores have a standard deviation of 10. Given the fixed mean of 50, a linear *T* score of 60 falls exactly 1 *SD* above the mean and a linear *T* score of 45 falls exactly 0.5 *SD* below the mean.
- Intelligence scores from the WISC have a standard deviation of 15. Given the fixed mean of 100, a WISC score of 115 falls exactly 1 *SD* above the mean and a WISC score of 92.50 falls exactly 0.5 *SD* below the mean.

10.2 Numerical example

The data set we will use for our numerical example is based on a sample of 250 students at a university where one of us teaches. The sample size we use here is large enough to allow us to meaningfully transform the raw scores to standard scores. It is composed of five quantitative variables representing raw scores on five personality dimensions: neuroticism, extraversion, openness, agreeableness, and conscientiousness. A portion of the data set is displayed in Figure 10.1.

As may be clear from a visual inspection of the data visible in the screenshot, students are exhibiting different values within each of the personality dimensions. However, which scores are relatively high and which are relatively low is not immediately apparent. Transforming these values to standardized scores will clarify matters.

10.3 Obtaining standardized scores: z scores

We will perform a z-score standardization on the variable assessing neuroticism. From the main *SAS Enterprise Guide* menu, select **Data ➜ Standardize Data**. This brings us to the **Task Roles** window. Drag **Neurotic** to the slot under **Analysis variables** in the rightmost panel. This is shown in Figure 10.2.

From the navigation panel on the far left, select **Standardize**. This brings us to the **Standardize** screen. As seen in Figure 10.3, we can set the standardized mean

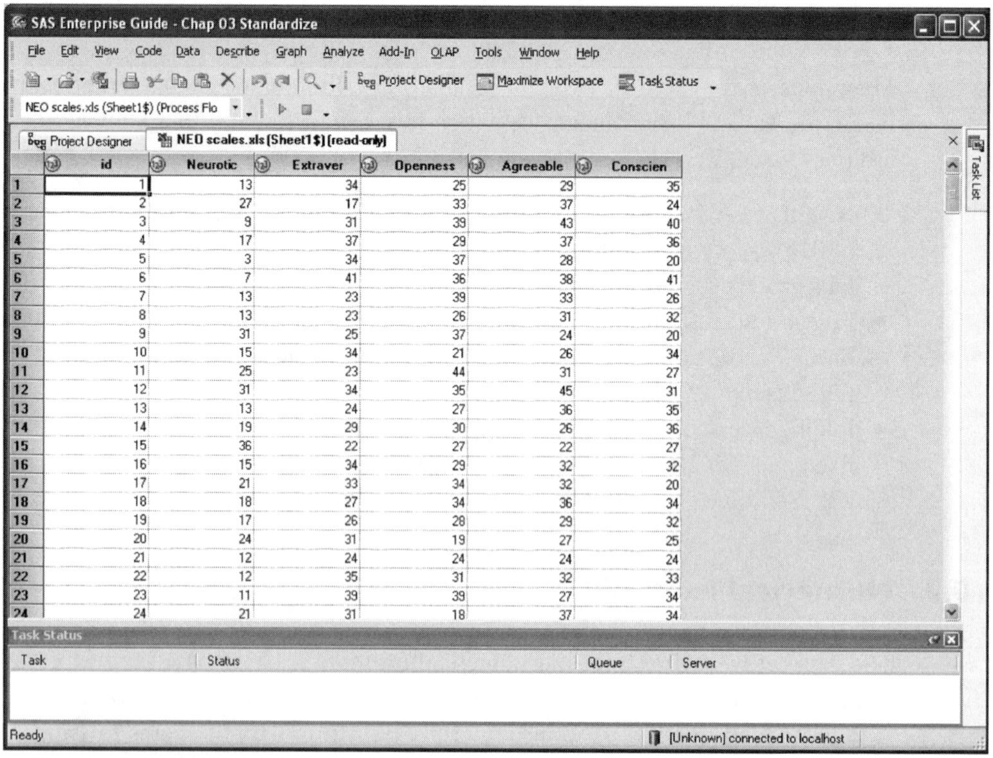

	id	Neurotic	Extraver	Openness	Agreeable	Conscien
1	1	13	34	25	29	35
2	2	27	17	33	37	24
3	3	9	31	39	43	40
4	4	17	37	29	37	36
5	5	3	34	37	28	20
6	6	7	41	36	38	41
7	7	13	23	39	33	26
8	8	13	23	26	31	32
9	9	31	25	37	24	20
10	10	15	34	21	26	34
11	11	25	23	44	31	27
12	12	31	34	35	45	31
13	13	13	24	27	36	35
14	14	19	29	30	26	36
15	15	36	22	27	22	27
16	16	15	34	29	32	32
17	17	21	33	34	32	20
18	18	18	27	34	36	34
19	19	17	26	28	29	32
20	20	24	31	19	27	25
21	21	12	24	24	24	24
22	22	12	35	31	32	33
23	23	11	39	39	27	34
24	24	21	31	18	37	34

Figure 10.1. A portion of the data set.

and standard deviation for the **Neurotic** variable (had we selected more variables, the same mean and standard deviation would be applied to each). The default standardization for *SAS Enterprise Guide* is a z score, and so the **New mean** is already set at 0 and the **New standard deviation** is already set at 1. We will keep these settings for **Neurotic**. Click **Run** to perform the transformation.

The result of the z-score transformation is shown in Figure 10.4 in the last column of the data set. *SAS Enterprise Guide* has named the new variable **stnd_Neurotic**. The values that are visible in the screenshot are all within ± 2 *SD* of the mean, which is not surprising as approximately 95% of the values in a normal distribution fall between ± 2. Nevertheless, more extreme values will appear, and examining the z-score values is a convenient way to spot outliers (extreme scores) in the data set, as we will see in Chapter 12.

We have generated some summary statistics for the standardized neuroticism variable as explained in Section 8.4. These are displayed in Figure 10.5. As we can see, the mean is very close to 0 (in calculator or computer notation, the expression "E–17" tells us to move the decimal 17 places to the left) and $SD = 1.00$.

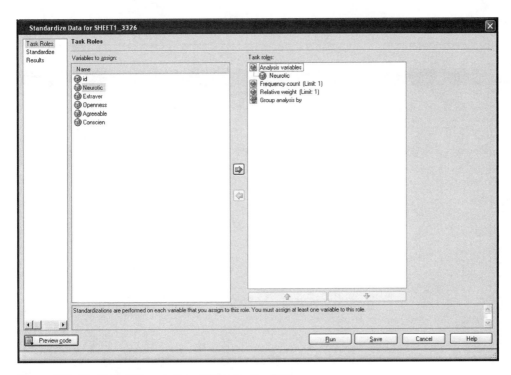

Figure 10.2. The **Task Roles** window of **Standardize Data**.

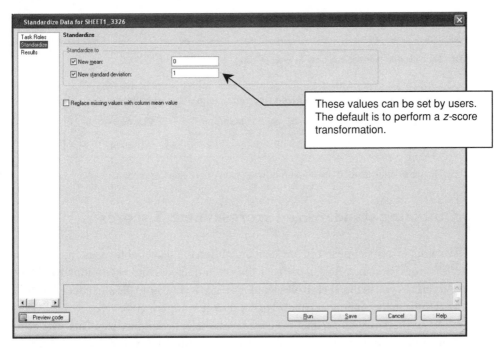

These values can be set by users. The default is to perform a *z*-score transformation.

Figure 10.3. The **Standardize** window.

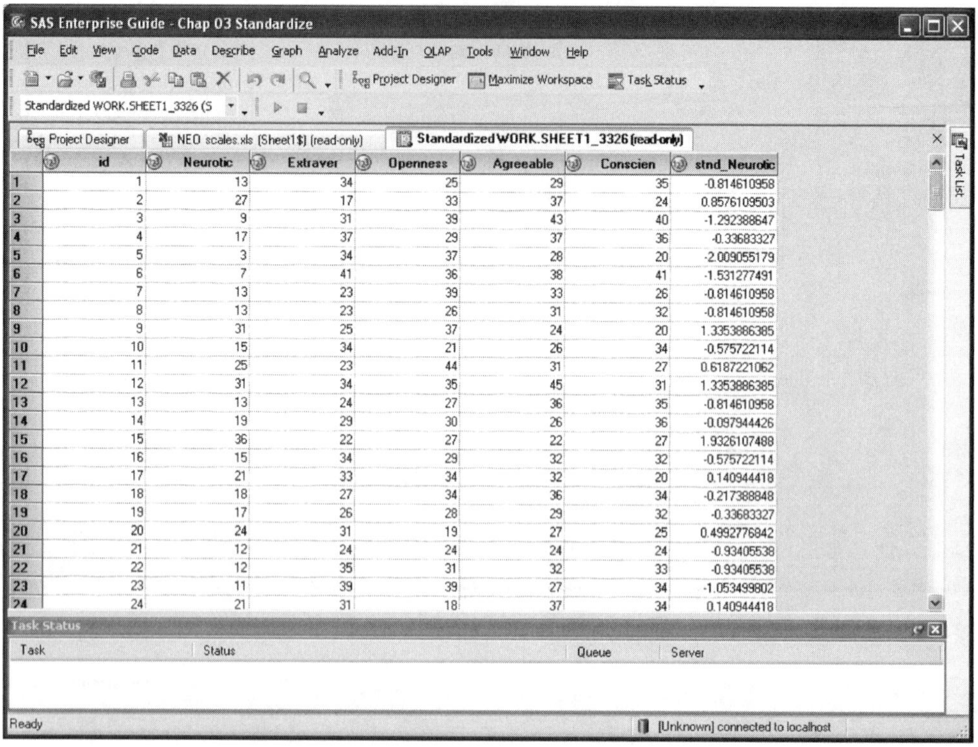

Figure 10.4. The variable **Neurotic** is now in z-score form.

Analysis Variable : stnd_Neurotic Standarized Neurotic: mean = 0 standard deviation = 1				
Mean	Std Dev	Minimum	Maximum	N
−2. 44249E−17	1. 000000	−2. 3673884	3. 2464994	250

Figure 10.5. The mean and standard deviation following the z-score transformation.

10.3   Obtaining standardized scores: linear *T* scores

We will perform a linear *T*-score standardization on the variable assessing extraversion. From the main *SAS Enterprise Guide* menu, select **Data → Standardize Data**. This brings you to the **Task Roles** window. Drag **Extraver** to the slot under **Analysis variables** in the rightmost panel. This is shown in Figure 10.6.

From the navigation panel on the far left, select **Standardize**. This will bring you to the **Standardize** window. As we can see in Figure 10.7, we have set the **New mean** at 50 and the **New standard deviation** at 10 for the linear *T*-score transformation. Click **Run** to perform the transformation.

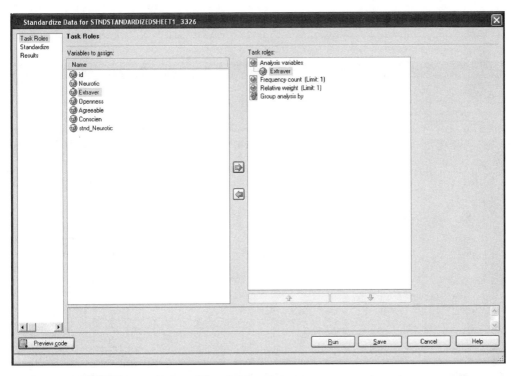

Figure 10.6. The **Task Roles** window of **Standardize Data**.

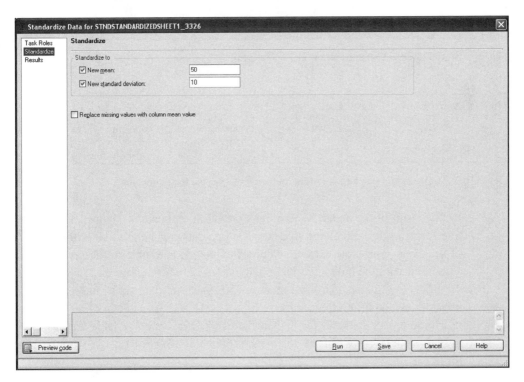

Figure 10.7. The **Standardize** window.

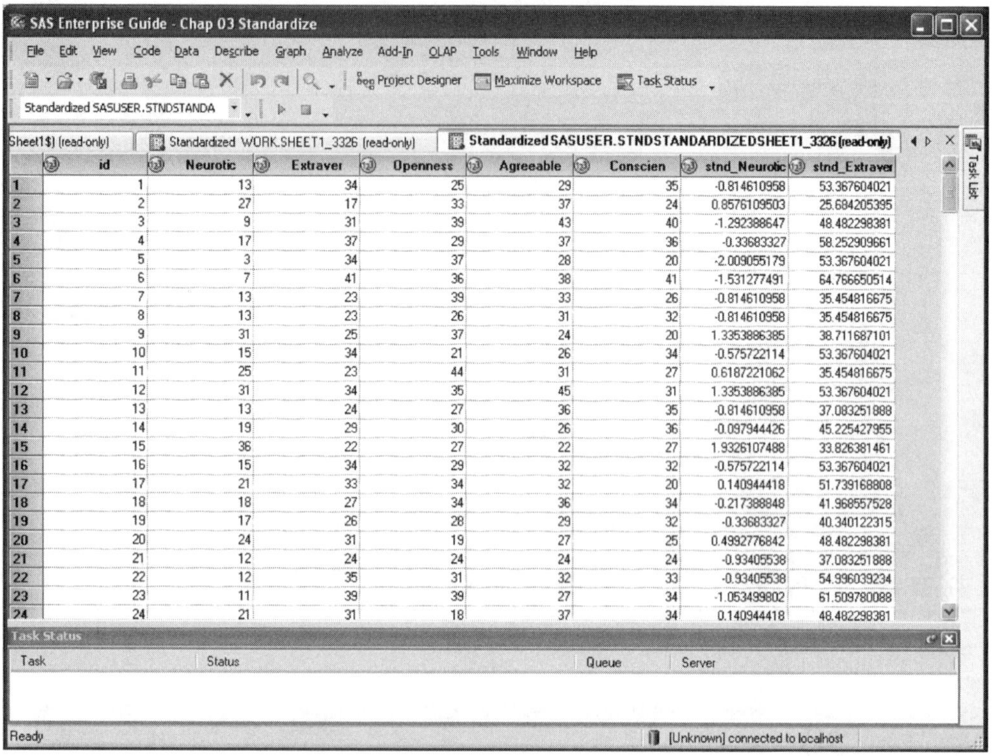

	id	Neurotic	Extraver	Openness	Agreeable	Conscien	stnd_Neurotic	stnd_Extraver
1	1	13	34	25	29	35	-0.814610958	53.367604021
2	2	27	17	33	37	24	0.8576109503	25.684205395
3	3	9	31	39	43	40	-1.292388647	48.482298381
4	4	17	37	29	37	36	-0.33683327	58.252909661
5	5	3	34	37	28	20	-2.009055179	53.367604021
6	6	7	41	36	38	41	-1.531277491	64.766650514
7	7	13	23	39	33	26	-0.814610958	35.454816675
8	8	13	23	26	31	32	-0.814610958	35.454816675
9	9	31	25	37	24	20	1.3353886385	38.711687101
10	10	15	34	21	26	34	-0.575722114	53.367604021
11	11	25	23	44	31	27	0.6187221062	35.454816675
12	12	31	34	35	45	31	1.3353886385	53.367604021
13	13	13	24	27	36	35	-0.814610958	37.083251888
14	14	19	29	30	26	36	-0.097944426	45.225427955
15	15	36	22	27	22	27	1.9326107488	33.826381461
16	16	15	34	29	32	32	-0.575722114	53.367604021
17	17	21	33	34	32	20	0.140944418	51.739168808
18	18	18	27	34	36	34	-0.217388848	41.968557528
19	19	17	26	28	29	32	-0.33683327	40.340122315
20	20	24	31	19	27	25	0.4992776842	48.482298381
21	21	12	24	24	24	24	-0.93405538	37.083251888
22	22	12	35	31	32	33	-0.93405538	54.996039234
23	23	11	39	39	27	34	-1.053499802	61.509780088
24	24	21	31	18	37	34	0.140944418	48.482298381

Figure 10.8. The variable **Extraver** is now in T-score form.

Analysis Variable : stnd_Extraver Standardized Extraver: mean = 50 standard deviation = 10				
Mean	**Std Dev**	**Minimum**	**Maximum**	**N**
50.0000000	10.0000000	22.4273350	71.2803914	250

Figure 10.9. The mean and standard deviation following the T-score transformation.

The result of the linear T-score transformation is shown in Figure 10.8. As was true for neuroticism, college students as a population generally fall within ± 2 *SD* of the mean. The most extreme value of extraversion visible in the screenshot is associated with the individual identified as Case 2, whose score of 25.68 is almost 2.5 *SD* below the standardized mean of 50. Save the data set to have these new variables available at a future time.

The summary statistics for the standardized extraversion variable are displayed in Figure 10.9. As we can see, the mean is 50 and the $SD = 10$, as we would expect for linear T scores.

11 Standardizing Variables Based on Existing Norms

11.1 Overview

Many measures developed by social and behavioral researchers, such as those of achievement, cognitive abilities, and personality, are published with a set of existing norms. Such norms are usually based on large and diverse nationally drawn samples. For our purposes, two statistical characteristics of such a normative sample are of interest to us: the mean and the standard deviation. In Chapter 10, we used the mean and standard deviation of the research sample as our base to compute the standard score; here, we discuss the procedure of computing standard scores based on the mean and standard deviation of the normative sample. This process is very similar to what was described in Chapter 7 when we computed a new variable, and so we will more quickly outline the steps that are needed; readers are referred to Section 7.3 for a more complete explanation of these steps.

11.2 Numerical example

We will use the same data set that we used in Chapter 10. The instrument used to measure the personality dimensions was the NEO Five-Factor Inventory (which measures five personality factors, namely neuroticism, extraversion, openness, agreeableness, and conscientiousness; see Costa & McCrae, 1991). We work with the personality factor of conscientiousness for this example. The combined male–female mean and standard deviation of the normative sample reported in the test manual (Costa & McCrae, 1992) is 34.57 and 5.88, respectively. NEO scores are ordinarily reported as linear T scores, and so we will compute these.

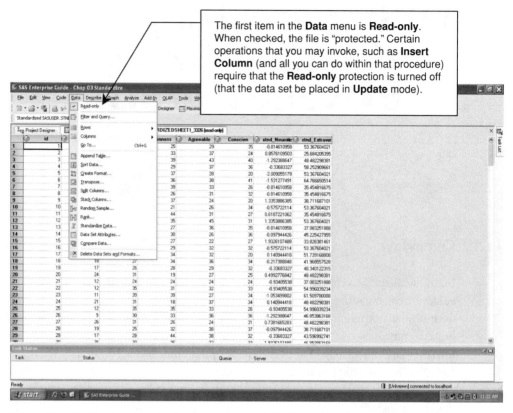

The first item in the **Data** menu is **Read-only**. When checked, the file is "protected." Certain operations that you may invoke, such as **Insert Column** (and all you can do within that procedure) require that the **Read-only** protection is turned off (that the data set be placed in **Update** mode).

Figure 11.1. The **Read-only** restriction on the data set is in place when opening a project.

11.3   Setting up the computing process

With the project open and the data set visible in the active window, select **Data →
Read-only** from the main *SAS Enterprise Guide* menu as shown in Figure 11.1 and
select the **Read-only** box. This will remove the **Read-only** restriction by switching
to the **Update** mode, allowing the data set to be modified by users. A dialog box
(see Figure 11.2) will ask you to confirm your choice; click the **Yes** push button.

Right-click the name of the variable at the top of the data column. As shown in
Figure 11.3, we have selected **Conscien**. Choose **Insert Column** from the drop-
down menu to reach the **Column Properties** dialog window.

The **General** window of **Insert Column** is shown in Figure 11.4. We have
created the name **Norm_Con** and given it the more complete label of **Normative
Conscientiousness**. Keep the rest of the defaults.

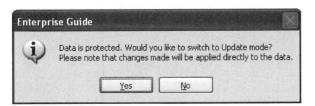

Figure 11.2. By clicking the **Read-only** restriction, you will void this restriction and are presented with a dialog box that will ask you to confirm your action.

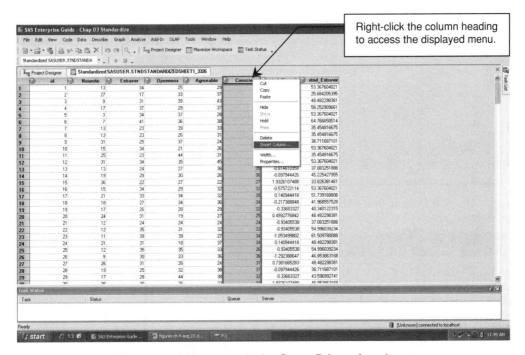

Figure 11.3. Right-click on the variable name and select **Insert Column** from the menu.

The **Expression** panel on the **General** screen is where users type in the algebraic transformation that is to be performed. To compute a linear *T* score, it is necessary to perform these arithmetic operations:

- Subtract the normative mean (34.57) from each person's score (**Conscien**);
- Divide the result of that subtraction by the normative standard deviation (5.88);
- Multiply that resulting value by 10, the linear *T*-score standard deviation;
- Add 50 to the last value to place the mean at 50.

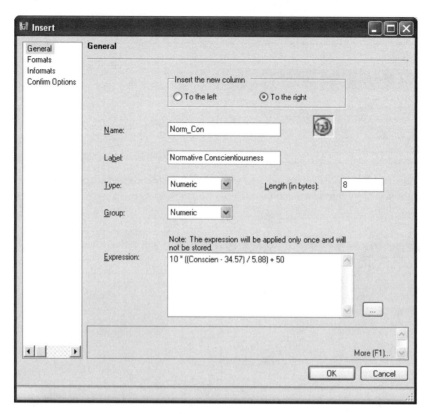

Figure 11.4. The **Column Properties** dialog window.

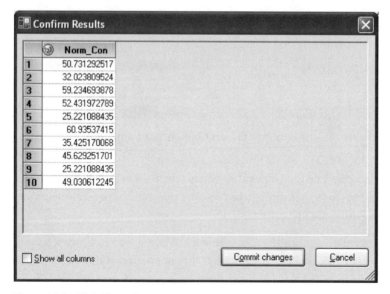

Figure 11.5. Click **Commit changes** to confirm the computation.

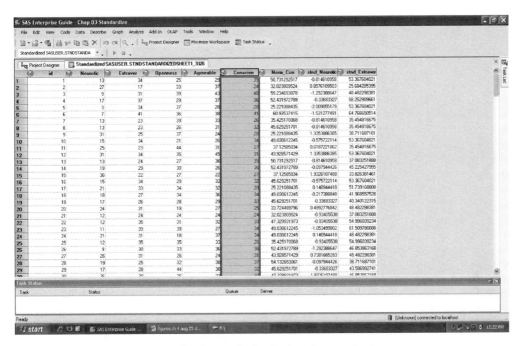

Figure 11.6. The data set now contains the standardized values for conscientiousness.

This computation can be performed by use of the following expression (which follows the format of the computer, not the mathematician):

$$10 * ((\text{Conscien} - 34.57)/5.88) + 50$$

Type this into the **Expression** panel as shown in Figure 11.4 and click **OK**.

11.4 Obtaining the standardized values

After clicking **OK**, providing all of the necessary information to *SAS Enterprise Guide*, you will be presented with the **Confirm Results** window (see Figure 11.5). Assuming the values in the preview window look approximately correct, click the **Commit changes** push button.

As shown in Figure 11.6, the data set now contains the standardized values for conscientiousness. Be sure to save the project if you wish to retain these results for future work.

Section V

Score Distribution Assumptions

12 Detecting Outliers

12.1 Overview

Outliers are extreme scores, ones that differ substantially from the majority of scores. Assuming that the extreme score is valid (i.e., it is not due to a measurement or transcription error), then it may indicate an unusual data-collection circumstance (e.g., the sale of hip-length boots was extraordinarily high in the year when the local river flooded) or an unusual case (e.g., one hospital in one city receives all gunshot victims and thus has an unusually high count of this type of trauma relative to other facilities). Because the outcome of some data-analysis procedures (e.g., regression) can be affected or distorted by the presence of outliers in the data set, especially with smaller sample sizes, it is useful for researchers to perform procedures to detect such values as one of the first steps in analyzing their data.

12.2 Specifying the boundary for an outlier

A z score indicates the direction and distance of a score from the mean in standard deviation units; it is computed like this: (score minus mean) divided by standard deviation. Most researchers think in terms of z scores when discussing outliers. However, how large a z score must be to "substantially" differ from its mates is not precisely agreed upon. Few authors draw a firm line in the sand, preferring instead to offer mild suggestions. Kirk (1995), for example, reports that some have suggested a z score of ± 2.5 might be a sufficiently large departure from the mean to be considered an outlier, but most other writers would consider that difference to not be substantial enough. Stevens (1999) has offered z-score cutoffs of ± 3 to ± 4

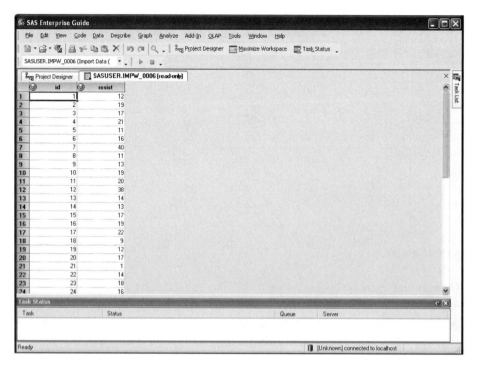

Figure 12.1. A portion of the data set.

but has indicated that the choice one makes should be at least partially guided by the maximum z score possible in the given data set. This maximum value, citing a study by Shiffler (1988), is $n - 1$ divided by the square root of n, where n is the size of the sample. A more complete discussion of this topic, demonstrating some of its complexity, may be found in Cohen, Cohen, West, and Aiken (2003).

12.3   Numerical example

We will use a data set consisting of a single measured variable, labeled **resist** in the data set, derived from the hypothetical records of 52 clients at a local medical clinic. These clients were tested for resistance to a certain variety of influenza, with higher scores reflecting greater resistance. Scores could range between 0 and 40. A portion of the data set is shown in Figure 12.1. Clients have identification numbers (**id**) in the data set in addition to their test score.

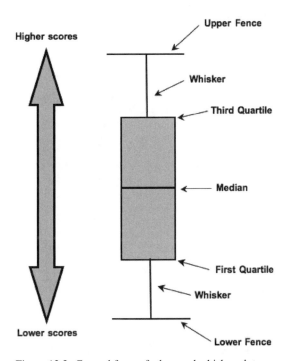

Figure 12.2. General form of a box and whisker plot.

12.4   The box and whisker plot

The general form of a box and whisker plot is displayed in Figure 12.2. It is based on quartiles and was devised by the prominent statistician John Tukey (1977). The lower and upper bounds of the box are the first and third quartile, respectively, with the median (midpoint) drawn as a line inside the box. Its whiskers extend from the box to the fences, which are placed at ± 1.5 interquartile range units. Translated to z scores, the fences correspond to z scores of approximately ± 2.6. Data points beyond the fences are suggestive of outliers under this criterion.

From the main *SAS Enterprise Guide* menu, select **Describe → Summary Statistics**. This brings you to the **Task Roles** window. Drag **resist** to the slot under **Analysis variables** in the rightmost panel as shown in Figure 12.3. Then, as seen in Figure 12.4, click **Plots** from the navigation panel on the far left and select **Box and whisker**. Click the **Run** push button.

The box and whisper plot is shown in Figure 12.5. *SAS Enterprise Guide* does not show the fences but they can be assumed to be at the end of the whiskers. As we

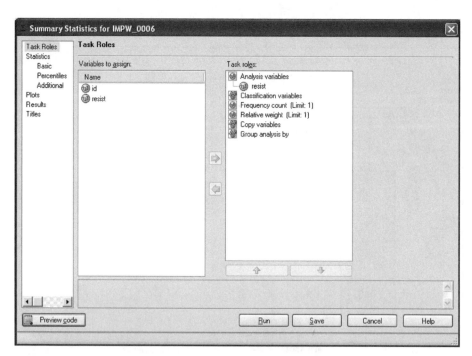

Figure 12.3. The **Task Roles** screen of **Summary Statistics**.

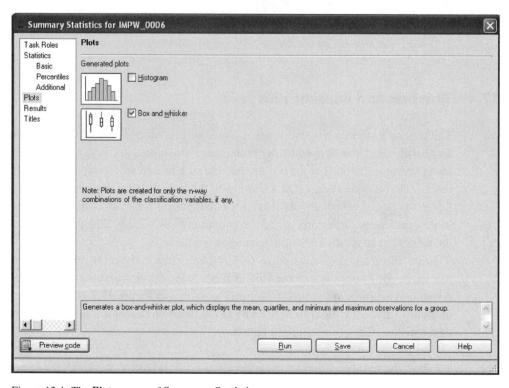

Figure 12.4. The **Plots** screen of **Summary Statistics**.

122

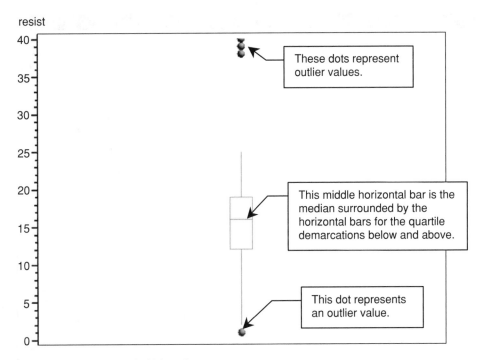

Figure 12.5. The box and whisker plot.

can see, there were data values (each data value could be associated with more than one client) beyond both the upper and lower fences; the higher data values are quite far from the main group of scores as the distances are drawn roughly proportional. The lower value is just beyond the lower fence, but we are approaching the lowest possible value (the floor) of the measurement instrument here, so we would need to be careful in our interpretation.

12.5 Transforming values to z scores

As we suggested in Section 12.2, it is useful to transform the values of the variable of interest into z scores based on the sample data to enable us to quickly judge how far a particular score falls from the mean. We therefore repeat the process discussed in Chapter 10 to accomplish this. Briefly, from the main *SAS Enterprise Guide* menu, select **Data → Standardize Data**. This brings you to the **Task Roles** window. Drag **resist** to the slot under **Analysis variables** in the rightmost panel as shown in Figure 12.6. From the navigation panel on the far left, select **Standardize**.

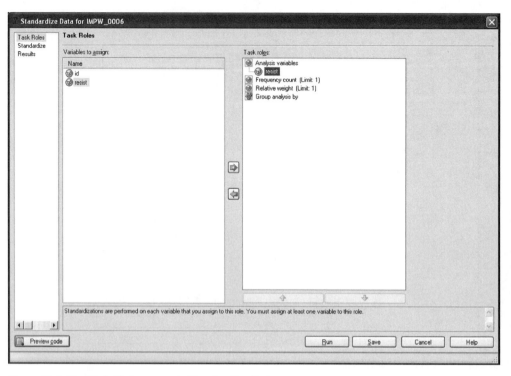

Figure 12.6. The **Task Roles** screen in **Standardize Data**.

Retain the settings for the **New mean** of 0 and the **New standard deviation** of 1 (see Figure 12.7). Click **Run** to perform the transformation.

The standardized values for **resist**, named by *SAS Enterprise Guide* as **stnd_resist**, are displayed in the rightmost data column in Figure 12.8. Save the project to retain these values.

Note that there are now three tabs appearing above the data grid: the project designer and two data sets. The first data set represents the file with which we started; the second is the data set with the standardized values included. It is this latter data set on which we want to base the next analysis.

12.6   Obtaining extreme values

To determine the values of the outliers pictured in the box and whisker plot, we can obtain what *SAS Enterprise Guide* calls *extreme values*. Make sure that the data set displaying the standardized values is selected (visible in the SAS

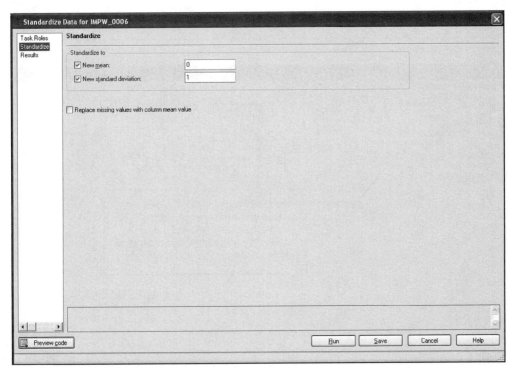

Figure 12.7. Setting the *z*-score standardization.

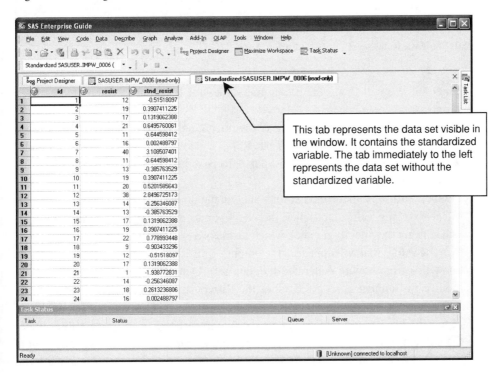

Figure 12.8. The data grid with the newly standardized variable.

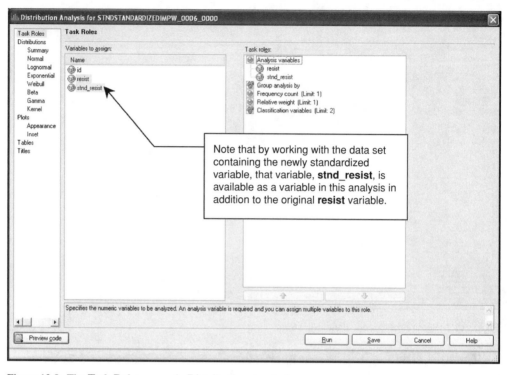

Figure 12.9. The **Task Roles** screen in **Distribution Analysis**.

window). We will then obtain extreme values for both the raw and standardized variables.

From the main *SAS Enterprise Guide* menu, select **Describe → Distribution Analysis**. This brings you to the **Task Roles** window. Drag **resist** to the slot under **Analysis variables** in the rightmost panel. Repeat this process for **stnd_resist**. This is shown in Figure 12.9.

Click **Tables** from the navigation panel on the far left. As shown in Figure 12.10, select **Extreme values** and click the checkbox to place a check mark there. That will activate the **Specify n** panel, which displays **5** as a default (this is the number of extreme values that will appear in the output). This is sufficient for our purposes (we know this from having generated the data set). Depending on your need, you can modify this number as required. Click the **Run** push button to perform the analysis.

The output for the unstandardized **resist** variable is shown in the two tables of Figure 12.11. The top table provides the five lowest and five highest values under the column heading **Value**. Also displayed under the column heading **Obs** are the case-identifying numbers (these are the line numbers in the data set) should you

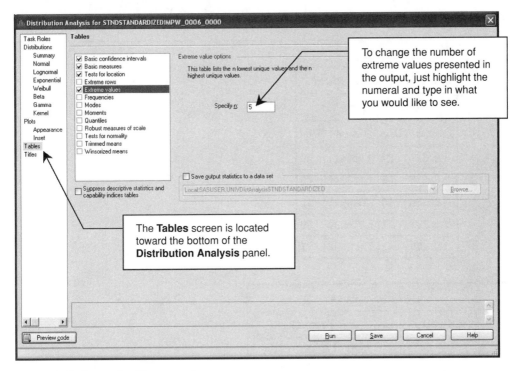

Figure 12.10. Requesting **Extreme values** output.

Extreme Observations			
Lowest		Highest	
Value	Obs	Value	Obs
1	21	23	29
2	48	25	26
2	30	38	12
7	27	39	36
8	42	40	7

Extreme Values					
Lowest			Highest		
Order	Value	Freq	Order	Value	Freq
1	1	1	19	23	1
2	2	2	20	25	1
3	7	1	21	38	1
4	8	1	22	39	1
5	9	2	23	40	1

Figure 12.11. Output for the variable **resist**.

Extreme Observations			
Lowest		Highest	
Value	Obs	Value	Obs
-1.93877	21	0.908411	29
-1.80936	48	1.167246	26
-1.80936	30	2.849673	12
-1.16227	27	2.979090	36
-1.03285	42	3.108507	7

Extreme Values					
Lowest			Highest		
Order	Value	Freq	Order	Value	Freq
1	-1.938773	1	19	0.908411	1
2	-1.809355	2	20	1.167246	1
3	-1.162268	1	21	2.849673	1
4	-1.032851	1	22	2.979090	1
5	-0.903433	2	23	3.108507	1

Figure 12.12. Output for the variable **stnd resist**.

have an interest in verifying the original data source. For example, the individuals represented by case numbers 30 and 48 each had **resist** scores of 2. The bottom table provides a frequency count of these extreme values. For example, two clients were associated with the **resist** score of 2.

Figure 12.12 provides the analogous output for **stnd_resist**. Note that because these values are z scores, we can make sense of the results much more quickly. We now see that the value clients 30 and 48 have in common is a z score of approximately -1.81. Note that *SAS Enterprise Guide* flagged these in the box and whisker plot as outliers even though they are closer than the traditional ± 2.6 z-score value associated at the position of the fences. Nonetheless, they do represent scores that are relatively different from the bulk of the distribution.

The most extreme scores in the present example are to be found toward the high end of the distribution, where three clients have values that are in the general range of a z score of 3.0. In some statistical analyses, some researchers might give consideration to removing some or all of these scores. Nevertheless, removing data from an analysis is serious business, and we are not for the purposes of the present example inclined to view their difference as sufficiently extreme to warrant that sort of action.

13 Assessing Normality

13.1 Overview

Many statistical procedures (e.g., analysis of variance) have as one underlying assumption that the variables to be analyzed are distributed in a manner best described by the normal curve (see Gamst et al., 2008). Most statistical analysis software packages are able to compute several different tests of normality, and it is common for researchers to perform such tests in the first stages of their data analysis.

13.2 The normality tests provided by SAS

When users select normality tests, *SAS Enterprise Guide* automatically computes and displays the results for four such tests: Shapiro–Wilk, Kolmogorov–Smirnov, Cramer–von Mises, and Anderson–Darling. We very briefly characterize each of these in the subsequent text.

13.2.1 Shapiro–Wilk

The Shapiro–Wilk test for normality is perhaps the most widely used test of the four computed by SAS. It is based on regression techniques. In its early version it was appropriate for sample sizes up to 50 (Shapiro & Wilk, 1965), but SAS has incorporated a modification proposed by Royston (1992) to extend the procedure to sample sizes up to about 2,000. Based on a review of the tests that are available, D'Agostino (D'Agostino, Belanger, & D'Agostino, 1990; D'Agostino & Stephens, 1986) concluded that, among several alternative normality tests (not available through SAS), the Shapiro–Wilk test was excellent.

13.2.2 Kolmogorov–Smirnov

The Kolmogorov–Smirnov test quantifies the differences between the observed and expected distribution by estimating the relative height of the distribution at many places. It works best with more than 2,000 cases. D'Agostino (1986) suggests that the test should not be used but Marascuilo and McSweeney (1977) do recommend it.

13.2.3 Cramer–von Mises

This is a variation of the Kolmogorov–Smirnov test. It uses squared differences in its calculation.

13.2.4 Anderson–Darling

This is another variation of the Kolmogorov–Smirnov test. Similar to the Cramer–von Mises test, it also uses squared differences in its calculation.

13.3 Numerical example

We will use a data set consisting of a single measured variable, **washfreq**, based on hypothetical survey responses from 66 consumers of a local utility company. The company wanted to learn how often per month families with one child under 10 years of age living in the household used their washers and dryers. A portion of the data set is shown in Figure 13.1. Customers were assigned identification numbers (**id**) in the data set in addition to their test score.

13.4 Obtaining the normality assessments

From the main *SAS Enterprise Guide* menu, select **Describe → Distribution Analysis**. This brings you to the **Task Roles** window. Drag **washfreq** to the slot under **Analysis variables** in the rightmost panel. This is shown in Figure 13.2.

Click **Tables** from the navigation panel on the far left. Select **Tests for normality** and click the checkbox to place a check mark there (see Figure 13.3). Click the **Run** push button to perform the analysis.

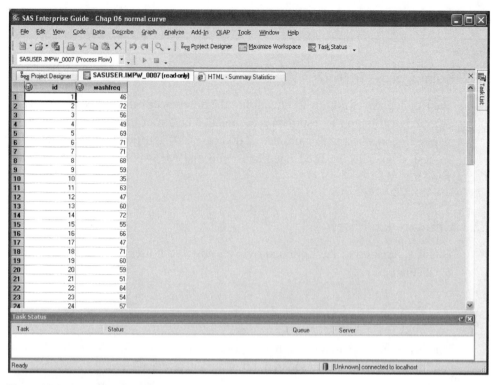

Figure 13.1. A portion of the data set.

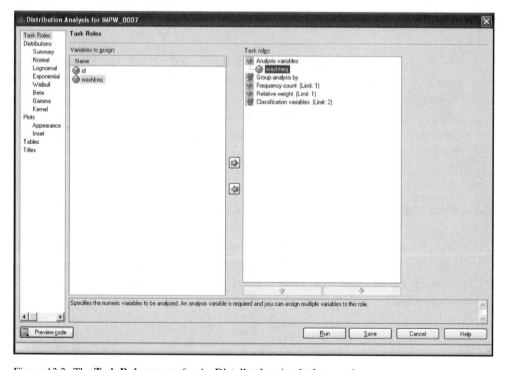

Figure 13.2. The **Task Roles** screen for the **Distribution Analysis** procedure.

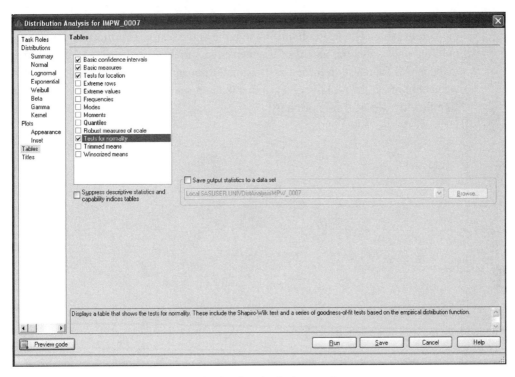

Figure 13.3. The **Tables** screen for the **Distribution Analysis** procedure.

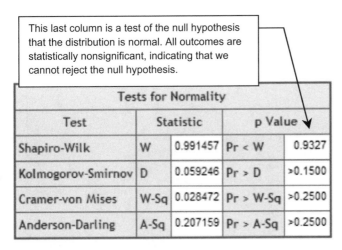

This last column is a test of the null hypothesis that the distribution is normal. All outcomes are statistically nonsignificant, indicating that we cannot reject the null hypothesis.

Tests for Normality				
Test	Statistic		p Value	
Shapiro-Wilk	W	0.991457	Pr < W	0.9327
Kolmogorov-Smirnov	D	0.059246	Pr > D	>0.1500
Cramer-von Mises	W-Sq	0.028472	Pr > W-Sq	>0.2500
Anderson-Darling	A-Sq	0.207159	Pr > A-Sq	>0.2500

Figure 13.4. The results of the normality tests.

The results of the analysis are shown in Figure 13.4. Each test occupies a row in the output table. The last column in the table is the test of significance against the null hypothesis that the values of the measured variable are distributed in a normal manner. All four tests returned a statistically nonsignificant result, indicating that we cannot reject the null hypothesis; that is, it appears that the distribution does not significantly depart from normality.

14 Nonlinearly Transforming Variables in Order to Meet Underlying Assumptions

14.1 Overview

Most of the statistical procedures we use are based on the assumption that the data are normally distributed, that there are no outliers potentially distorting the results of the analyses, and, if there are two or more distributions involved in the analysis, that the sets of scores have comparable variances (the assumption of homogeneity of variance). If these assumptions are violated, one option available to researchers is to transform the data to force the values to come closer to meeting the assumptions.

Chapter 11 discussed standardizing variables based on existing norms, which is one form of transformation. Standardizing a variable (e.g., to z or linear T scores) is an example of a *linear transformation*, that is, one preserving the characteristics of the distribution. Thus, a distribution whose values are skewed remains so following the raw scores being converted to z scores. In the present chapter, we discuss transformations that are performed with the intention of modifying the shape of the distribution. These types of transformations are known as *nonlinear transformations*.

14.2 Notes on transformations

To transform data is to perform certain types of mathematical operations on the scores of a variable for each case in the data set. We do this by computing a new variable in much the same way as we showed in Chapter 7 when we computed new variables and in Chapter 11 when we discussed standardizing a variable based on external norms. The operations we discuss here change the "spacing" between the new scores after the transformation; thus, these transformations are defined as nonlinear.

There are advantages and disadvantages to performing nonlinear transformations. For example, a transformation to the natural logarithm of the original value may drive a positively skewed distribution closer to normality but at the same time render the natural log values relatively uninterpretable. Because it can be thought of as a double-edged sword, the use of transformations has stimulated a certain amount of controversy in the research and statistical literature. It does appear that a majority of users generally advocate the use of transformations, but even those who endorse this practice urge its judicious use. Very readable nontechnical discussions of this topic can be found in Kirk (1995), Meyers et al. (2006), Osborne (2002), and Wheater and Cook (2000).

Generally, the effects of nonlinear transformations are most easily understood in terms of affecting the skewness of a distribution, although such transformations will generally also affect kurtosis. If skewness is reduced in one or more distributions that are being compared, it will also tend to make their variances more comparable, thus dealing with both normality and homogeneity of variance at the same time. Our focus in this chapter is on reducing the skewness of a single distribution.

14.3   Examples of nonlinear transformations

14.3.1 Positive skew

Positively skewed distributions have distribution tails on their right side pointing toward the positive (higher) end of continuum. Three commonly cited transformations to reduce positive skewness, in order of their impact, are as follows: square root transformation, log transformation, and reflected inverse transformation.

In a square root transformation, we compute the square root of the variable's values, creating a corresponding new score on a new variable for each case in the data set. This transformation can be used to reduce moderate positive skewness. One of its limitations is that we cannot take the square root of a negative number. Another feature of the square root transformation is that taking the square root of a value that is less than 1.00 produces a larger value than the original, whereas taking the square root of a value that is greater than 1.00 produces a smaller value than the original. To thwart these and other problems, Kirk (1995) has recommended adding the constant of 1 to all scores in the transformation process if there are values of less than 10 in the distribution and if they are all positive. If there are negative numbers, then a value should be added to bring all values above 1.00.

In a log transformation, we compute the logarithm of the variable's values, creating a corresponding new score on a new variable for each case in the data set.

It can be used to reduce substantial positive skewness. Logs can be computed with reference to different bases, the most commonly used being base 10, base 2, and natural logs (where the constant e of 2.7182818 is the base). One limitation of this transformation is that logs of negative numbers and of numbers less than 1.00 are undefined; to remedy this, a constant such as 1 (or whatever value must balance the negative numbers in the distribution) must be added to the original scores in the transformation process under those circumstances.

In a reflected inverse transformation, we compute the reciprocal (1/score) of the variable's values, creating a corresponding new score on a new variable for each case in the data set. It can be used to reduce excessive positive skewness. One limitation of this transformation is that inverses make originally small numbers large and originally large numbers small, thus reversing the normal order of scores. To prevent this reordering, we typically multiply the variable values by -1 (to *reflect* them) before taking the reciprocal. Hence, this is called a *reflected* inverse transformation.

14.3.2 Negative skew

Negatively skewed distributions have distribution tails on their left side pointing toward the negative (lower) end of continuum. Two commonly cited transformations to reduce negative skewness, in order of their impact, are as follows: square transformation and cubed transformation.

In a square transformation, we compute the square of the variable's values, creating a corresponding new score on a new variable for each case in the data set. In a cubed transformation, we compute the cube of the variable's values, creating a corresponding new score on a new variable for each case in the data set.

14.4 Numerical example

We have generated a sample of yearly income data (in thousands of dollars) for a hypothetical set of 166 patients brought in for emergency services at a local county hospital one Saturday night in June. A portion of the data set is shown in Figure 14.1.

We have constructed the distribution for the variable **income** in the data set such that is noticeably positively skewed. The descriptive statistics and histogram, produced in the **Summary Statistics** procedure, are shown in Figures 14.2 and 14.3, respectively. Note that the distribution has a skewness value of approximately 1.70, which we can consider to be sufficiently large for our purposes in this chapter. The

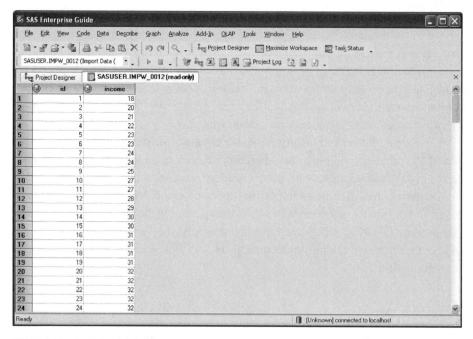

Figure 14.1. A portion of the data set.

Analysis Variable: income income				
Mean	Std Dev	N	Skewness	Kurtosis
73.9638554	55.5505657	166	1.7024856	2.6000592

Figure 14.2. Basic descriptive statistics.

histogram produced in the **Summary Statistics** procedure has grouped the income scores; nonetheless, we can easily see the degree of positive skew in the histogram.

14.5   Transformation strategy

We will compute the three transformations described in Section 14.3.1 to correct positive skewness. Specifically, we will do the following:

- We will compute the square root of **income** in the data set, using the preexisting format available in SAS.

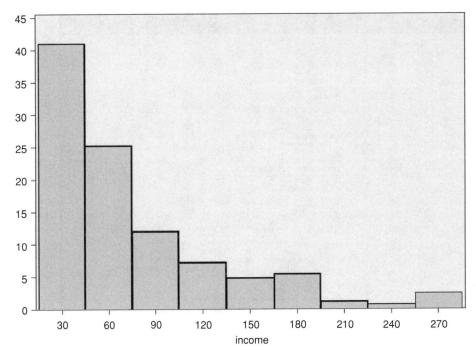

Figure 14.3. The histogram for the **income** variable.

- We will perform two logarithmic transformations of **income**, one to base 10 and one to the natural log base, using the preexisting formats available in SAS.
- We will perform a reflected inverse transformation. To make it clear what we are doing here, we will first reflect the variable by multiplying **income** by −1.00, creating a reflected variable to use as an intermediate step toward our goal. Then we will compute the reciprocal of the reflected variable (1.00 divided by the reflected variable).

14.6 Switch to Update mode

As described in Chapter 7, navigate the path **Data → Read-only** from the main *SAS Enterprise Guide* menu and select the **Read-only** box. This will remove the **Read-only** restriction by switching to the **Update** mode, allowing the data set to be modified by users. Click **Yes** to confirm.

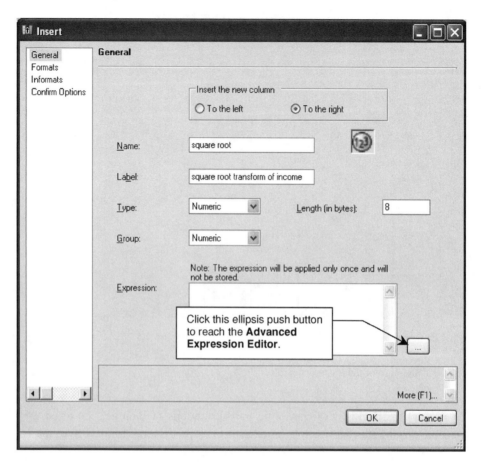

Figure 14.4. The **Properties** dialog window.

14.7 Setting up the computing process

14.7.1 Square root transformation

Right-click the name of the variable at the top of the data column for **income** and select **Insert Column** from the drop-down menu. This brings us to the **General** screen of the **Insert Column** procedure, which is shown in Figure 14.4. We have created the name **square root** and the label **square root transform of income**. Click the little ellipsis (three-dot) push button.

Clicking the little ellipsis (three-dot) push button brings us to the **Advanced Expression Editor** shown in Figure 14.5. We enter the dialog window on the **Data** tab. Click the **Functions** tab, which will change the screen to that shown in Figure 14.6.

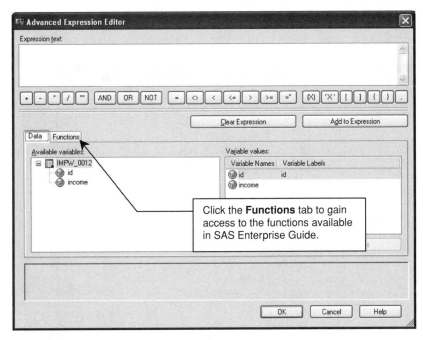

Figure 14.5. The initial **Advanced Expression Editor** screen.

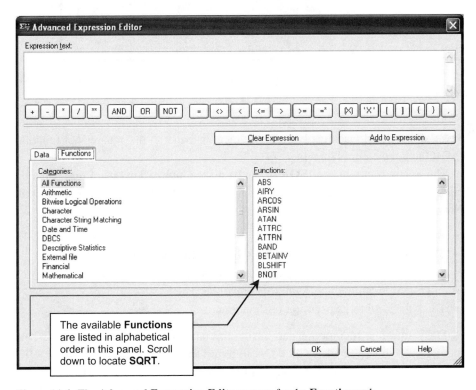

Figure 14.6. The **Advanced Expression Editor** screen for the **Functions** tab.

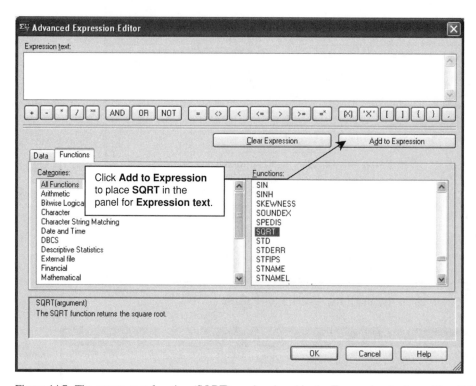

Figure 14.7. The square root function (**SQRT**) can be placed in the **Expression text** panel by clicking the **Add to Expression** push button.

Scroll down the alphabetically ordered functions panel to the square root function (**SQRT**) as shown in Figure 14.7.

The square root function (**SQRT**) can be placed in the **Expression text** panel by clicking the **Add to Expression** push button. This has been done in Figure 14.8. Now follow these steps:

- Select the **Data** tab.
- Delete the expression <**numValue**> in the **Expression text** panel.
- Keep your cursor inside the parentheses after deleting <**numValue**>.
- Highlight **income** in the **Available variables** panel.
- Click the **Add to Expression** push button.

Make sure that **income** appears inside the parentheses following **SQRT**. This may be seen in Figure 14.9. Click **OK** to return to the **General** screen. Click **OK**, click **Commit changes** on the **Confirm Results** screen (see Figure 14.10), and view

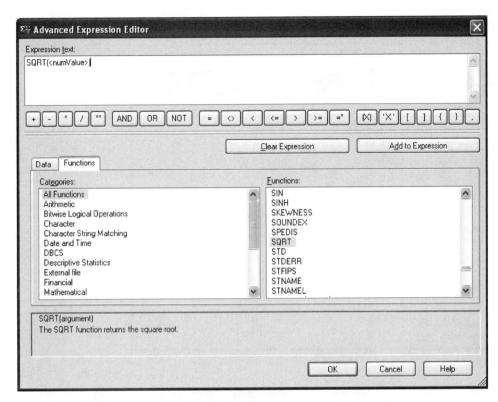

Figure 14.8. The **Expression text** panel now has the square root function.

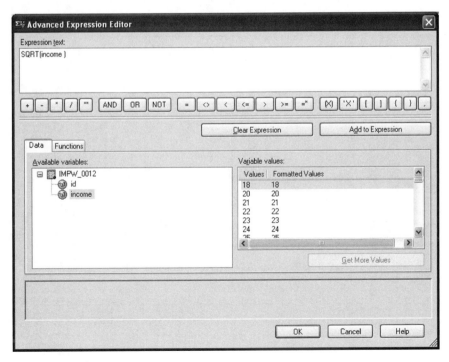

Figure 14.9. We are ready to compute the square root of the **income** variable.

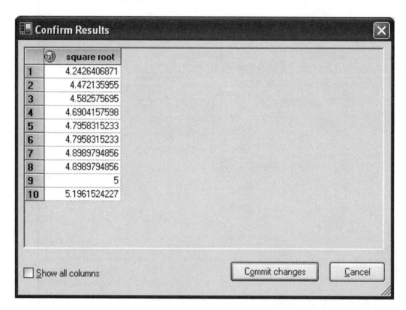

Figure 14.10. Commit to the computation.

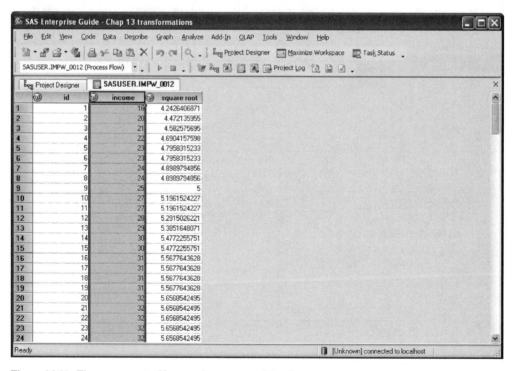

Figure 14.11. The square root of **income** is now part of the data set.

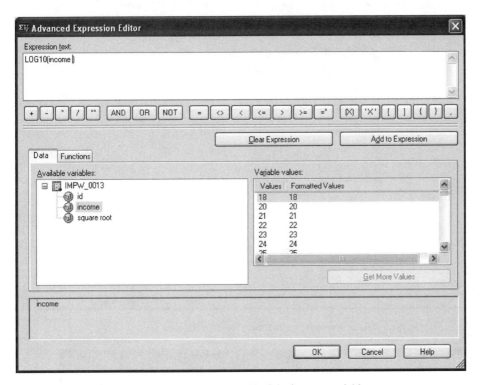

Figure 14.12. Expression for computing log base 10 of the **income** variable.

the outcome as shown in Figure 14.11. As we can see on the first row of the data set, for example, the square root of 18 is 4.2426406871.

14.7.2 Log base 10 transformation

The process of transforming **income** to a log base 10 is the same as we just described. Right-click the column named **square root** to insert a column next to it and navigate to the **Advanced Expression Editor** screen. Here we select the function symbolized as **LOG10**. The **Expression text** should look like what we have in Figure 14.12 with **income** clicked into the parentheses. Completing the computation results in this transformation being added to the data set (see Figure 14.13).

14.7.3 Natural log transformation

The natural log transformation is done in precisely the same manner as described for the log base 10 transformation. The function is symbolized as **LOG**, and the

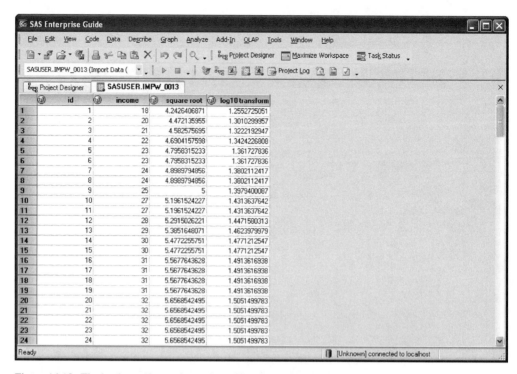

Figure 14.13. The log base 10 transformation of **income** is now in the data set.

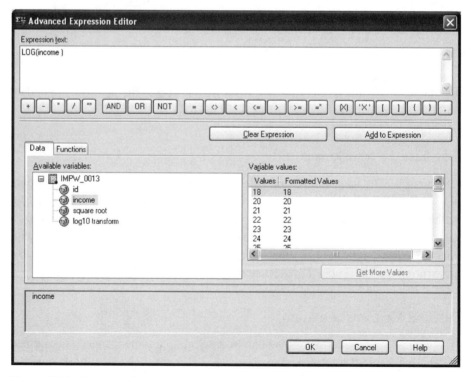

Figure 14.14. Expression for computing the natural log of **income**.

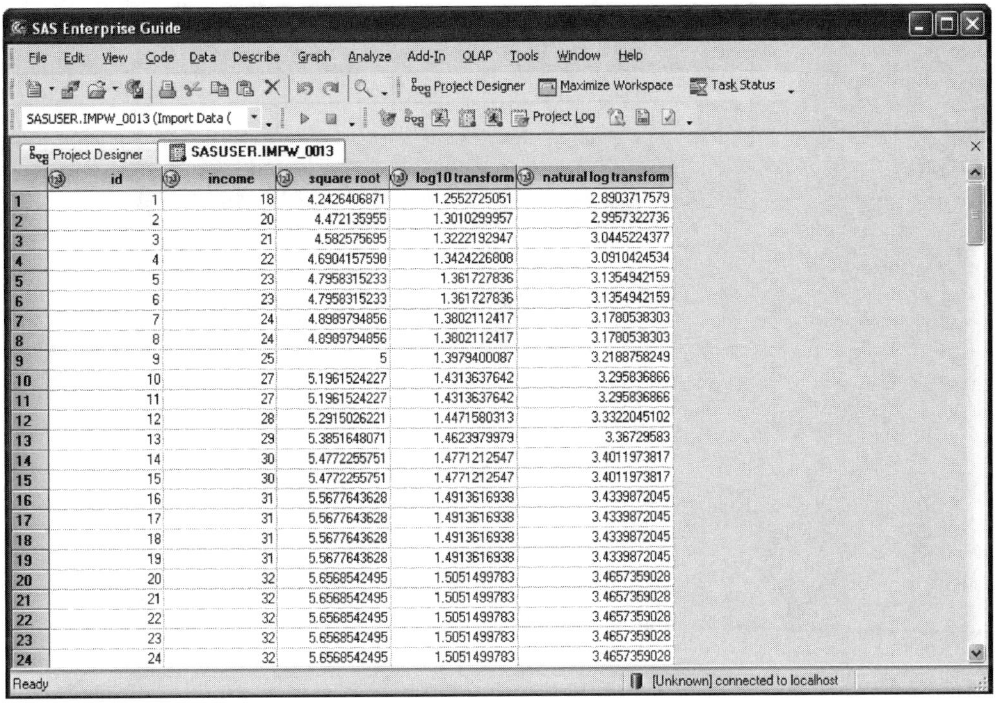

	id	income	square root	log10 transform	natural log transfom
1	1	18	4.2426406871	1.2552725051	2.8903717579
2	2	20	4.472135955	1.3010299957	2.9957322736
3	3	21	4.582575695	1.3222192947	3.0445224377
4	4	22	4.6904157598	1.3424226808	3.0910424534
5	5	23	4.7958315233	1.361727836	3.1354942159
6	6	23	4.7958315233	1.361727836	3.1354942159
7	7	24	4.8989794856	1.3802112417	3.1780538303
8	8	24	4.8989794856	1.3802112417	3.1780538303
9	9	25	5	1.3979400087	3.2188758249
10	10	27	5.1961524227	1.4313637642	3.295836866
11	11	27	5.1961524227	1.4313637642	3.295836866
12	12	28	5.2915026221	1.4471580313	3.3322045102
13	13	29	5.3851648071	1.4623979979	3.36729583
14	14	30	5.4772255751	1.4771212547	3.4011973817
15	15	30	5.4772255751	1.4771212547	3.4011973817
16	16	31	5.5677643628	1.4913616938	3.4339872045
17	17	31	5.5677643628	1.4913616938	3.4339872045
18	18	31	5.5677643628	1.4913616938	3.4339872045
19	19	31	5.5677643628	1.4913616938	3.4339872045
20	20	32	5.6568542495	1.5051499783	3.4657359028
21	21	32	5.6568542495	1.5051499783	3.4657359028
22	22	32	5.6568542495	1.5051499783	3.4657359028
23	23	32	5.6568542495	1.5051499783	3.4657359028
24	24	32	5.6568542495	1.5051499783	3.4657359028

Figure 14.15. The natural log transformation of **income** is now in the data set.

Expression text with **income** in the parentheses is shown in Figure 14.14. Completing the computation results in this transformation being added to the data set (see Figure 14.15).

14.7.4 Reflecting the income variable

We will perform the reflected inverse transformation in two stages. First, we will reflect the income variable by multiplying it by –1; second, we will take its reciprocal. Again, the computation to reflect **income** in the data set is akin to what we have already done. The exception is that there is no function we can select to perform the operation, but writing the function ourselves is pretty simple. When we first arrive at the **Advanced Expression Editor** after completing the **General** dialog screen of the **Insert Column** procedure, we remain on the **Data** tab. Select **income**, click **Add to Expression** to move **income** into the **Expression text** panel, and type in * **–1** (alternatively, you can click the asterisk button just below the panel for the **Expression text** and then type in the value of **–1**) as shown in Figure 14.16.

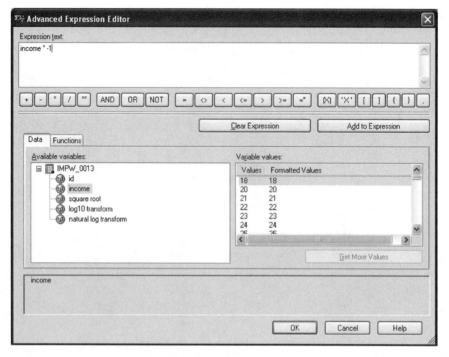

Figure 14.16. We multiply **income** by −1 to reflect it.

Completing the computation results in this transformation being added to the data set, as we can see in Figure 14.17.

14.7.5 Computing the reflected inverse transformation

To compute the reflected inverse transformation, we repeat the steps outlined for reflecting **income**, except that we enter a different expression into the **Expression text** panel: we type in **1 /** into the **Expression text** panel and then click **reflected income** as shown in Figure 14.18. *SAS Enterprise Guide* has added a couple of extra characters to the name but so long as the software has done this we are not concerned. Completing the computation results in this transformation being added to the data set, as we can see in Figure 14.19.

14.8   Evaluating the effects of our transformations

To determine the effectiveness of our transformations in removing the positive skewness from **income**, we perform another **Summary Statistics** analysis on the

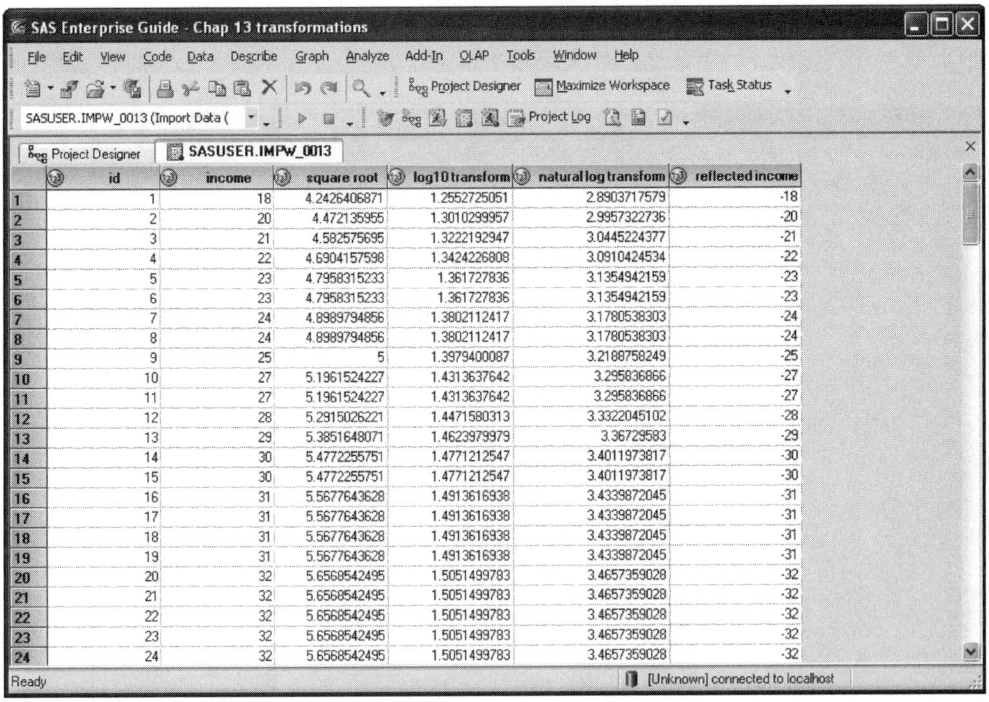

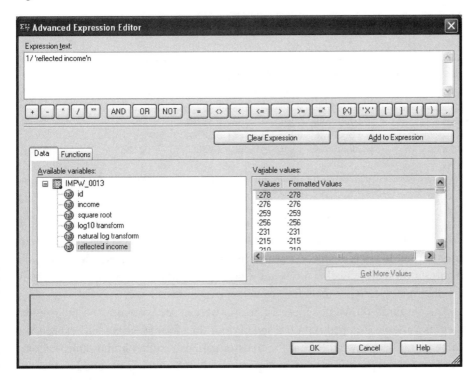

Figure 14.17. **Income** has now been reflected.

Figure 14.18. Computing **reflected income**.

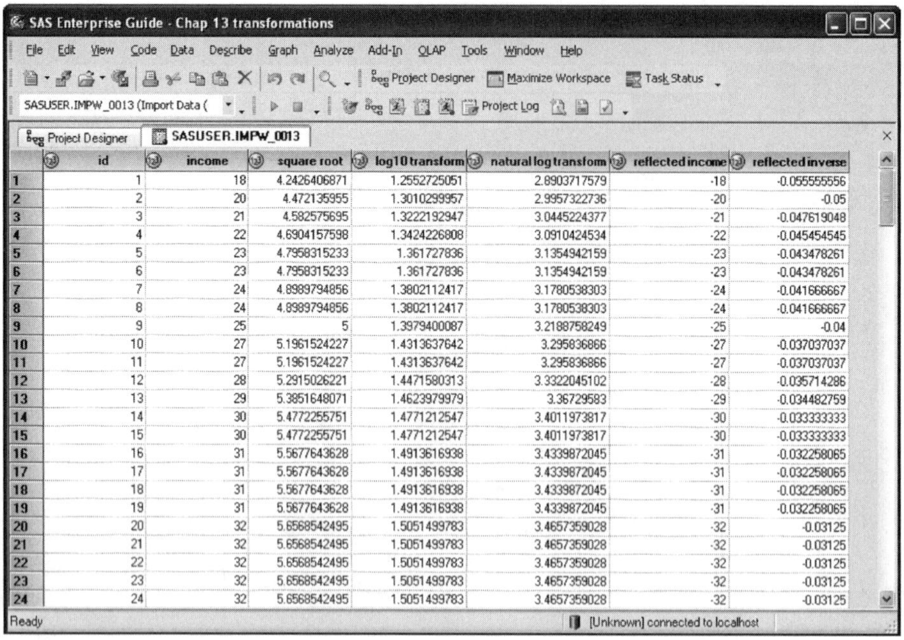

	id	income	square root	log10 transform	natural log transfom	reflected income	reflected inverse
1	1	18	4.2426406871	1.2552725051	2.8903717579	-18	-0.055555556
2	2	20	4.472135955	1.3010299957	2.9957322736	-20	-0.05
3	3	21	4.582575695	1.3222192947	3.0445224377	-21	-0.047619048
4	4	22	4.6904157598	1.3424226808	3.0910424534	-22	-0.045454545
5	5	23	4.7958315233	1.361727836	3.1354942159	-23	-0.043478261
6	6	23	4.7958315233	1.361727836	3.1354942159	-23	-0.043478261
7	7	24	4.8989794856	1.3802112417	3.1780538303	-24	-0.041666667
8	8	24	4.8989794856	1.3802112417	3.1780538303	-24	-0.041666667
9	9	25	5	1.3979400087	3.2188758249	-25	-0.04
10	10	27	5.1961524227	1.4313637642	3.295836866	-27	-0.037037037
11	11	27	5.1961524227	1.4313637642	3.295836866	-27	-0.037037037
12	12	28	5.2915026221	1.4471580313	3.3322045102	-28	-0.035714286
13	13	29	5.3851648071	1.4623979979	3.36729583	-29	-0.034482759
14	14	30	5.4772255751	1.4771212547	3.4011973817	-30	-0.033333333
15	15	30	5.4772255751	1.4771212547	3.4011973817	-30	-0.033333333
16	16	31	5.5677643628	1.4913616938	3.4339872045	-31	-0.032258065
17	17	31	5.5677643628	1.4913616938	3.4339872045	-31	-0.032258065
18	18	31	5.5677643628	1.4913616938	3.4339872045	-31	-0.032258065
19	19	31	5.5677643628	1.4913616938	3.4339872045	-31	-0.032258065
20	20	32	5.6568542495	1.5051499783	3.4657359028	-32	-0.03125
21	21	32	5.6568542495	1.5051499783	3.4657359028	-32	-0.03125
22	22	32	5.6568542495	1.5051499783	3.4657359028	-32	-0.03125
23	23	32	5.6568542495	1.5051499783	3.4657359028	-32	-0.03125
24	24	32	5.6568542495	1.5051499783	3.4657359028	-32	-0.03125

Figure 14.19. The reflected inverse transformation is now part of the data set.

Variable	Label	Mean	Std Dev	N	Skewness	Kurtosis
income	income	73.9638554	55.5505657	166	1.7024856	2.6000592
square root		8.1254787	2.8264067	166	1.1277090	0.5514926
log10 transform		1.7736689	0.2760718	166	0.5888473	–0.5330073
natural log transform		4.0840236	0.6356787	166	0.5888473	–0.5330073
reflected inverse		–0.0200504	0.0108141	166	–0.5306076	0.0081267

Figure 14.20. Basic descriptive statistics for the original **income** variable and the various transformations.

transformed variables. We include the original income variable in this analysis for easy reference. Select **Data ➔ Read-only** to protect the data set. Then drag **income**, **square root**, **log10 transform**, **natural log transform**, and **reflected inverse** to the **Analysis variables** panel and repeat the steps necessary (see Section 8.5) to obtain the descriptive statistics including skewness and kurtosis.

The output is shown in Figure 14.20. As we can see, skewness on the original **income** variable dropped with the square root transformation but still exceeded a value of 1.00. The two different log transformations resulted in the same outcome and reduced the skewness down to approximately 0.58, which is a good result. The reflected inverse transformation changed the original skewness the most, overshooting the zero mark to finish at −0.53 but as good a result as the log transforms.

Kurtosis improved as well, from an original 2.60 on **income** (which is relatively peaked) down to a value of less than 1.00 with all of the transforms, but the reflected inverse transformation yielded a kurtosis value of close to zero. Generally, either of the two log transformations or the reflected inverse transformation would appear to be quite satisfactory solutions to our positively skewed example distribution.

Section VI

Correlation and Prediction

15 Bivariate Correlation: Pearson Product–Moment and Spearman Rho Correlations

15.1 Overview

Correlation in statistical terms is a way to assess the degree of relationship or association that is observed between variables. *Bivariate correlation* focuses on the relationship between two (*bi-*) variables (*-variate*). Behavioral and social research almost always is concerned about the relationship of two or more variables, and so correlation plays a central role in such ventures.

15.2 Some history

Sir Francis Galton, the late 19th-century geographer, meteorologist, and statistician, was perhaps best known for his study of the inheritance of both physical and intellectual characteristics. As early as 1875, he distributed packets of sweet pea seeds to seven of his friends. Each packet contained seeds of uniform weight, but the weight of the seeds varied across packets. These friends were asked to plant the seeds, raise several generations of the plants, and then send the last generation of seeds back to Galton (Stanton, 2001). Upon graphing the results of this experiment he discovered that relatively heavier- and relatively lighter-weighted parent seeds ultimately produced seeds of less extreme weight. Later, Galton, on the basis of some physical characteristics of people and their family history, determined that both taller than average and shorter than average men have family and offspring who deviate less from the mean than they do. Galton presented this latter work in 1886 as the framework for introducing the concept of regression "towards the level of mediocrity" (Galton, 1886, p. 492) – what we now call regression toward the mean.

From this regression framework, Galton (1888) provided a quantitative measure of something he labeled as *co-relation*, and he devised an index of the degree to which covariation of two measures was observed in a data set. He named this index *regression* (based on his 1886 publication) and symbolized it as *r*. Galton's colleague and biographer, Karl Pearson, elaborated on and formalized the computation of this corelation measure in the following decade (Pearson, 1896), giving us what we now call the Pearson product–moment coefficient, more informally referred to as the Pearson *r*.

Building from the Pearson correlation coefficient, Sir Charles Spearman (1904b) suggested several variations on it, including a couple based on scores that were rank ordered. Spearman suggested that the chief advantage of what he called the *Rank method*, which carried over to his *method of rank differences*, was that there was reduction of the "accidental error" (Spearman, 1904b, p. 81); this is what we now call the effect of outliers.

15.3   The two correlation coefficients of interest here

This chapter focuses on obtaining two correlation coefficients from *SAS Enterprise Guide*, the Pearson product–moment correlation coefficient, often abbreviated as the Pearson *r*, and the Spearman rho correlation coefficient.

15.3.1 The Pearson *r*

The Pearson *r* is probably the best known and most widely used measure of correlation. It is also the foundation for many more complex statistical procedures (e.g., multiple regression, factor analysis). The Pearson correlation is designed to describe the degree to which two quantitative variables are linearly related. Note that if two variables are related quite strongly but not in a linear manner, such as in a purely quadratic manner (e.g., a U-shaped function), the Pearson *r* will return a value near zero.

The value of the Pearson *r* can vary between zero and 1; values closer to zero represent weaker relationships and values closer to 1 represent stronger relationships. Positive values indicate a direct relationship (e.g., higher values of one variable are associated with higher values of the other variable); negative values indicate an inverse relationship (e.g., higher values of one variable are associated with lower values of the other variable). The strength of the relationship between the two variables is indexed by r^2.

In the data set, each case has a value on each variable. By virtue of this, bivariate correlations can be pictured in a scatterplot. In such a plot, one variable (variable y) is placed on the y axis and the other (variable x) is placed on the x axis. Each data point represents the coordinate of a single case's x and y scores. The set of data points comprise the plot. A straight line of best fit estimated through the least squares method (where the squared deviation from the line is minimal) is known as the line of regression.

15.3.2 The Spearman Rho

Everything we said in Section 15.3.1 about the Pearson r can be said about the Spearman rho except that the scores used in the computation for the Spearman correlation are ranked values. Because it is applied to ranked data, the Spearman rho is classified as a nonparametric and distribution-free statistic, a class of statistical methods testing no hypothesis about the value of a population parameter (Marascuilo & McSweeney, 1977) and making no assumptions about the shape of the population distributions (Agresti & Finlay, 2009).

The Spearman rho is an approximation to the Pearson r and in fact is the Pearson r that would be computed on the rank values (Guilford & Fruchter, 1978). It will ordinarily return a lower value than the Pearson r.

15.4 Numerical example

Assume that our data set from a hypothetical study consists of 140 students at a local private middle school who were recruited by a Center for Media Studies in a nearby state. Over a 2-week period, researchers determined how many hours of television the children watched during the weekdays (named **tvhours** in the data set). They measured the children on several other variables, but for this example we will focus on one other variable: the children's grade point average (named **gpa** in the data set), in which 4.0 is an "A," 3.7 is an "A–," 3.3 is a "B+," and so on. A portion of the data set is shown in Figure 15.1. Students were assigned identification numbers (**id**) in the data set.

15.5 Setting up the correlation analysis

From the main *SAS Enterprise Guide* menu, select **Analyze → Multivariate → Correlations**. This brings you to the **Task Roles** screen. Drag **tvhours** to the slot

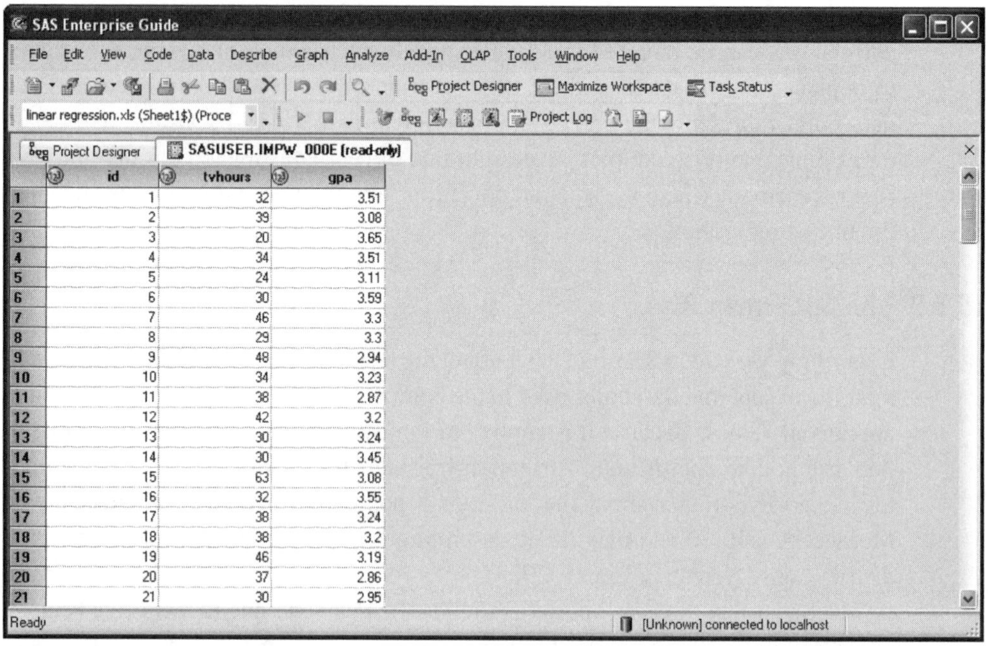

	id	tvhours	gpa
1	1	32	3.51
2	2	39	3.08
3	3	20	3.65
4	4	34	3.51
5	5	24	3.11
6	6	30	3.59
7	7	46	3.3
8	8	29	3.3
9	9	48	2.94
10	10	34	3.23
11	11	38	2.87
12	12	42	3.2
13	13	30	3.24
14	14	30	3.45
15	15	63	3.08
16	16	32	3.55
17	17	38	3.24
18	18	38	3.2
19	19	46	3.19
20	20	37	2.86
21	21	30	2.95

Figure 15.1. A portion of the data set.

under **Analysis variables** in the rightmost panel. Repeat this for **gpa**. This is shown in Figure 15.2.

Click **Options** from the navigation panel on the far left (see Figure 15.3). Check both **Pearson** and **Spearman** under **Correlation types**.

Click **Results** from the navigation panel on the far left. As shown in Figure 15.4, check the box for **Create a scatter plot for each correlation pair**. Then click the **Run** push button to perform the analysis.

15.6 The correlation output

Figure 15.5 displays the statistical output produced by SAS. Descriptive statistics are presented in the upper table of **Simple Statistics**. We obtain the mean, standard deviation, median, minimum, and maximum in the output.

The Pearson correlation coefficient is shown in the little table of correlations below the **Simple Statistics** table. The table is "square" such that each variable is listed in both the rows and columns; thus, the correlation between the two variables in this example is shown twice. The value of the Pearson r is shown as −0.456543.

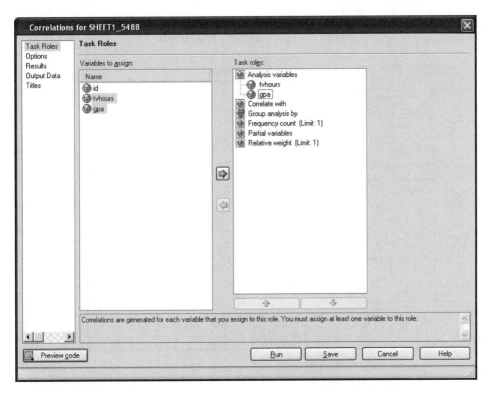

Figure 15.2. The **Task Roles** screen of the **Correlations** procedure.

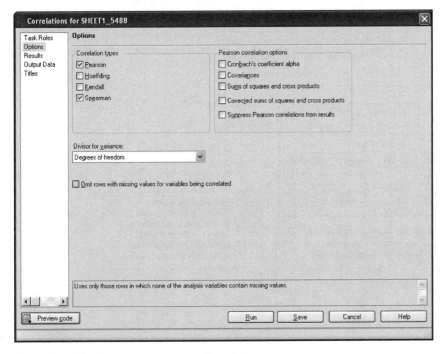

Figure 15.3. The **Options** screen for the **Correlations** procedure.

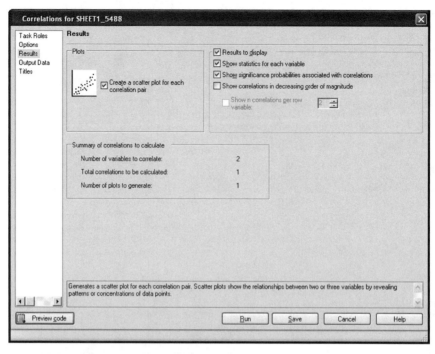

Figure 15.4. The **Results** screen for the **Correlations** procedure.

2 Variables:	tvhours gpa

To change the number of extreme values presented in the output, just highlight the numeral and type in what you would like to see.

Simple Statistics							
Variable	N	Mean	Std Dev	Median	Minimum	Maximum	Label
tvhours	140	38.27143	10.41709	38.00000	20.00000	74.00000	tvhours
gpa	140	3.30629	0.25464	3.30000	2.49000	3.90000	gpa

Pearson Correlation Coefficients, N = 140 Prob > |r| under H0: Rho=0		
	tvhours	gpa
tvhours tvhours	1.00000	-0.46543 <.0001
gpa gpa	-0.46543 <.0001	1.00000

The correlation values are given in a square matrix format. Probability values assuming the null hypothesis is true are provided directly under the correlation values.

Spearman Correlation Coefficients, N = 140 Prob > |r| under H0: Rho=0		
	tvhours	gpa
tvhours tvhours	1.00000	-0.40943 <.0001
gpa gpa	-0.40943 <.0001	1.00000

Figure 15.5. The correlation coefficients in the output.

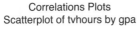

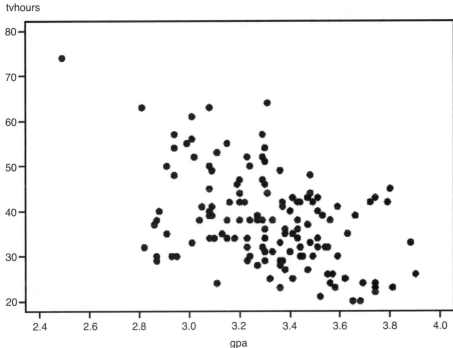

Figure 15.6. The scatterplot.

Its probability of occurrence if the null hypothesis is true is shown just below the numerical value; here, the Pearson r is statistically significant ($p < .0001$ is less than our alpha level of $\alpha = .05$). We may therefore conclude that children who watch more television have lower grade point averages.

The Spearman rho correlation table appears below the Pearson r table. It is structured in the same manner. Here, the Spearman correlation shown of -0.40943 is a bit lower than the Pearson, but is still statistically significant against an alpha level of $\alpha = .05$.

The scatterplot is shown in Figure 15.6. It suggests a linear relationship between the two variables.

16 Simple Linear Regression

16.1 Overview

Simple linear regression is a procedure that fits a linear function (a straight line) to predict one quantitatively measured variable based on the values of another quantitatively measured or dichotomously coded variable. The function is a *least squares* solution in that the sum of the squared distances between the data points and the linear function (the residuals) is the minimum value possible; this fitting process is technically referred to as *ordinary least squares*.

As you probably know, simple linear regression is intimately related to the Pearson correlation coefficient (the standardized regression coefficient is the Pearson r). The name of this procedure is very descriptive of its nature:

- It is called *simple* because there is only one predictor variable.
- It is called *linear* because the function on which the prediction is based is linear; that is, a straight line of best fit is imposed on the data.
- It is called *regression* because it is a prediction procedure.

16.2 Naming the classes of variables

In simple linear regression there are two measured variables. They are known by a variety of names.

The following terms have been applied to the variable that is being predicted. Among the most commonly used are these: *dependent variable*, *criterion variable*, and *outcome variable*. The following terms have been applied to the variable used

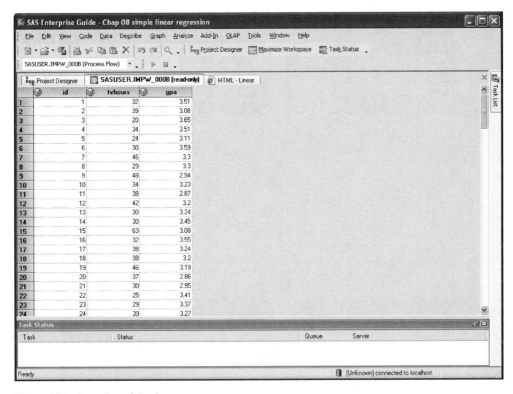

Figure 16.1. A portion of the data set.

as the basis of prediction. Among the most commonly used are these: *independent variable*, *predictor variable*, and *explanatory variable*.

16.3 Numerical example

Our data set is the same one we used in Chapter 15, as it will demonstrate the interface between the Pearson correlation and simple linear regression. Briefly, it consists of 140 students at a local private middle school who were studied by a Center for Media Studies in a nearby state. Because the study was conducted by a media center that was focused on media variables (e.g., looking for factors predicting exposure to certain media), in this example we will attempt to predict the amount of television viewing (named **tvhours** in the data set) on the basis of the children's grade point average (named **gpa** in the data set); these were the two variables used in the example of the Pearson *r*. A portion of data set is shown in Figure 16.1. Students were assigned identification numbers (**id**) in the data set.

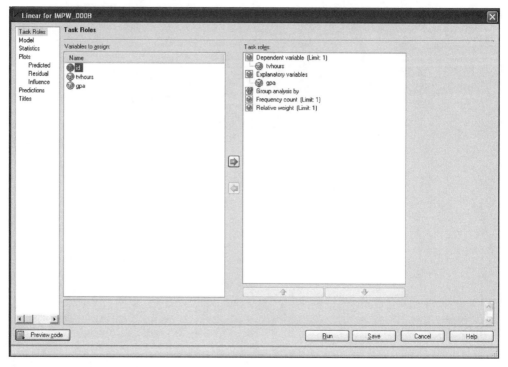

Figure 16.2. The **Task Roles** screen for the **Linear Regression** procedure.

16.4 Setting up the regression solution

From the main *SAS Enterprise Guide* menu, select **Analyze → Regression → Linear**. This brings you to the **Task Roles** window. Drag **tvhours** to the slot under **Dependent variable** in the rightmost panel. Then drag **gpa** to the slot under **Explanatory variables** in the rightmost panel. This is shown in Figure 16.2.

Click **Model** from the navigation panel on the far left (see Figure 16.3). The default for *SAS Enterprise Guide* is the full model, which is fine for us. There are other choices included on the pulldown menu.

Click **Statistics** from the navigation panel on the far left. As shown in Figure 16.4, select **Standardized regression coefficients** under **Details on estimates**. Then select under **Correlations** both **Partial correlations** and **Semi-partial correlations**.

Select **Predicted** under **Plots** from the navigation panel on the far left. Check **Observed vs independents** (see Figure 16.5) to obtain a scatterplot with the fitted regression line. Then click the **Run** push button to perform the analysis.

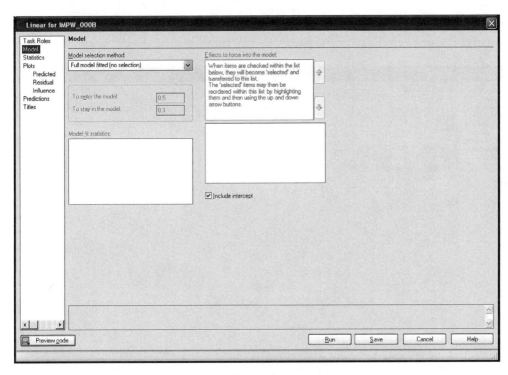

Figure 16.3. The **Model** screen for the **Linear Regression** procedure.

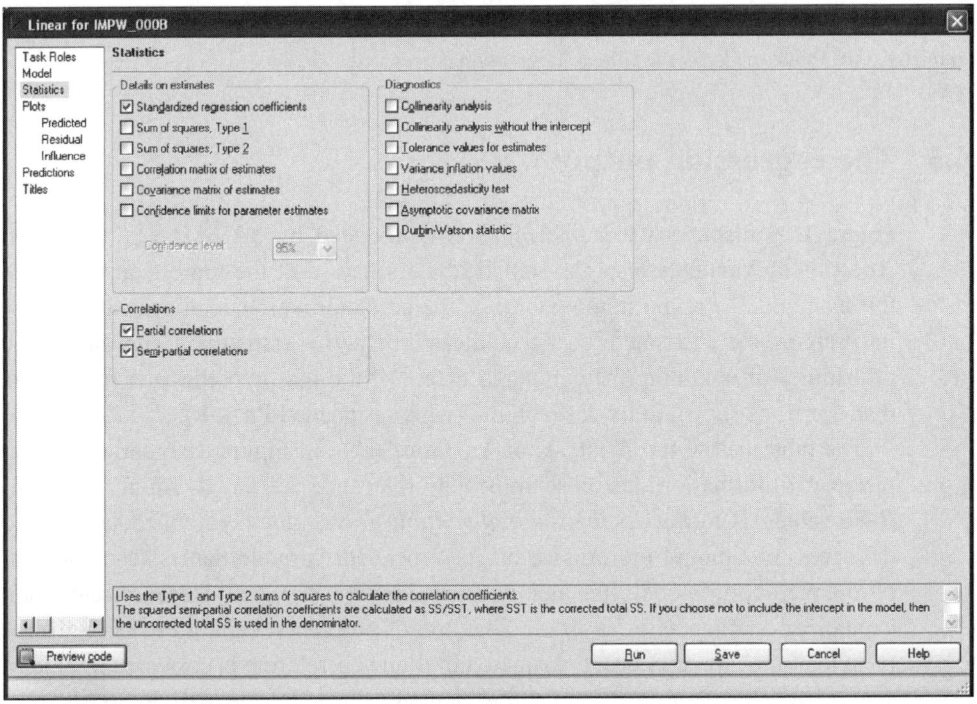

Figure 16.4. The **Statistics** screen for the **Linear Regression** procedure.

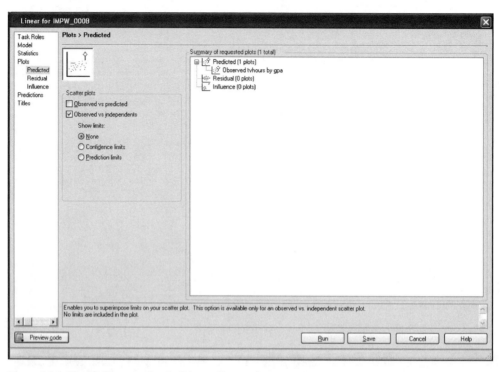

Figure 16.5. The **Plots** screen for the **Linear Regression** procedure.

16.5   The regression output

Figure 16.6 displays the statistical model produced by SAS. The table labeled **Analysis of Variance** tests the statistical significance of the regression model. In this example, the regression model (i.e., the predictor weighted as indicated below intercepting the *y* axis at a location indicated below) is statistically significant; the probability of obtaining the computed *F* ratio if the null hypothesis is true is less than .0001, as shown in the last column (which is headed **Pr > F**).

The table below the **Analysis of Variance** table in Figure 16.6 shows several pieces of information. Of most immediate relevance are the **R-Square** and **Adj R-Sq** values. **R-Square** is the *squared multiple correlation* (symbolized as R^2) and describes the amount of variance of the dependent variable that is accounted for by the prediction model; its value is approximately $R^2 = .22$. Because regression capitalizes on chance (error in the direction of prediction cannot be distinguished from legitimate prediction), the squared multiple correlation is corrected to at least somewhat adjust for this. This adjustment is shown by the **Adj R-Sq** statistic.

Number of Observations Read	140
Number of Observations Used	140

Analysis of Variance					
Source	DF	Sum of Squares	Mean Square	F Value	Pr > F
Model	1	3267.50575	3267.50575	38.16	<.0001
Error	138	11816	85.62449		
Corrected Total	139	15084			

Root MSE	9.25335	R-Square	0.2166
Dependent Mean	38.27143	Adj R-Sq	0.2109
Coeff Var	24.17822		

Parameter Estimates											
Variable	Label	DF	Parameter Estimate	Standard Error	t Value	Pr > |t|	Standardized Estimate	Squared Semi-partial Corr Type I	Squared Partial Corr Type I	Squared Semi-partial Corr Type II	Squared Partial Corr Type II
Intercept	Intercept	1	101.22452	10.22075	9.90	<.0001	0	.	.	.	.
gpa	gpa	1	-19.04043	3.08225	-6.18	<.0001	-0.46543	0.21663	0.21663	0.21663	0.21663

Figure 16.6. The model generated by the regression procedure.

In this example, the adjustment is minor, reducing the R-square value down to approximately $R^2 = .21$; thus, approximately 21% of the variance of television viewing can be predicted from the students' grade point average.

As for the other entries in the table, we can briefly tell you what they are:

- **Root MSE** is the *root mean square error*. It is the square root of the mean square error in the summary table above (the square root of 85.62449 with all of its unseen decimal values is 9.25335).
- **Dependent Mean** is the mean of the dependent variable.
- **Coeff Var** is the *coefficient of variation*. It is computed by multiplying the ratio of the root mean square error divided by the mean of the dependent variable by 100. In this case, the value is $100 \times (9.25335/38.27143)$ or 100×0.241782, which equals 24.17822 (see Section 23.6 for a somewhat fuller description of this statistic).

The bottom table in Figure 16.6 presents the regression model in both raw score and standardized form. This model is the equation for the straight line that has been fit to the data by using the least squares method. The raw score equation

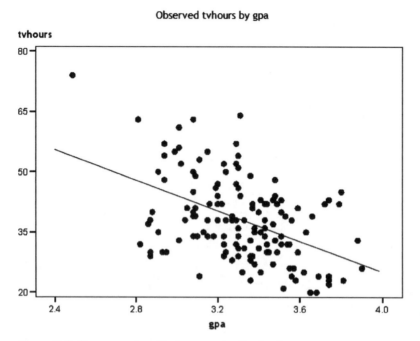

Figure 16.7. The scatterplot with the regression line in place.

is composed of an intercept (where the line intersects the y axis) and a weight or coefficient associated with the predictor variable. The value for the intercept is given in the first row under the column label of **Parameter Estimate**, where we note that the y intercept for the model is 101.22452 in this example. SAS tests the statistical significance of the intercept by using a t test as discussed in Chapter 20 (the t value and the probability of its occurrence if the null hypothesis is true are under the columns labeled **t Value** and **Pr > |t|**, respectively). In this model, the intercept is significant, that is, it is statistically different from a value of zero. The raw score coefficient is labeled as **Parameter Estimate**; in our example, it has a value of -19.04043 and is statistically different from a value of zero.

In the standardized score equation, the regression line intercepts the y axis at a value of zero and thus drops out of the equation. This is shown by the entry of **0** in the cell under the column labeled **Standardized Estimate**. The standardized regression coefficient is also known as a *beta weight*; its outcome for **gpa** is shown under the column labeled **Standardized Estimate**. The beta value in the model is -0.46543. In simple linear regression, this standardized estimate is the Pearson correlation coefficient, which you will recognize as the value we obtained in Chapter 15. As we can see, the predictor of **gpa**, tested via a t test, was statistically significant; its

t Value was computed to be -6.18 and its probability of being obtained if the null hypothesis is true, shown in the column named **Pr > |t|**, is $< .0001$ and is lower than our alpha level of $\alpha = .05$.

Note that **gpa** has a negative coefficient, indicating an inverse relationship with the dependent variable; thus we learn that increasingly higher grades were predictive of increasingly less television viewing. In fact, given the raw score coefficient associated with grade point average of -19.04043 in the regression solution (the model), we can even more specifically say the following:

> Television viewing decreased by about 19 hours for every full increment of gain of grade point average (e.g., from a grade point average of 2.0 to a grade point average of 3.0) exhibited by the students.

Figure 16.7 shows the scatterplot with the regression line fitted. This is the same scatterplot that we obtained in the correlation procedure. Here, we see the line of best fit. The amount of "scatter" surrounding the regression line gives a visual sense of what it means to account for about 21% of the variance of **tvhours** (the adjusted R-square value was approximately $R^2 = .21$).

17 Multiple Linear Regression

17.1 Overview

Multiple linear regression is a direct extension of simple linear regression. We still use a straight line (linear) function based on ordinary least squares to predict a dependent variable. The only difference here is that multiple (more than one) quantitative or dichotomously coded predictors are used. It is common practice to generate the model (solution) by entering all the variables in a single step; this is sometimes called the *standard* or *simultaneous* method. However, other methods that call for entering (or entering and then removing) the variables in stages or steps can be used as well; *SAS Enterprise Guide* provides several on a drop-down menu that offer a range of method choices. We will focus here on the standard method.

17.2 Numerical example

We will use an extension of the example presented in Chapter 16 in which we wished to predict the number of hours that students watched television over 10 weekdays. In addition to grade point average (**gpa** in the data set) that we used as a variable in Chapters 15 and 16, we will also use the number of pages submitted by the students when they completed their reports (**rep_size** in the data set), the number of hours the children were in childcare during that 10-day weekday period (**childcare hrs** in the data set), and the number of hours per week the children used the Internet to interact with the Web site established by the school (**internet hrs** in the data set) to access school-related assignment and instructor materials.

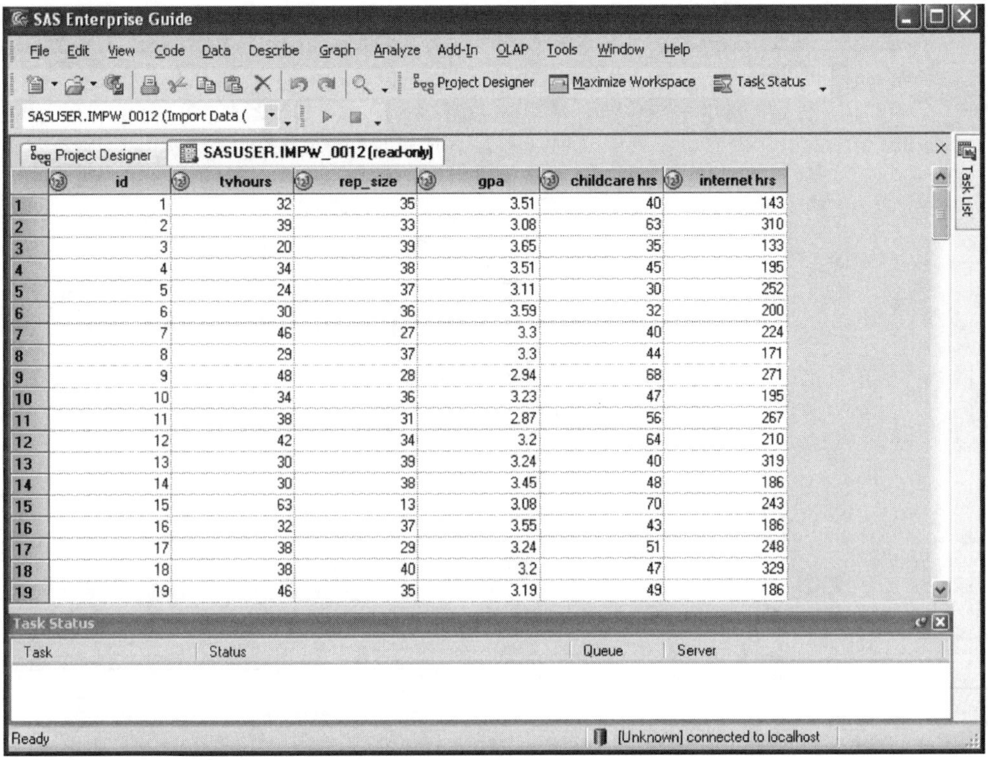

	id	tvhours	rep_size	gpa	childcare hrs	internet hrs
1	1	32	35	3.51	40	143
2	2	39	33	3.08	63	310
3	3	20	39	3.65	35	133
4	4	34	38	3.51	45	195
5	5	24	37	3.11	30	252
6	6	30	36	3.59	32	200
7	7	46	27	3.3	40	224
8	8	29	37	3.3	44	171
9	9	48	28	2.94	68	271
10	10	34	36	3.23	47	195
11	11	38	31	2.87	56	267
12	12	42	34	3.2	64	210
13	13	30	39	3.24	40	319
14	14	30	38	3.45	48	186
15	15	63	13	3.08	70	243
16	16	32	37	3.55	43	186
17	17	38	29	3.24	51	248
18	18	38	40	3.2	47	329
19	19	46	35	3.19	49	186

Figure 17.1. A portion of the data set.

A portion of the data set is shown in Figure 17.1. Students were assigned identification numbers (**id**) in the data set.

17.3 Viewing the correlations

It is useful to examine the Pearson correlations between the variables in advance of performing the regression analysis. From the main *SAS Enterprise Guide* menu, select **Analyze → Multivariate → Correlations**. This brings you to the **Task Roles** window. Drag all of the variables (except for **id**) to the slot under **Analysis variables** in the rightmost panel. This is shown in Figure 17.2. Then click the **Run** push button to perform the analysis.

Figure 17.3 presents the correlation matrix of the variables in the regression analysis. Because it is a square matrix, the same values appear in the upper (above the diagonal) and lower (below the diagonal) portions of the array. Each cell displays

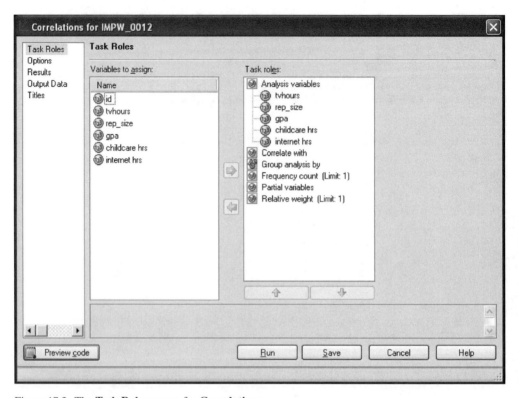

Figure 17.2. The **Task Roles** screen for **Correlations**.

the Pearson correlation coefficient as the top entry, the probability of obtaining that correlation by chance alone if the null hypothesis is true as the middle entry, and the sample size used for the calculation as the bottom entry.

All of the variables are significantly correlated with each other. Both **rep_size** and **childcare hrs** are quite highly correlated and are also highly correlated with the dependent variable **tvhours**; although this is not especially desirable in that the two predictor variables may be redundant, we will nonetheless include both in the regression analysis as their combined effect in the model is of interest.

17.4   Setting up the regression solution

From the main *SAS Enterprise Guide* menu, select **Analyze → Regression → Linear**. This brings you to the **Task Roles** window. Drag **tvhours** to the slot under **Dependent variable** in the rightmost panel. Then drag all of the remaining

Correlation Analysis

The CORR Procedure

5 Variables:	tvhours rep_size gpa childcare hrs internet hrs

Simple Statistics							
Variable	N	Mean	Std Dev	Sum	Minimum	Maximum	Label
tvhours	140	38.27143	10.41709	5358	20.00000	74.00000	tvhours
rep_size	140	32.44286	7.00901	4542	5.00000	40.00000	rep_size
gpa	140	3.30629	0.25464	462.88000	2.49000	3.90000	gpa
childcare hrs	139	51.41007	11.72314	7146	26.00000	85.00000	childcare hrs
internet hrs	140	216.82143	52.50560	30355	100.00000	367.00000	internet hrs

Pearson Correlation Coefficients Prob > |r| under H0: Rho=0 Number of Observations					
	tvhours	rep_size	gpa	childcare hrs	internet hrs
tvhours tvhours	1.00000 140	-0.69957 <.0001 140	-0.46543 <.0001 140	0.79823 <.0001 139	0.28286 0.0007 140
rep_size rep_size	-0.69957 <.0001 140	1.00000 140	0.43159 <.0001 140	-0.64037 <.0001 139	-0.31110 0.0002 140
gpa gpa	-0.46543 <.0001 140	0.43159 <.0001 140	1.00000 140	-0.47669 <.0001 139	-0.28510 0.0006 140
childcare hrs childcare hrs	0.79823 <.0001 139	-0.64037 <.0001 139	-0.47669 <.0001 139	1.00000 139	0.26127 0.0019 139
internet hrs internet hrs	0.28286 0.0007 140	-0.31110 0.0002 140	-0.28510 0.0006 140	0.26127 0.0019 139	1.00000 140

Figure 17.3. The correlations of the variables in the regression analysis.

variables (except for **id**) to the slot under **Explanatory variables** in the rightmost panel. This is shown in Figure 17.4.

The **Model** is set for the full model as the default for *SAS Enterprise Guide* and is fine for us. We therefore do not need to deal with that screen (see Section 16.4 for a description of it). Click **Statistics** from the navigation panel on the far left. As shown in Figure 17.5, select **Standardized regression coefficients** under

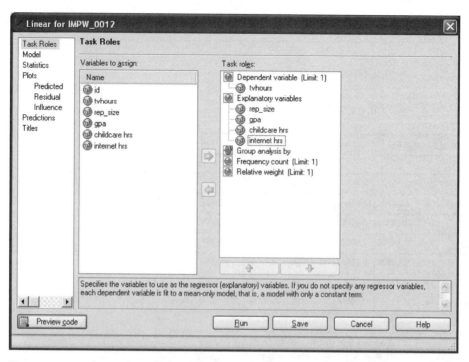

Figure 17.4. The **Task Roles** screen for the **Linear Regression** procedure.

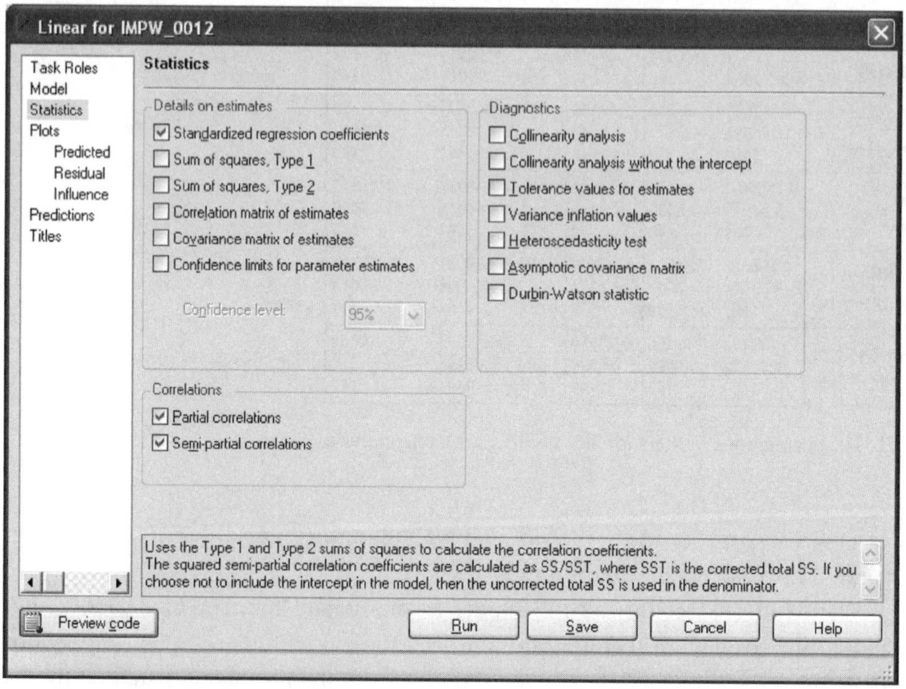

Figure 17.5. The **Statistics** screen for the **Linear Regression** procedure.

Model: Linear_Regression_Model
Dependent Variable: tvhours tvhours

Number of Observations Read	140
Number of Observations Used	139
Number of Observations with Missing Values	1

Analysis of Variance					
Source	**DF**	**Sum of Squares**	**Mean Square**	**F Value**	**Pr > F**
Model	4	10567	2641.66606	78.38	<.0001
Error	134	4516.48686	33.70513		
Corrected Total	138	15083			

Root MSE	5.80561	**R-Square**	0.7006
Dependent Mean	38.26619	**Adj R-Sq**	0.6916
Coeff Var	15.17165		

Figure 17.6. An overview of the model.

Details on estimates. Then select under **Correlations** both **Partial correlations** and **Semi-partial correlations**. Click **Run** to perform the analysis.

17.5   The regression output

The output is structured in the same way as that described in Chapter 16, and so we will deal with only the highlights here. The tables shown in Figure 17.6 display the general information concerning the regression model produced by SAS. The analysis of variance indicates that the model is statistically significant; that is, it accounts for a statistically significant portion of the variance of the dependent variable **tvhours**. In this fictitious data set, a rather large amount (approximately 70%) of **tvhours** variance is accounted for ($R^2 = .7006$; adjusted $R^2 = .6916$).

17.5.1 The statistically significant predictors

The model parameters (intercept and the regression coefficients for the predictors) based on the ordinary least squares method are shown in Figure 17.7. We determine from the table that with all of the variables used in combination to predict **tvhours**,

								Squared	Squared	Squared	Squared
								Semi-partial	Partial	Semi-partial	Partial
Variable	Label	DF	Parameter Estimate	Standard Error	t Value	Pr > |t|	Standardized Estimate	Corr Type I	Corr Type I	Corr Type II	Corr Type II
Intercept	Intercept	1	33.19735	10.08253	3.29	0.0013	0	.	.	.	.
rep_size	rep_size	1	-0.44801	0.09442	-4.75	<.0001	-0.30144	0.48938	0.48938	0.05031	0.14386
gpa	gpa	1	-2.31090	2.27608	-1.02	0.3118	-0.05634	0.03299	0.06461	0.00230	0.00763
childcare hrs	childcare hrs	1	0.51026	0.05736	8.90	<.0001	0.57218	0.17770	0.37205	0.17684	0.37129
internet hrs	internet hrs	1	0.00469	0.01005	0.47	0.6416	0.02360	0.00048625	0.00162	0.00048625	0.00162

Parameter Estimates

Figure 17.7. The parameters of the model.

only **childcare hrs** and **rep_size** are statistically significant contributors to the model. We can thus say the following concerning these variables:

- Given that **childcare hrs** has a raw score coefficient of 0.51026, we can say that, controlling for all the other variables, television viewing increased by about half an hour (about 0.5 hours) for every hour of increased childcare.
- Given that **rep_size** has a raw score coefficient of −0.44801, we can say that, controlling for all the other variables, television viewing decreased by almost half an hour (about 0.45 hours) for every page produced by the children for their reports.

17.5.2 The predictors not reaching statistical significance

The two remaining variables, **gpa** and **internet hrs**, did not reach statistical significance as predictors. Although one might naively be inclined to dismiss these variables as viable predictors, that would be incorrect. We know from the correlation analysis that all of the potential predictors in the model were significantly related to **tvhours**. In fact, we intentionally used **gpa** and **tvhours** in Chapters 15 and 16 to illustrate bivariate correlation and simple linear regression, respectively. Furthermore, we determined that, when used in isolation, **gpa** was a significant predictor of **tvhours**.

The lesson to be learned is that each variable *on its own* was perfectly capable of significantly predicting **tvhours** (because each was significantly correlated with it). The key here is that these variables were *not* on their own but were rather used as a set. It was in this particular combination that **gpa** and **internet hrs** were "overshadowed" by the other two predictors (i.e., they were doing the same prediction as **childcare hrs** and **rep_size** and were therefore providing redundant or nonrelevant additional information); it is possible that if **gpa** and **internet hrs** were members of a different combination of independent variables, these two variables might very well turn out to be statistically significant predictors.

18 Simple Logistic Regression

18.1 Overview

Logistic regression is conceptually analogous to linear regression in that a single dependent variable is predicted from either a single predictor (simple logistic regression) or multiple predictors (multiple logistic regression) based on a prediction model. It is also permissible to use both quantitatively measured and dichotomously (binary) coded variables as predictors. Our example for this chapter involves a single quantitatively measured predictor variable.

18.2 Some differences between linear and logistic regression

Although the two regression methods are conceptually similar, the differences between linear and logistic regression are important. Three of the most salient differences are as follows:

- In linear regression, the dependent variable is quantitatively measured; in logistic regression, the dependent variable is categorical. We will limit ourselves to a dichotomously coded dependent variable.
- In linear regression, a straight line function is fitted to the data set by using an ordinary least squares method; in logistic regression, a logistic function (an S-shaped function) is fitted to the data set by using a maximum likelihood estimation procedure.
- In linear regression the value of the quantitatively measured dependent variable is predicted; in logistic regression the dependent variable is categorical and what is predicted is the likelihood that a case with a certain value or values on the predictor(s) is a member of a particular group (the reference group).

18.3   Two notable features of logistic regression

18.3.1 Coding of the binary dependent variable

Although the specific coded values for dichotomous variables may be completely arbitrarily assigned in theory, in logistic regression it is important to thoughtfully determine which group is assigned which code. In accord with Hosmer and Lemeshow (2000), we suggest using values of 1 and 0. One value is assigned to the group you wish to use as the reference or focal group, and the other code is assigned to the comparison group to which you want to compare the reference group.

Consider a study in which you want to predict that a person will purchase a hybrid automobile (as opposed to any other type of car). The reference or focal group of this dependent variable is then the individuals who would purchase the hybrid. Because purchasing a hybrid is the focus of the study, the people who did so are coded as 0. Further, because we wish to compare them to those who purchased other types of cars, the people in this latter group are coded as 1.

18.3.2 The focus is on the odds ratio

The outcome of most interest to researchers using logistic regression is the odds ratio. It is a value associated with each predictor allowing us to make a statement based on the predictor variable regarding the odds of a case being coded as 0 on the dependent variable. For example, given an obtained odds ratio of 1.25 with price of gas predicting hybrid purchase, the following is an example of how to interpret an odds ratio: "For every price increase of 10 cents per gallon, the odds of people purchasing a hybrid automobile increases by 1.25."

18.4   Numerical example

This hypothetical study, funded by the Feline Study Institute, wished to predict whether people would identify themselves as either a "cat person" or a "dog person." In the data set this variable is named **sas person type**, with the characterization of cat person coded as 0 (this establishes cats as the reference group in SAS) and that of dog person coded as 1. For this study, the individuals who were asked what kind of person they were also completed a brief inventory measuring the strength of their social dominance behavior (**dominance** in the data set), with higher scores indicating greater dominance. The intent of the study was to predict if people were

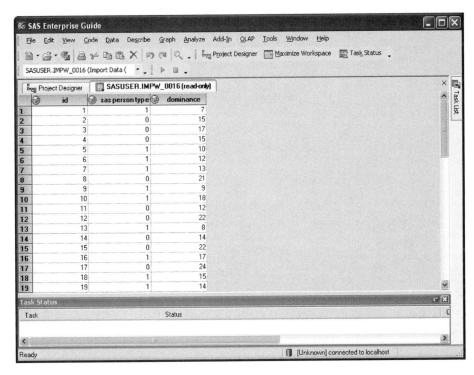

Figure 18.1. A portion of the data set.

cat folks based on their dominance score. A portion of the data set is shown in Figure 18.1.

18.5   Setting up the logistic regression solution

From the main *SAS Enterprise Guide* menu, select **Analyze → Regression → Logistic**. This brings us to the **Task Roles** window. Drag **sas person type** to the slot under **Dependent variable** in the rightmost panel. Then drag **dominance** to the slot under **Quantitative variables** in the rightmost panel. This is shown in Figure 18.2.

Click **Model** from the navigation panel on the far left. The window opens on the **Effects** tab as shown in Figure 18.3. Note that **dominance** appears in the panel for **Class and quantitative variables**. Variables listed in this panel are potential predictors. To place **dominance** in the model, click it. This action will activate the **Main, Cross,** and **Polynomial** bars in the area between panels. Click the **Main** push

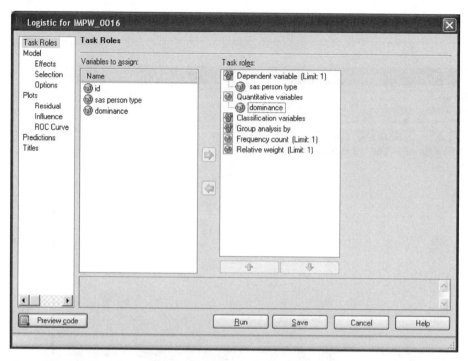

Figure 18.2. The **Task Roles** screen of the **Logistic Regression** procedure.

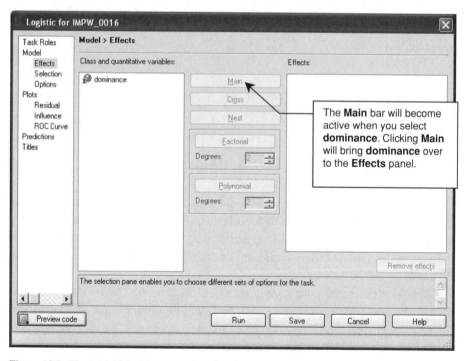

The **Main** bar will become active when you select **dominance**. Clicking **Main** will bring **dominance** over to the **Effects** panel.

Figure 18.3. The initial **Model** screen of the **Logistic Regression** procedure.

180

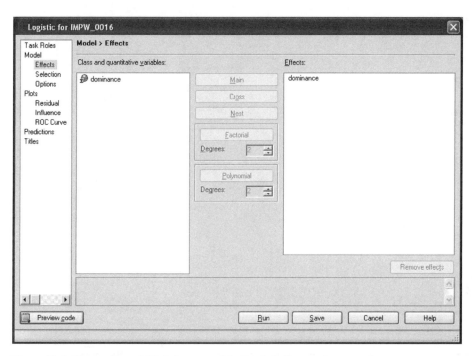

Figure 18.4. The configured **Model** screen of the **Logistic Regression** procedure.

button to place **dominance** in the far right **Effects** panel, as shown in Figure 18.4. This will cause SAS to evaluate the effects of **dominance** as a *main effect* in the analysis (akin to a main effect in analysis of variance).

Under **Model** in the navigation panel, click **Options**. Select under **Statistics** both **Hosmer and Lemeshow goodness-of-fit test** and **Generalized R-squared** (see Figure 18.5). Then click the **Run** push button to perform the analysis.

18.6 The logistic regression output

Figure 18.6 provides information about how well the model performed in predicting how people characterized themselves. The lower table labeled **Testing Global Null Hypothesis** uses a chi-square procedure to test the statistical significance of the model, analogous to the analysis of variance procedure for linear regression. All three tests agree in indicating that our prediction of people's characterization is better than chance, assuming an alpha level of $\alpha = .05$; for example, the **Likelihood Ratio** is associated with a probability level (**Pr > ChiSq**) of .0001.

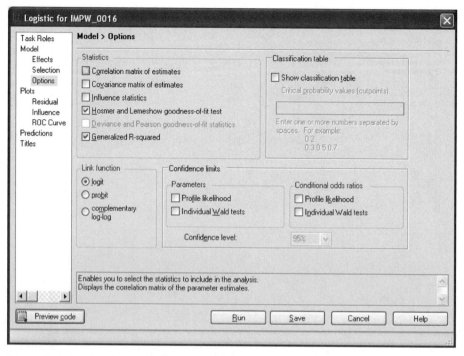

Figure 18.5. The **Options** screen of the **Logistic Regression** procedure.

R-Square	0.4123	Max-rescaled R-Square	0.5498

Testing Global Null Hypothesis: BETA=0			
Test	Chi-Square	DF	Pr > ChiSq
Likelihood Ratio	31.8967	1	<.0001
Score	25.2637	1	<.0001
Wald	14.1123	1	0.0002

Figure 18.6. How well the model performed.

The top table in Figure 18.6 indicates the effectiveness of prediction. Although a true *R*-square value cannot be computed, so-called pseudo *R*-square values can be estimated (Meyers et al., 2006). *SAS Enterprise Guide* provides two such estimates. What is named **R-Square** in the table, with a value of .4123, is the Cox and Snell estimate. The statistic named **Max-rescaled R-Square**, with a value of .5498, is the Nagelkerke estimate. Both are interpreted in the same way as an *R*-square

Partition for the Hosmer and Lemeshow Test					
		sas person type = 0		sas person type = 1	
Group	Total	Observed	Expected	Observed	Expected
1	8	0	0.39	8	7.61
2	10	3	1.66	7	8.34
3	3	0	0.79	3	2.21
4	8	3	2.98	5	5.02
5	7	3	3.47	4	3.53
6	7	6	4.77	1	2.23
7	8	6	7.13	2	0.87
8	9	9	8.83	0	0.17

Hosmer and Lemeshow Goodness-of-Fit Test		
Chi-Square	DF	Pr > ChiSq
5.7284	6	0.4543

Figure 18.7. Results of the Hosmer and Lemeshow test.

from linear regression: each estimates the amount of dependent variable variance accounted for by the model. For example, based on the Nagelkerke pseudo R-square value, we would say that the model accounted for approximately 55% of the variance of how people characterized themselves. These two R-square measures are not interchangeable – researchers need to be specific about what they report and use for interpretation.

The lower table in Figure 18.7 presents the results of the omnibus Hosmer and Lemeshow test. Very briefly, this test assesses whether the predicted probabilities of how people characterized themselves based on the model match the observed probabilities. A chi-square statistic is used to test this, and a nonsignificant result means that the model predictions and the data are in accord (this is a desirable outcome).

In the upper table the data set has been divided into portions (eight segments or groups in this case) representing increasing likelihoods of respondents identifying themselves as cat people (first set of columns) and decreasing likelihoods of respondents identifying themselves as dog people (last set of columns). The observed and expected count (frequency) for each type of person is shown for each segment.

The test for the overall (omnibus) model based on all of the segments combined is what we saw in the lower table. With eight segments for the two types of people,

Analysis of Maximum Likelihood Estimates					
Parameter	DF	Estimate	Standard Error	Wald Chi-Square	Pr > ChiSq
Intercept	1	-7.5659	1.9933	14.4064	0.0001
dominance	1	0.5031	0.1339	14.1123	0.0002

Odds Ratio Estimates		
Effect	Point Estimate	95% Wald Confidence Limits
dominance	1.654	1.272 2.150

Figure 18.8. The details of the model.

we have 6 degrees of freedom, or 6 *df* (we lose 1 *df* for each person type). Thus, the omnibus chi-square is tested with 6 *df*.

Figure 18.8 shows the details of the model. The logistic regression coefficient for **dominance** is listed under the **Estimate** column in the upper table (the coefficient value is 0.5031), and it indicates the amount of change expected in the log odds when there is a 1-unit change in the predictor variable. It is statistically significant, informing us that **dominance** is a statistically significant predictor of how people characterize themselves. However, it is the odds ratio that is most intuitively interpreted, and that is shown in the lower table in the column named **Point Estimate**. The odds ratio of 1.654 signifies that an increase of 1 point on the scale measuring dominance increases the odds of respondents characterizing themselves as "cat people" by better than one and a half times (specifically, 1.654 times).

19 Multiple Logistic Regression

19.1 Overview

Multiple logistic regression is a direct extension of simple logistic regression. A logistic (S-shaped) function is used to predict a categorical variable from information provided by two or more predictor variables. As is true for multiple linear regression, it is common practice to generate the model (solution) by entering all the variables in a single step; this is sometimes called the *standard* or *simultaneous* method. However, other methods call for entering (or entering and then removing) the variables in stages or steps; there are many ways to accomplish this, and *SAS Enterprise Guide* provides several on a drop-down menu. We will focus here on the standard method predicting a binary dependent variable.

Everything we said in Chapter 18 regarding simple logistic regression is applicable here. One noteworthy feature of the analysis concerns the coding of binary predictor variables.

19.2 Coding of binary predictor variables

In Section 18.3.1 of the previous chapter, we discussed coding the dichotomous *dependent* variable. The default coding scheme used by *SAS Enterprise Guide* presumes that for the dependent variable the group we wish to use as the reference group is coded as 0 and that the comparison group to which we want to compare the reference group is coded as 1.

The coding scheme for the *predictor* binary variables has to be just the reverse of the scheme used for the dependent variable. Specifically, *SAS Enterprise Guide* presumes that the group we wish to use as the reference group is coded as 1 and that the comparison group to which we want to compare the reference group is coded as 0. This may actually be the more commonly used coding scheme in other statistical packages. For example, the SPSS logistic regression procedure treats the code of 1 as designating the focal group for all binary variables, whether they are dependent or predictor variables. Thus, if we wished to focus on the purchasing tendencies of female shoppers in our narrative of the results, then we would code female as 1 for the sex-of-consumer predictor variable.

19.3   Numerical example

We will carry over and extend our example from simple logistic regression. Recall that we wished to predict whether people would identify themselves as a "cat person" or a "dog person." In the data set this variable is named **sas person type** with the characterization of cat person coded as 0 and that of dog person coded as 1. We intentionally identify person type with the SAS software package as a cue to help readers remember that the focal group of the *dependent* variable is coded as 0 (because the binary *predictor* variable we use will code the focal group as 1).

For this example, we continue to use the strength of social dominance behavior, that is, **dominance** in the data set from the Chapter 18 example, as a quantitatively measured predictor. We add here the binary predictor of **sex**. The group in this example about which we wish to be the focus of our narrative is female; thus, in the data set individuals of the female sex are coded as 1 and those of the male sex are coded as 0. A portion of the data set is shown in Figure 19.1.

19.4   Setting up the logistic regression solution

From the main *SAS Enterprise Guide menu*, select **Analyze → Regression → Logistic**. This brings you to the **Task Roles** window. Drag **sas person type** to the slot under **Dependent variable** in the rightmost panel. Drag **dominance** and then **sex** to the slot under **Quantitative variables** in the rightmost panel. This is shown in Figure 19.2.

Click **Model** from the navigation panel on the far left. The window opens on the **Effects** tab as shown in Figure 19.3. Note that **dominance** and **sex** appear in the panel for **Class and quantitative variables**. Variables listed in this panel are potential predictors. To place **dominance** in the model, click it. This action will activate the **Main**, **Cross**, and **Polynomial** bars in the area between panels. Click the **Main** push button to place **dominance** in the far right **Effects** panel. Repeat this

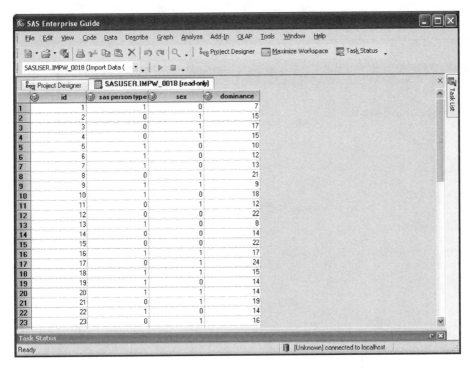

Figure 19.1. A portion of the data set.

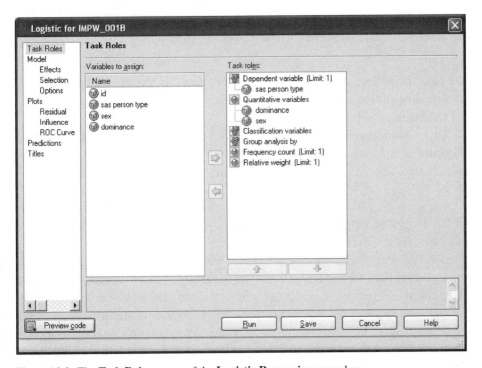

Figure 19.2. The **Task Roles** screen of the **Logistic Regression** procedure.

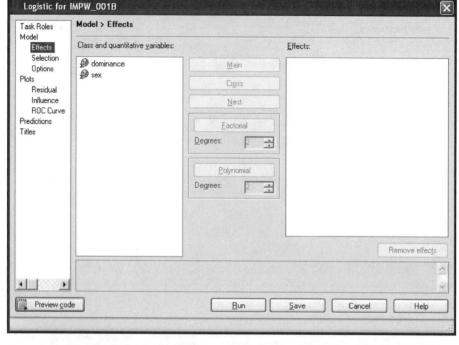

Figure 19.3. The initial **Model** screen of the **Logistic Regression** procedure.

for **sex**. This is shown in Figure 19.4. This will cause SAS to evaluate the effects of **dominance** and **sex** as *main effects* in the analysis (akin to main effects in analysis of variance).

Under **Model** in the navigation panel, click **Options**. Select under **Statistics** both **Hosmer and Lemeshow goodness-of-fit test** and **Generalized R-squared** (see Figure 19.5). Then click the **Run** push button to perform the analysis.

19.5   The logistic regression output

Figure 19.6 provides information about how well the model performed in predicting how people characterized themselves. The lower table labeled **Testing Global Null Hypothesis** uses a chi-square procedure to test the statistical significance of the model, analogous to the analysis of variance procedure for linear regression. All three tests agree in indicating that our prediction of people's characterization is better than chance, assuming an alpha level of $\alpha = .05$; for example, the **Likelihood Ratio** is associated with a probability level (**Pr > ChiSq**) of .0001.

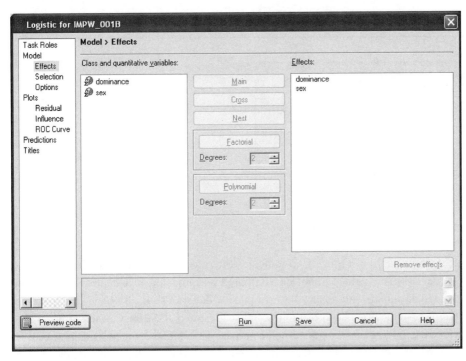

Figure 19.4. The configured **Model** screen of the **Logistic Regression** procedure.

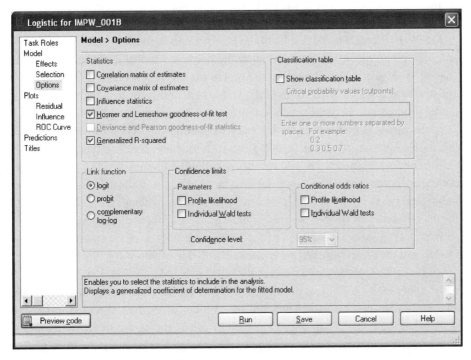

Figure 19.5. The **Options** screen of the **Logistic Regression** procedure.

R-Square	0.5307	Max-rescaled R-Square	0.7075

Testing Global Null Hypothesis: BETA=0			
Test	Chi-Square	DF	Pr > ChiSq
Likelihood Ratio	45.3851	2	<.0001
Score	33.8327	2	<.0001
Wald	16.8129	2	0.0002

Figure 19.6. How well the model performed.

The top table in Figure 19.6 indicates the effectiveness of prediction. Although a true R-square value cannot be computed as indicated in Chapter 18, so-called pseudo R-square values can be estimated (Meyers et al., 2006). *SAS Enterprise Guide* provides two such estimates. What is named **R-Square** in the table, with a value of .5307, is the Cox and Snell estimate. The statistic named **Max-rescaled R-Square**, with a value of .7075, is the Nagelkerke estimate. Both estimate the amount of dependent variable variance accounted for by the model. In our example, based on the Nagelkerke pseudo R-square value, we would say that the model accounted for approximately 71% of the variance of how people characterized themselves.

Figure 19.7 presents the results of the Hosmer and Lemeshow test. As discussed in Chapter 18, this test assesses whether the predicted probabilities of how people characterized themselves based on the model match the observed probabilities. A chi-square statistic is used to test this, and a nonsignificant result means that the model predictions and the data do not differ (this is a desirable outcome).

In the upper table the data set has been divided into portions (nine segments in this case). The observed and expected count (frequency) for each type of person is shown for each segment. The test for the overall model based on all of the segments combined is shown in the lower table. The result is not statistically significant, indicating a match between the predicted and observed values. With nine segments for the two types of people, we have 7 *df* (we lose 1 *df* for each person type).

Figure 19.8 shows the details of the model. We now have two predictors in the model, and the effects of each are evaluated with the effects of the other statistically controlled. The logistic regression coefficients are listed under the **Estimate** column in the upper table. As we can see, the coefficients for **dominance** and **sex** are 0.5037 and 2.8348, respectively, and indicate the amount of change expected in the log odds when there is a 1-unit change in each of the predictor variables. Both are statistically significant ($p = .0007$ and $p = .0012$, respectively) under the **Pr > ChiSq** column.

Partition for the Hosmer and Lemeshow Test					
		sas person type = 0		sas person type = 1	
Group	Total	Observed	Expected	Observed	Expected
1	6	0	0.07	6	5.93
2	6	0	0.28	6	5.72
3	8	1	0.88	7	7.12
4	6	1	1.19	5	4.81
5	7	4	3.10	3	3.90
6	6	4	4.55	2	1.45
7	5	5	4.42	0	0.58
8	7	6	6.58	1	0.42
9	9	9	8.94	0	0.06

Hosmer and Lemeshow Goodness-of-Fit Test		
Chi-Square	DF	Pr > ChiSq
2.7178	7	0.9098

Figure 19.7. Results of the Hosmer and Lemeshow test.

Analysis of Maximum Likelihood Estimates					
Parameter	DF	Estimate	Standard Error	Wald Chi-Square	Pr > ChiSq
Intercept	1	-8.9817	2.3805	14.2358	0.0002
dominance	1	0.5037	0.1480	11.5839	0.0007
sex	1	2.8348	0.8761	10.4691	0.0012

Odds Ratio Estimates		
Effect	Point Estimate	95% Wald Confidence Limits
dominance	1.655	1.238 2.212
sex	17.027	3.058 94.823

Figure 19.8. The details of the model.

The odds ratios are the outcomes that are most often interpreted when the results of multiple logistic regression are reported, and those are shown in the lower table in the **Point Estimate** column. The odds ratio for a **dominance** of 1.655 signifies that an increase of 1 point on the scale measuring dominance increases the odds of respondents characterizing themselves as "cat people" by better than one and a half times (specifically, 1.655 times) when the effects of **sex** are controlled for. This is virtually the same odds ratio as obtained in the Chapter 18 analysis where **dominance** was the only predictor. The reason for this is that the predictive work done by the two predictors are rather independent of each other.

A more dramatic result as shown in the model is the odds ratio for **sex**. With female individuals coded as 1 to make them the subject of the narrative, the odds ratio of 17.027 can be interpreted as indicating that female individuals are approximately 17 times more likely to characterize themselves as cat people than are male individuals when the effects of **dominance** are controlled for.

Section VII

Comparing Means:
The *t* Test

20 Independent-Groups *t* Test

20.1 Overview

The independent-groups *t* test is a procedure to determine if the means of exactly two independent distributions are significantly different. Because a one-way between-subjects analysis of variance (ANOVA) design is the general case of the independent-groups *t* test, and because $t^2 = F$, it is common practice to defer to the ANOVA for two-group as well as multigroup designs. However, the *t* test is well worth covering in statistics courses, and we believe it is of sufficient importance to cover in this book as well.

20.2 Some history

William Sealy Gosset, a chemist and mathematician, was hired in 1899 by the Guinness Brewing Company. As Salsburg (2001) tells the story, in the context of monitoring the brewing of that beer, Gosset developed several statistical innovations that he wished to publish in the professional literature. However, to protect trade secrets, the company prohibited its employees from publishing their work. Gosset therefore devised a pseudonym with the help of Karl Pearson so that he could disseminate his work in Pearson's *Biometrika*. The pseudonym that they devised was the name *Student*, and in 1908 Student published an article describing a new statistical test and its distribution. The letter *t* was selected by Gosset and Pearson as the name of the test and distribution because it was the last letter of the word *Student*.

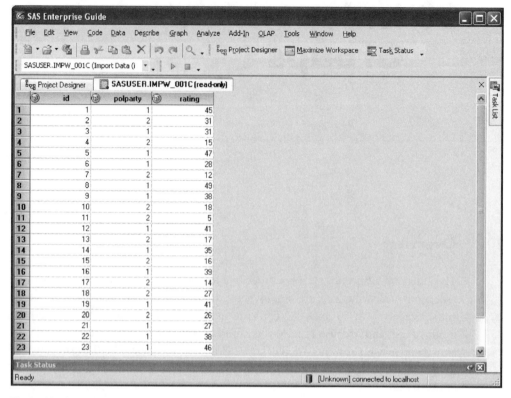

Figure 20.1. A portion of the data set.

20.3 Numerical example

To test the proposition that beauty or truth is in the eye of the beholder, a hypothetical sample of political activists was recruited who acknowledged themselves to be long-term members of either the Democratic or Republican party. In this study, political party is the *independent variable*; in the data set, it is called **polparty**; Democrats are coded as 1 and Republicans are coded as 2. All participants then listened to a speech given by a prominent Democratic politician, and they were asked to rate it by using a 50-point scale in which higher values represented better ratings. The variable denoting these scores is called **rating** in the data set, and it is the *dependent variable*. The question addressed by this research is whether or not there is a difference in the way that the Democrats and Republicans evaluated the speech. A portion of the data set is shown in Figure 20.1.

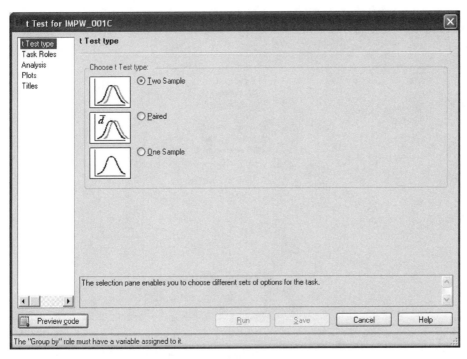

Figure 20.2. The **t Test type** screen of the **t Test** procedure.

20.4   Setting up the analysis

From the main *SAS Enterprise Guide* menu, select **Analyze → ANOVA → t Test**. The initial window, shown in Figure 20.2, is named **t Test type**, and it asks us to identify the kind of *t* test we wish to perform. The default of **Two Sample** is what we want for the data we have here. It is already selected, and so we can click on **Task Roles** in the navigation panel to reach the **Task Roles** screen. Drag **rating** to the slot under **Analysis variables** in the rightmost panel. Then drag **polparty** to the slot under **Group by**. This is shown in Figure 20.3. Finally, click the **Run** push button to perform the analysis.

20.5   The *t*-test output

The upper **Statistics** table of Figure 20.4 displays the descriptive statistics produced by SAS. These include the means and their confidence limits (noted as **CL**), the

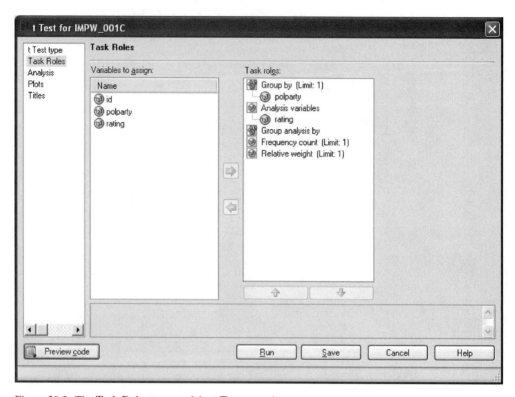

Figure 20.3. The **Task Roles** screen of the **t Test** procedure.

			Statistics							
Variable	polparty	N	Lower CL Mean	Mean	Upper CL Mean	Lower CL Std Dev	Std Dev	Upper CL Std Dev	Std Err	Minimum	Maximum
rating	1	13	34.56	38.846	43.132	5.0861	7.0928	11.708	1.9672	27	49
rating	2	13	13.289	17.615	21.942	5.1339	7.1594	11.818	1.9856	5	31
rating	Diff (1-2)		15.462	21.231	27	5.5643	7.1262	9.9136	2.7951		

		T-Tests			
Variable	Method	Variances	DF	t Value	Pr > |t|
rating	Pooled	Equal	24	7.60	<.0001
rating	Satterthwaite	Unequal	24	7.60	<.0001

		Equality of Variances			
Variable	Method	Num DF	Den DF	F Value	Pr > F
rating	Folded F	12	12	1.02	0.9747

The **Folded F** is a ratio of the larger of the two variances divided by the smaller of the two variances.

Figure 20.4. The output of the **t Test** procedure.

standard deviations, and the standard errors. We can see in the table, for example, that the mean rating of the speech by Democrats (**polparty** = 1) was 38.846 and the mean rating of the speech by Republicans (**polparty** = 2) was 17.615.

The bottom table gives the results of the comparison of group variances. One of the assumptions underlying the *t* test is that the group variances are equal (not significantly different); this is known as *homogeneity of variance*. We tested this assumption as part of the analysis by using what SAS labels as a **Folded F** procedure. In computing a folded *F*, the larger of the two variances is divided by the smaller of the two variances (Davis, 2007), producing an *F* ratio (see Chapter 23) whose lowest possible value is 1.00. The results of the **Folded F** procedure indicated that the two variances were comparable (**Pr > F = 0.9747**).

The middle table provides the *t*-test results, which are provided for the case in which the group variances are equal and in which the variances are unequal. Our data meet the equal variances assumption, and so we can read from the first row of the table (labeled as **Pooled**). Based on 24 *df*, the computed *t* value of 7.60 is statistically significant (**Pr > |t| < .0001**). Looking at the two means, we can therefore conclude that the speech of a prominent Democratic politician was more favorably evaluated by Democrats than by Republicans.

20.6 Magnitude of the effect

The procedure just described addressed the issue of whether or not the two means were significantly different. We determined that they were. However, it is then appropriate to ask about the magnitude of the effect, something that is not directly computed by *SAS Enterprise Guide* but is increasingly emphasized in the professional literature (see Gamst et al., 2008). Thus we briefly conclude this chapter by presenting two indexes assessing effect magnitude: eta squared and Cohen's *d*.

20.6.1 Eta squared

Eta is a correlation coefficient. Applied to the independent *t*-test design, it represents the correlation between the dependent and the independent variables. Eta squared in the present context is interpreted as the *strength of the effect*: the amount of variance in the dependent variable (speech ratings) accounted for by the independent variable (political party). Values of eta squared of $\eta^2 = .09$, .14, and .22 can be interpreted, at least in isolation, as weak, medium, and strong (Meyers et al., 2006).

Eta squared may be computed as follows in an independent *t*-test design (Hays, 1981):

$$\eta^2 = t^2/(t^2 + \text{degrees of freedom}).$$

For the present results, that is, $t = 7.60$ and 24 *df*, the eta-square value is $\eta^2 = 57.76$ divided by $(57.76 + 24)$, or $57.76/81.76$, or .706, and represents a strong effect. Thus, approximately 70% of the variance of the speech ratings can be explained by the political party of the raters.

20.6.2 Cohen's *d*

Jacob Cohen (1969, 1977, 1988) suggested looking at the potency of the treatment effect by examining what he called *effect size*. He proposed that the mean difference can be judged relative to the standard deviations of the groups. In his guidelines for interpreting the value of *d*, Cohen proposed that, all else equal, values of $d = 0.2$, 0.5, and 0.8 can be thought of as small, medium, and large effect sizes, respectively. For example, if the mean difference spans a distance of almost a full 1 *SD*, then the means of the two groups can be quite easily distinguished and so we would judge the effect size to be large.

Cohen's *d* may be computed as follows:

Cohen's *d* = absolute mean difference/average standard deviation.

For the present results, the standard deviations are 7.0928 and 7.1594. With equal group sizes, the average is 7.1261. The mean difference is 38.846 – 17.615, or 21.231. Cohen's *d* is therefore equal to 21.231 divided by 7.1261, or 2.979. This would be judged as a very large effect size, and we would conclude that political party is a very important factor in factors determining the evaluation of a political speech; that is, we would conclude that beauty was indeed in the eyes of the beholder.

21 Correlated-Samples *t* Test

21.1 Overview

In addition to being applied to independent groups as shown in Chapter 20, the *t* test can also be used to test the statistical significance of mean differences when the two sets of scores represent the same cases, that is, when each case in the sample contributes a score on each of two variables. It is on this basis that the *x* and *y* variables are said to be linked or correlated (at least from a data-collection standpoint).

21.2 Relation to bivariate correlation

The correlated *t* test and Pearson correlation are intimately related. The following are two aspects of this relationship:

- The data set is structured in the same way. Specifically, each case in the data set is associated with two scores.
- The calculation of the *t* value takes into account the correlation between the scores (see Ferguson & Takane, 1989).

The correlated *t* test and Pearson correlation differ primarily in terms of the aspect of the data on which each focuses:

- The Pearson correlation identifies the degree of relationship or covariation that exists between the two sets of scores. In making such an evaluation, the differences between the means is completely irrelevant.

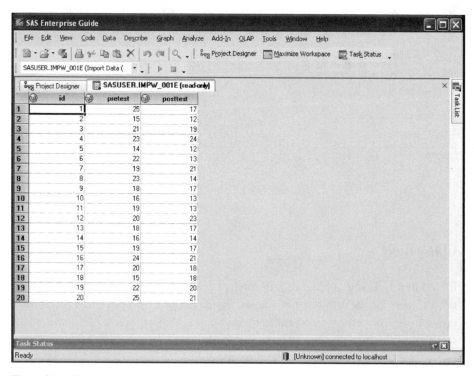

Figure 21.1. The data set.

- The *t* test focuses on mean differences; that is, it focuses on the relative differences in the magnitudes of the scores in each condition.

21.3 Numerical example

The hypothetical study we use as an example deals with an experimental medical treatment. In a portion of the clinical trials phase of the research, 20 patients diagnosed with advanced congestive heart failure agreed to receive Drug H. Ignoring for this example patients in any control group, the patients on whom we are focusing are tested before the beginning of treatment for congestive heart failure; these scores are named **pretest** in the data set. Higher values signify more intense symptoms. After receiving the drug and waiting an appropriate amount of time, the patients are again tested; these scores are named **posttest** in the data set. The data set is shown in Figure 21.1.

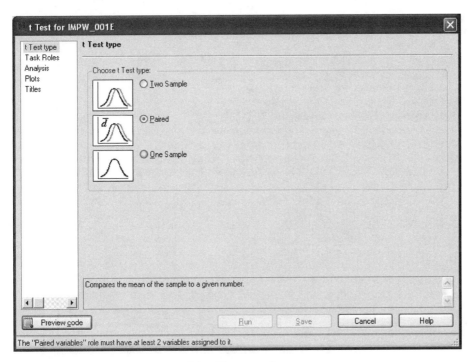

Figure 21.2. The **t Test type** screen of the **t Test** procedure.

21.4   Setting up the analysis

From the main *SAS Enterprise Guide* menu, select **Analyze → ANOVA → t Test**. The initial window, shown in Figure 21.2, is named **t Test type**, and it asks us to identify the kind of *t* test we wish to perform. Select **Paired**. Click on **Task Roles** in the navigation panel to reach the **Task Roles** window. Drag **pretest** and **posttest** to the slot under **Paired variables** in the rightmost panel. This is shown in Figure 21.3. Finally, click the **Run** push button to perform the analysis.

21.5   The *t*-test output

The upper **Statistics** table of Figure 21.4 displays the descriptive statistics produced by SAS. Descriptive statistics for the computed mean difference include the value of the mean difference and its confidence limits (noted as **CL**), its standard deviation, and its standard error.

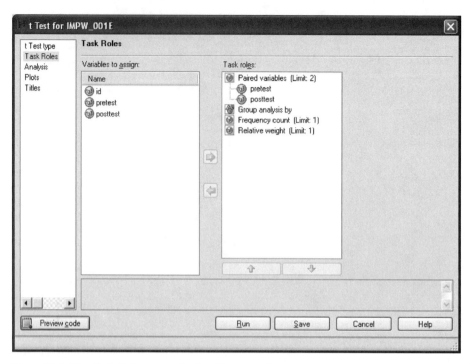

Figure 21.3. The **Task Roles** screen in the **t Test** procedure.

t Test

The TTEST Procedure

Statistics									
Difference	N	Lower CL Mean	Mean	Upper CL Mean	Lower CL Std Dev	Std Dev	Upper CL Std Dev	Std Err	Minimum	Maximum
pretest - posttest	20	0.8752	2.5	4.1248	2.6402	3.4717	5.0707	0.7763	-3	9

T-Tests			
Difference	DF	t Value	Pr > |t|
pretest - posttest	19	3.22	0.0045

Figure 21.4. The output for the **t Test** procedure.

The bottom table provides the *t*-test results for the evaluation of the mean difference. Based on 19 *df*, the computed *t* value of 3.22 is statistically significant (**Pr > |t| = 0.0045**). Given that the value of **pretest – posttest** is a positive 2.5, we know that scores significantly dropped from the pretreatment baseline to the posttreatment measurement; in other words, patients exhibited less intense symptoms for congestive heart failure following treatment with Drug H.

21.6 Magnitude of the effect

21.6.1 Pearson correlation squared

Because the correlated *t* test is intimately tied to the Pearson correlation, we can use the Pearson correlation squared to assess the strength of the relationship between the pretest and the posttest. Using the process described in Chapter 15, we obtain a Pearson product–moment correlation of approximately $r = .53$, which in turn yields a Pearson correlation squared value of approximately $r^2 = .28$. We may therefore say that Drug H can impact approximately 28% of the congestive heart failure symptomatology measured by the medical test. In this context, that would probably be taken as a particularly strong effect.

21.6.2 Cohen's *d*

Computing Cohen's *d* requires knowledge of the means and standard deviations of the two sets of scores, information not provided by the **t Test** procedure of *SAS Enterprise Guide*. However, using the procedures described in Chapter 8, we can determine that the pretest mean and standard deviation are 19.70 and 3.404, respectively, and that the posttest mean and standard deviation are 17.20 and 3.722, respectively. Cohen's *d*, which is applicable to correlated *t* tests as well as independent-groups *t* tests (Cohen, 1988), can be computed to be 0.70. In isolation, this value would be considered to represent a medium-tending-toward-large effect size. Given the context of treatment for congestive heart failure, such an effect size would likely be considered by medical researchers to be exceptionally large.

22 Single-Sample *t* Test

22.1 Overview

A third and much less widely used application of the *t* test focuses on a situation in which we have data from a single sample and want to determine if it is likely that the sample had been drawn from a population whose parameter (typically a mean) is specified. Here are two examples of occasions in which we might employ such a test (the second based on an example used by Runyon, Coleman, & Pittenger, 2000).

First, the nationwide incidence for infectious disease D is known. Call this the population mean or parameter. The 17 townships surrounding city C appear to have a higher incidence of the disease. We can record the incidence values for these 17 townships, giving us a sample of 17 cases. We can then ask if the mean of the sample is significantly different from the population parameter.

Second, a researcher wishes to determine if the four-alternative multiple-choice questions in a reading comprehension exam contain cues to the correct answer. She therefore administers the test questions without the reading passages to 23 students who are instructed to answer the questions as best they can. If nothing but chance was in play, students should score 25% correct, and that is the population parameter of relevance. The percentage correct for the 23 students comprises the distribution of scores.

22.2 The general approach

The conceptual strategy used to evaluate the question of whether the sample mean and population mean significantly differ is, very briefly, as follows:

- The standard error of the sample mean is computed.
- A confidence interval corresponding to the alpha level used by researchers is then computed from the standard error. For example, under an alpha level of $\alpha = .05$, we would compute a 95% confidence interval.
- We would then determine where the population parameter fell with respect to the confidence interval: If it fell inside the interval we would judge the sample mean and the population parameter to be not significantly different; if it fell outside the interval we would judge the sample mean and the population parameter to be significantly different.
- This determination is made by means of a *t* test. The null hypothesis is that the sample mean is equivalent to the population parameter.

22.3 Numerical example

The hypothetical study we use as an example follows up on the second example provided in Section 22.1. The variable **percent corr** in the data set indexes the percentage correct a given student scored on the set of test questions. The data set is shown in Figure 22.1.

22.4 Setting up the analysis

From the main *SAS Enterprise Guide* menu, select **Analyze → ANOVA → t Test**. The initial window, shown in Figure 22.2, is named **t Test type**, and it asks us to identify the kind of *t* test we wish to perform. Select **One Sample**.

Click on **Task Roles** in the navigation panel to reach the **Task Roles** window. Drag **percent corr** to the slot under **Analysis variables** in the rightmost panel. This is shown in Figure 22.3.

Next, select **Analysis** in the navigation panel. In the **Null hypothesis** panel, we type in the population parameter against which we are testing. In this example, the value we type is **25**. The **Confidence level** is already set at 95%, and we opt for the default **Equal tailed** strategy. Click the **Run** push button to perform the analysis (see Figure 22.4).

22.5 The *t*-test output

The upper table of Figure 22.5 displays the descriptive statistics for the sample, including the mean, its confidence limits (noted as **CL**), its standard deviation,

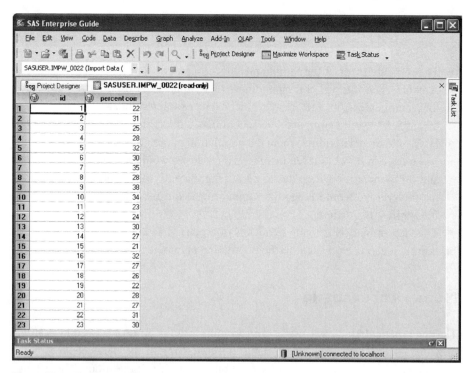

Figure 22.1. The data set.

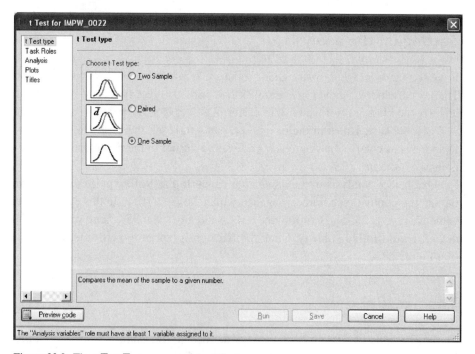

Figure 22.2. The **t Test Type** screen of the **t Test** procedure.

208

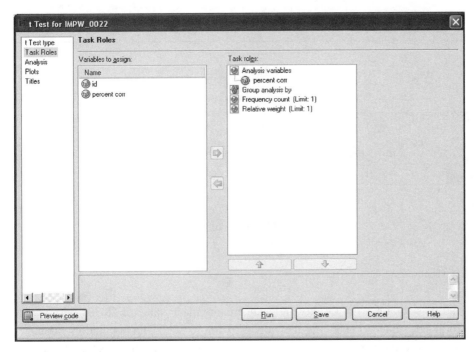

Figure 22.3. The **Task Roles** screen of the **t Test** procedure.

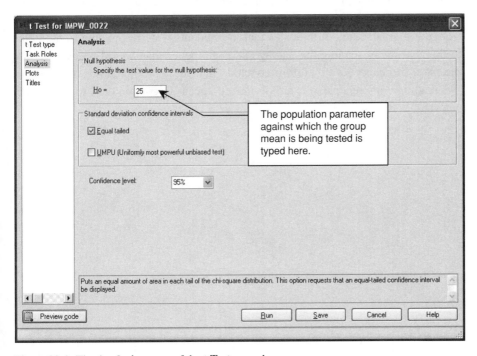

Figure 22.4. The **Analysis** screen of the **t Test** procedure.

t Test

The TTEST Procedure

Statistics									
Variable	N	Lower CL Mean	Mean	Upper CL Mean	Lower CL Std Dev	Std Dev	Upper CL Std Dev	Std Err	Minimum	Maximum
percent corr	23	26.408	28.304	30.2	3.3907	4.3842	6.2052	0.9142	21	38

T-Tests			
Variable	DF	t Value	Pr > |t|
percent corr	22	3.61	0.0015

Figure 22.5. The results of the analysis.

and its standard error. Of most relevance is the mean value of 28.304 with a 95% confidence interval spanning the values 26.408 to 30.2. The population parameter of 25 therefore lies outside of this range, immediately informing us that the sample mean is statistically different from the population parameter.

The bottom table provides the *t*-test results. Based on 22 *df*, the computed *t* value of 3.61 is statistically significant (**Pr > |t| = 0.0015**). This confirms what was clear from the first table, and it indicates that the students were responding to the items in the absence of reading the passage at a rate better than would be expected on the basis of chance; we therefore conclude that the multiple-choice questions in this reading comprehension exam do indeed appear to contain cues to the correct answer.

Section VIII

Comparing Means: ANOVA

23 One-Way Between-Subjects ANOVA

23.1 Overview

Analysis of variance (ANOVA) is a family of research and statistical designs allowing us to determine if the means of two or more distributions are significantly different. Each of the next four chapters focuses on a separate ANOVA design.

23.2 Naming of ANOVA designs

There are three important pieces of information that are contained in the name of each ANOVA design: the number of independent variables in the design, the number of levels contained in each independent variable, and an indication of the type of independent variables that are included in the design.

23.2.1 The number of independent variables

It is possible to have any number of independent variables in an ANOVA design, although each additional variable that is added substantially escalates the logistics of the data collection. In this chapter and in Chapter 25, we discuss designs containing one independent variable; in Chapters 24 and 26, we discuss designs containing two independent variables.

We communicate the number of independent variables by speaking of n-way designs where n is the count of independent variables. For example, a one-way design contains a single independent variable and a two-way design contains two independent variables.

23.2.2 The number of levels of the independent variables

It is also especially useful when there is more than one independent variable to include an indication of the number of levels of each. By convention, we assume that the independent variables are combined factorially, that is, that all of the combinations of the levels of each independent variable are represented in the data collection. Thus, a 2×3 design tells us that there are two independent variables, one having two levels and the other having three levels, for a total of six conditions. We could then also call the design a 2×3 factorial design.

23.2.3 Identifying the type of independent variables in the design

Independent variables can be of one of two types: between-subjects independent variables or within-subjects independent variables.

A *between-subjects* design requires that the scores for the different levels of the independent variable are derived from different cases. A one-way between-subjects design is an extension of the t test for independent groups. We discuss between-subjects designs in this chapter and in Chapter 24.

A *within-subjects* design, also called a *repeated-measures* design, requires that the scores for the different levels of the independent variable(s) are provided by the same cases. A one-way within-subjects design is an extension of the t test for correlated groups. We discuss within-subjects designs in Chapter 25. A *mixed* design contains at least one between-subjects and at least one within-subjects variable. We discuss a two-way mixed design in Chapter 26.

23.3 Some history

The technique of ANOVA can be directly attributed to the creativity of Sir Ronald Aylmer Fisher. As described by Salsburg (2001), it was during the time that Fisher worked at the Rothamsted Agricultural Experimental Station from 1919 to 1933 that he developed this statistical innovation. Rothamsted was the oldest agricultural research institute in the United Kingdom, established in 1837 to study the effects of nutrition and soil types on plant fertility. The researchers at the station had been experimenting for the better part of a century with different kinds of fertilizers by using a single fertilizer product on the entire field during a single year and measuring, together with a variety of other variables such as rainfall and temperature, the crop yield for that year. The institute used a different fertilizer in the next year, a different one the year following, and so forth. They then attempted to compare fertilizers across years while taking into account differences in temperature, rainfall, and other environmental variables.

Fisher (1921a) was able to demonstrate that, despite the elaborate mathematical treatment of the data by those who worked at the station before him, one could not draw any reliable conclusions from all of that work (Salsburg, 2001). He fixed things by changing the way in which the agricultural experiments were done (Salsburg, 2001). Under Fisher, Rothamsted now compared the effects of fertilizers within a single year by using all of them simultaneously on different nearby plots. To mostly control for local conditions within the field, Fisher would take a block of plots and randomly assign fertilizers to them. Any differences between the fertilizers in terms of crop yield, aggregated over the entire field of crops, could then be attributed to the product and not to one area receiving more rainfall or having better drainage than another. Not only did Fisher practically invent a powerful, elegant, and relatively simple experimental procedure, he produced the statistical technique to analyze the data collected through such a procedure. This technique was the ANOVA (as well as the analysis of covariance, or ANCOVA). He laid the groundwork and documentation for this work as well as the experimental design innovations through a series of what are now considered to be classic publications (Fisher, 1921b, 1925, 1935a; Fisher & Eden, 1927; Fisher & Mackenzie, 1923).

The statistic that is computed in the ANOVA procedure is an F ratio. It was originally not Fisher himself who designated this ratio by the letter F but rather George W. Snedecor at Iowa State University. To honor Fisher, whom he knew personally and very much respected, Snedecor in the first edition of his *Statistical Methods* book (Snedecor, 1934) proposed that the letter F should be used as the symbol for the final ratio that is computed in ANOVA. Needless to say, this suggestion was universally adopted.

23.4 Numerical example

Individuals who worked at computer stations all day were recruited for a study on improving cardiovascular health. These participants were randomly assigned to one of four exercise groups. This is the single *between-subjects* independent variable in the study; it is labeled **exercise** in the data set, and it has the following four levels or groups associated with it: bicycling (coded as 1 in the data set), walking (coded as 2 in the data set), dance (coded as 3 in the data set), and weight lifting (coded as 4 in the data set). Participants spent 30 minutes per day for 6 weeks engaged in the activity called for by the program.

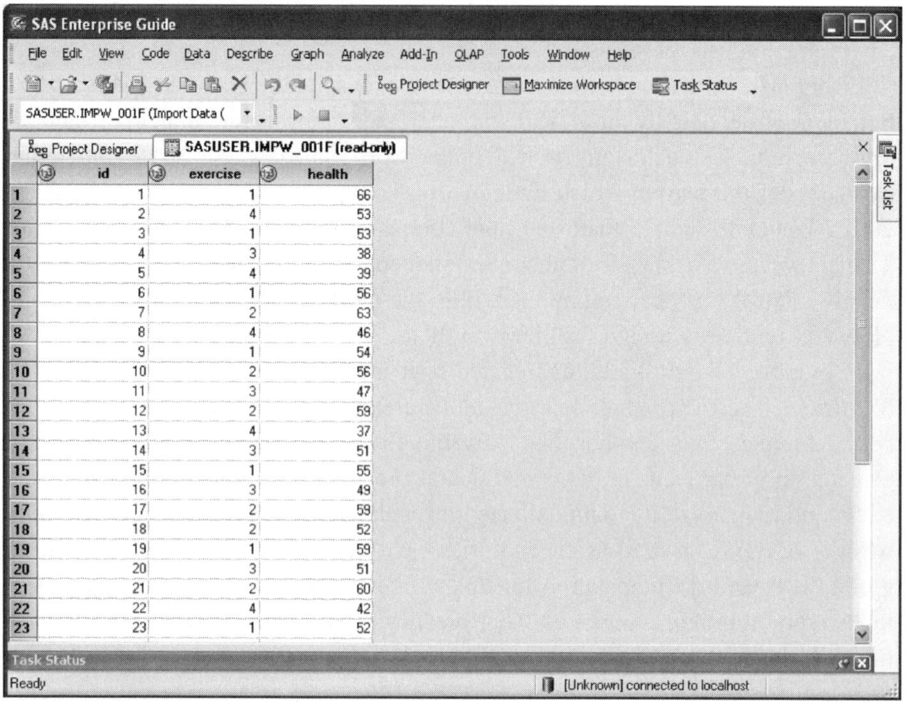

	id	exercise	health
1	1	1	66
2	2	4	53
3	3	1	53
4	4	3	38
5	5	4	39
6	6	1	56
7	7	2	63
8	8	4	46
9	9	1	54
10	10	2	56
11	11	3	47
12	12	2	59
13	13	4	37
14	14	3	51
15	15	1	55
16	16	3	49
17	17	2	59
18	18	2	52
19	19	1	59
20	20	3	51
21	21	2	60
22	22	4	42
23	23	1	52

Figure 23.1. A portion of the data set.

A composite measure, based on blood pressure, blood cholesterol level, and inflammatory markers from a blood test, served as the dependent variable. This composite measure could range from 20 to 70, with higher scores representing better cardiovascular health. Those whose scores from an initial screening were around 35 were selected to participate in this study. At the end of the 6 weeks of activity, participants were again measured for cardiovascular health and their scores were recorded; this is the dependent variable and is labeled **health** in the data set. A portion of the data set is shown in Figure 23.1.

23.5 Setting up the analysis

From the main *SAS Enterprise Guide* menu, select **Analyze ➔ ANOVA ➔ One-Way ANOVA**. This SAS procedure is specialized to analyze one-way between-subjects ANOVA designs. Drag **health** to the slot under **Dependent variables** in the rightmost panel. Then drag **exercise** to the slot under **Independent variable**. This is shown in Figure 23.2.

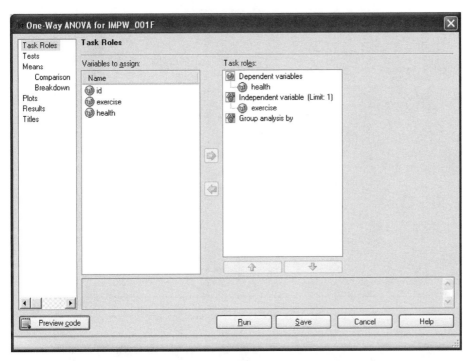

Figure 23.2. The **Task Roles** screen of the **One-Way ANOVA** procedure.

Click **Tests** from the navigation panel on the far left (see Figure 23.3). This screen deals with the assumption of homogeneity of variance. Under **tests for equal variance** are three tests: **Bartlett's test**, **Brown Forsythe test**, and **Levene's test**. We have checked all three so you can see the output. Toward the top of the screen is a checkbox for **Welch's variance-weighted ANOVA**, an alternative to the Fisher ANOVA when the assumption of equal variances is not met. We have checked it but will use this output only if the homogeneity tests indicated that the assumption is violated; if the variances are not significantly different, we will take the output from the Fisher procedure as our result.

Select **Means** from the navigation panel. This brings us to the **Comparison** screen as shown in Figure 23.4. Because we have more than two groups in the analysis, a statistically significant F ratio would indicate that significant mean differences exist between the groups but would not specify where those lie. Thus, some post-ANOVA comparison procedure must be performed to remove the ambiguity. An extensive treatment of this topic can be found in Gamst et al. (2008).

The simplest of these post-ANOVA comparison procedures to perform in *SAS Enterprise Guide* are the **post hoc** tests, and it is on this **Means** > **Comparison** screen that we identify which, if any, post hoc means comparison procedure we

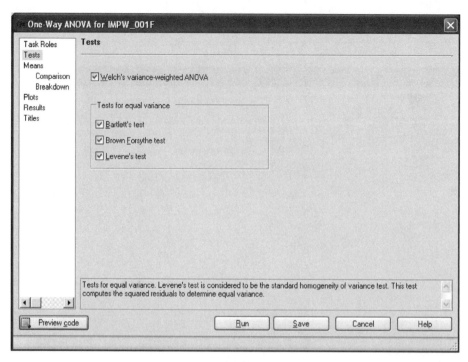

Figure 23.3. The **Tests** screen for the **One-Way ANOVA** procedure.

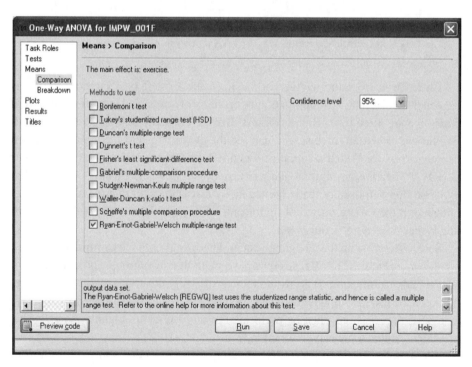

Figure 23.4. The **Comparisons** tab of the **Means** screen for the **One-Way ANOVA** procedure.

218

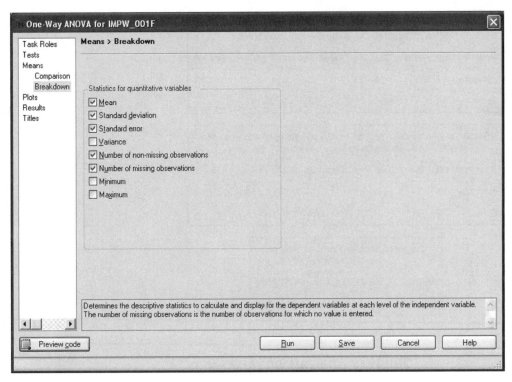

Figure 23.5. The **Breakdown** tab of the **Means** screen for the **One-Way ANOVA** procedure.

wish to use should a statistically significant F ratio be obtained. In anticipation of a statistically significant F ratio we make our selection, the **Ryan-Einot-Gabriel-Welsch multiple-range test**. This test is described in Gamst et al. (2008) and is recommended by many respected authors (e.g., Howell, 1997; Keppel & Wickens, 2004). We will use the Tukey post hoc test, another widely recommended procedure, in our simple effects analyses in the next several chapters.

Selecting **Breakdown** from the navigation panel brings us to the screen shown in Figure 23.5. Here we are able to specify the descriptive statistics we wish to obtain for each group. We have checked **Mean**, **Standard deviation**, **Standard error**, **Number of non-missing observation**s, and **Number of missing observations**. Then click the **Run** push button to perform the analysis.

23.6   The ANOVA output

Figure 23.6 shows the results of the homogeneity of variance tests. None of the tests yielded a statistically significant outcome. Thus, we can treat the assumption of

Levene's Test for Homogeneity of health Variance ANOVA of Squared Deviations from Group Means					
Source	DF	Sum of Squares	Mean Square	F Value	Pr > F
exercise	3	686.7	228.9	0.15	0.9306
Error	32	49699.7	1553.1		

Brown and Forsythe's Test for Homogeneity of health Variance ANOVA of Absolute Deviations from Group Medians					
Source	DF	Sum of Squares	Mean Square	F Value	Pr > F
exercise	3	1.8889	0.6296	0.04	0.9881
Error	32	472.7	14.7708		

Bartlett's Test for Homogeneity of health Variance			
Source	DF	Chi-Square	Pr > ChiSq
exercise	3	0.5409	0.9098

Figure 23.6. Results of the homogeneity of variance tests.

One-Way Analysis of Variance
Results
Means and Descriptive Statistics

exercise	Mean of health	Std. Dev. of health	Std. Error of health	Number of non-missing values for health	Number of missing values for health
.	51.0556	8.14842	1.35807	36	0
1	57.3333	4.52769	1.50923	9	0
2	56.8889	5.75423	1.91808	9	0
3	48.3333	4.66369	1.55456	9	0
4	41.6667	5.00000	1.66667	9	0

Figure 23.7. Descriptive statistics for the groups.

homogeneity of variance as having been met and we can ignore the Welch ANOVA that we ran just in case we had unequal variances.

Figure 23.7 displays the descriptive statistics that we had specified on the **Means > Breakdown** screen. The top row of the table summarizes the sample as a whole; the remaining rows are specific to the groups.

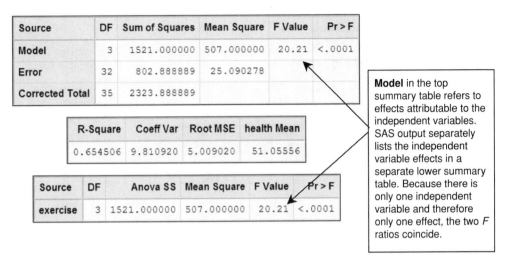

Source	DF	Sum of Squares	Mean Square	F Value	Pr > F
Model	3	1521.000000	507.000000	20.21	<.0001
Error	32	802.888889	25.090278		
Corrected Total	35	2323.888889			

R-Square	Coeff Var	Root MSE	health Mean
0.654506	9.810920	5.009020	51.05556

Source	DF	Anova SS	Mean Square	F Value	Pr > F
exercise	3	1521.000000	507.000000	20.21	<.0001

Model in the top summary table refers to effects attributable to the independent variables. SAS output separately lists the independent variable effects in a separate lower summary table. Because there is only one independent variable and therefore only one effect, the two *F* ratios coincide.

Figure 23.8. The summary table for the ANOVA.

Figure 23.8 shows the results for the omnibus ANOVA procedure. The top table addresses the "overall" model, which in this case is the effect of the independent variable of **exercise**; this is highlighted in the bottom table. The **exercise** variable is statistically significant; the **R-Square** value in the middle table is an eta-square value and tells us that approximately 65% of the variance in **health** is explained by **exercise**. The result would be written as follows: $F(3, 32) = 20.21, p < .05, \eta^2 = .654$.

The other entries in the middle table were discussed in Section 16.5. Briefly, they can be understood as follows:

- **Root MSE** is the *root mean square error*. It is the square root of the mean square error in the summary table above (the square root of 25.090278 with all of its unseen decimal values is 5.009020).
- **health Mean** is the overall or grand mean of the dependent variable **health** with a value of 51.05556.
- **Coeff Var** is the *coefficient of variation*. It is computed by multiplying the ratio of the root mean square error divided by the mean of the dependent variable by 100. In this case, the value is $100 \times (5.009020/51.05556)$ or 100×0.098109, which equals 9.810920. The coefficient of variation is an index of the relative fit of the model (the general linear model in the case of ANOVA) that is independent of the unit of measurement of the dependent variable, and it can be used to compare models. The model with the lower coefficient of variation would represent a relatively better fit.

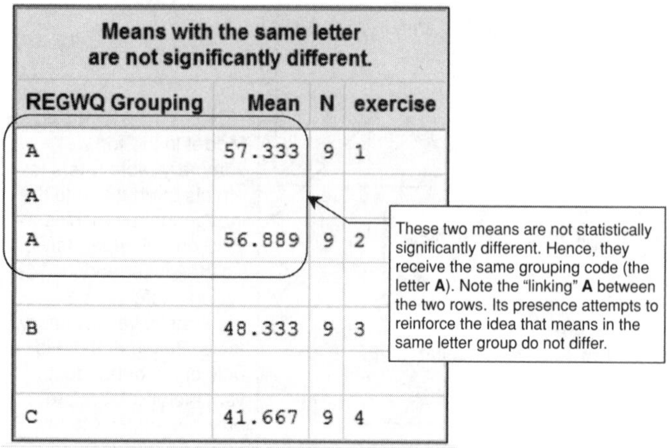

Means with the same letter are not significantly different.			
REGWQ Grouping	**Mean**	**N**	**exercise**
A	57.333	9	1
A			
A	56.889	9	2
B	48.333	9	3
C	41.667	9	4

These two means are not statistically significantly different. Hence, they receive the same grouping code (the letter **A**). Note the "linking" **A** between the two rows. Its presence attempts to reinforce the idea that means in the same letter group do not differ.

Figure 23.9. Results of the post hoc test for mean comparisons.

With a statistically significant effect of the independent variable, we can examine the outcome of our post hoc test. This is shown in Figure 23.9. The last three columns show, in order, the group means, the sample size, and the group codes (recall that bicycling, walking, dancing, and weight lifting were coded as 1, 2, 3, and 4, respectively).

The heart of the results is contained in the first column. Letters are used by *SAS Enterprise Guide* to depict sets of scores that are significantly different; any group means given the same letter designation are not significantly different. In the results, the groups coded 1 and 2 are each designated as **A** and are thus comparable; SAS reinforces this by placing a "joining" **A** between the rows to help users visualize the outcome. The results of the **Ryan-Einot-Gabriel-Welsch test** indicate that all group means are significantly different except those of Groups 1 and 2. In short, and given that higher scores index better cardiovascular health, we can say that participants benefited most (and equally) from bicycling and walking, benefited less from dancing, and benefited least from lifting weights.

24 Two-Way Between-Subjects Design

24.1 Overview

In this chapter we discuss how to perform a 2×2 between-subjects ANOVA. The advantage of combining two independent variables into a single design is that we not only evaluate the differences between the levels of each variable separately, called *main effects*, but we also evaluate the unique combinations of the levels of the variables, called an *interaction* effect. Detailed explanations of interaction effects can be found in a variety of sources (e.g., Agresti & Finlay, 2009; Gamst et al., 2008; Runyon et al., 2000). Here is a very brief one:

- A *main effect* addresses the differences between the means of the levels of a single independent variable. In factorial designs, the main effect means are averages across all of the other independent variables in the study. In Figure 24.1, the main effect of A is evaluated by comparing the mean of a_1 with the mean of a_2, and the main effect of B is evaluated by comparing the mean of b_1 with the mean of b_2.
- An *interaction effect* of A and B (the $A \times B$ interaction) addresses the differences in patterns of means between the levels of one independent variable across the levels of the other independent variable. For example, we contrast the pattern of a_1b_1 and a_1b_2 with the pattern of a_2b_1 and a_2b_2. If those patterns differed, that is, if the patterns did not reflect a parallel relationship, then we would have a significant interaction effect; if those patterns were the same (if they were parallel), then there would be no significant interaction effect.

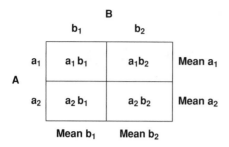

Figure 24.1. A 2 × 2 factorial design.

24.2 Omnibus and simple effects analysis

There are three effects of interest in this design: the main effect of A, the main effect of B, and the $A \times B$ interaction. These effects are presented in the summary table produced by SAS in what is ordinarily termed the *omnibus* or overall ANOVA. Depending on the outcome of this analysis, follow-up or simplifying analyses may be needed. These contingencies are summarized as follows:

- If a main effect is statistically significant and if that factor has more than two levels, a statistically significant F ratio indicates that there is a mean difference in the set of means. To determine where those significant mean differences lie, it is necessary to perform a multiple-comparisons procedure. We have shown how to accomplish this in Chapter 23.
- If the interaction is statistically significant, it signals that the pattern of cell means across a_1 is different than the pattern across a_2 (it also signals that the pattern of cell means across b_1 is different than the pattern across b_2). To determine where those significant mean differences lie, it is necessary to perform analyses of *simple effects*. We show how to perform this analysis in the present chapter.

24.3 Numerical example

The numerical example we use here represents a hypothetical 2 × 2 between-subjects factorial design. Researchers were interested in evaluating the effectiveness of massage therapy in treating lower back pain. Twenty-eight clients selected from a waiting list and who agreed to participate in a Pain Relief Study were administered either massage therapy (coded as 1) or a sham laser treatment control (coded as 2) twice a week for 6 weeks. This independent variable was named **therapy type** in the data set. The other independent variable was the degree of pain clients experienced

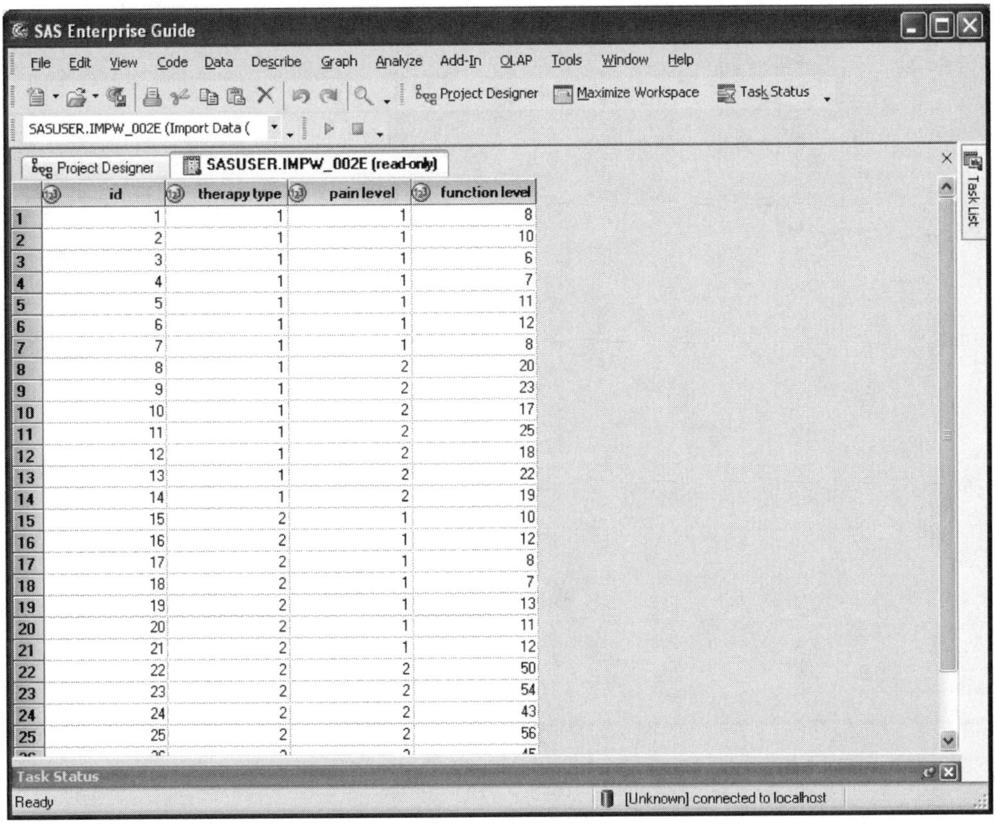

	id	therapy type	pain level	function level
1	1	1	1	8
2	2	1	1	10
3	3	1	1	6
4	4	1	1	7
5	5	1	1	11
6	6	1	1	12
7	7	1	1	8
8	8	1	2	20
9	9	1	2	23
10	10	1	2	17
11	11	1	2	25
12	12	1	2	18
13	13	1	2	22
14	14	1	2	19
15	15	2	1	10
16	16	2	1	12
17	17	2	1	8
18	18	2	1	7
19	19	2	1	13
20	20	2	1	11
21	21	2	1	12
22	22	2	2	50
23	23	2	2	54
24	24	2	2	43
25	25	2	2	56

Figure 24.2. A portion of the data set.

at the start of treatment, named **pain level** in the data set. Clients were classified as experiencing either mild pain (coded as 1) or moderate pain (coded as 2). Following the 6 weeks of treatment, all clients were tested on their ease of movement, level of dysfunction, and other factors. These measures were combined into a composite variable, named **function level** in the data set, that served as the dependent variable. Higher values represent poorer levels of functioning. A portion of the data set is shown in Figure 24.2.

24.4 Setting up the analysis

24.4.1 The omnibus analysis

Select **Analyze → ANOVA → Linear Models**. The window for this procedure opens on the **Task Roles** tab; this is highlighted in the navigation panel in the

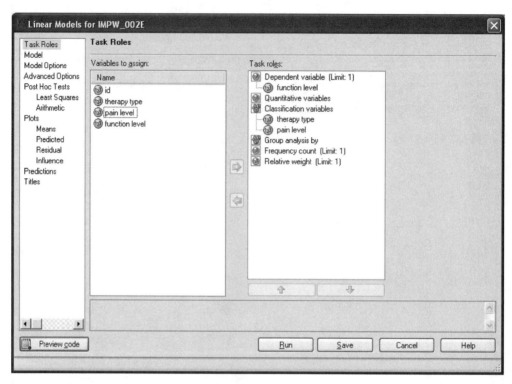

Figure 24.3. The **Task Roles** screen of the **Linear Models** procedure is configured.

left portion of the window. Highlight **function level** and drag it to the icon for
the **Dependent variable**. Then drag **therapy type** and **pain level** to the icon for
Classification variables. When finished, your screen should look similar to that
shown in Figure 24.3.

Click on the **Model** tab. The variables **therapy type** and **pain level** appear in
the **Class and quantitative variables** panel. Highlighting the single variable of
therapy type activates the **Main** bar (see Figure 24.4). Click the **Main** bar to place
therapy type in the **Effects** panel. Then do the same with **pain level**. This will
specify the two main effects for the model.

To specify the interaction, highlight **therapy type** and, while depressing the
Control key, highlight **pain level**; both variables as well as the **Cross** and **Factorial**
bars should now be highlighted (see Figure 24.5). Clicking the **Cross** (or **Factorial**)
bar while the two are highlighted will cause the two variables to be brought over to
the **Effects** panel as an interaction effect. The final configuration of this screen is
shown in Figure 24.6.

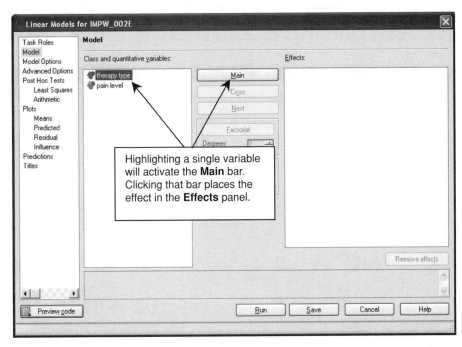

Figure 24.4. Highlighting a single variable activates the **Main** bar, which, when clicked, places the variable in the **Effects** panel.

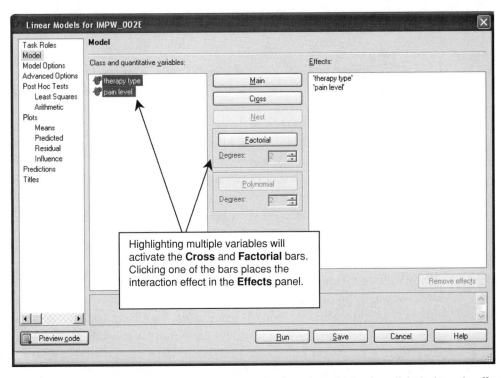

Figure 24.5. Highlighting multiple variables activates the **Cross** bar, which, when clicked, places the effects for the interaction of those variables in the **Effects** panel.

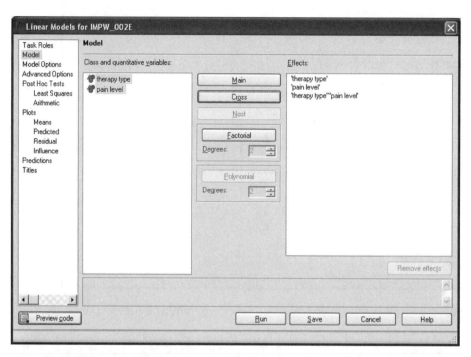

Figure 24.6. The final configuration of the **Model** screen of the **Linear Models** procedure.

Click on the **Model Options** tab. The panel of interest for us, labeled **Sum of squares to show**, is shown in Figure 24.7. There are four options representing different strategies for calculating the terms of the sum of squares in the ANOVA. Generally, ANOVA is an application of the general linear model in which the effects of interest (main effects and interaction effects) are used as weighted predictors of the dependent variable in a linear regression model. As such, the effects of the predictors are adjusted or statistically controlled for the effects of the other predictors in the model. The four types of sum of squares shown in the **Model Options** window represent different strategies by which the adjustment (statistical control) is accomplished. Very briefly, these are as follows.

- *Type I sum of squares*: This strategy is also known as hierarchical partitioning. The effects in the design are prioritized as follows: covariates, main effects, two-way interactions, three-way interactions, and so on if there are interaction effects (i.e., if there are two or more independent variables). Each effect in the model is adjusted only for the effects lower in priority to it in the model.
- *Type II sum of squares*: Effects are adjusted for those other effects that do not contain it. It is commonly used for ANOVA models with main effects only.

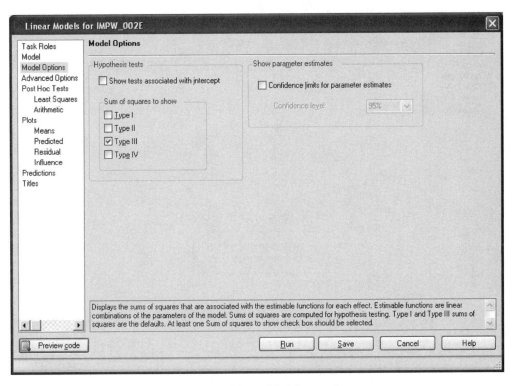

Figure 24.7. The **Model Options** screen of the **Linear Models** procedure.

- *Type III sum of squares*: Effects are adjusted for all other effects in the model. This strategy yields values that are not affected by unequal cell frequencies. It is probably the most commonly used strategy.
- *Type IV sum of squares*: This strategy is applicable for designs that have missing cells.

For our ANOVA, we have selected the checkbox for **Type III** sums of squares. Most statistical software applications treat this strategy as their default.

We next select the **Post Hoc Tests** tab, which places us automatically in the **Least Squares** screen. *Least squares* means are unweighted means in that "they represent the average of the group means without taking into account the sample sizes on which those means were based" (Gamst et al., 2008, p. 189). The **Least Squares** screen is where we would be able to obtain the least squares means. When groups differ in sample size, the least squares means are different from the observed means (the means that we would arithmetically compute by adding scores and dividing by sample size). In the present example, our group sizes are

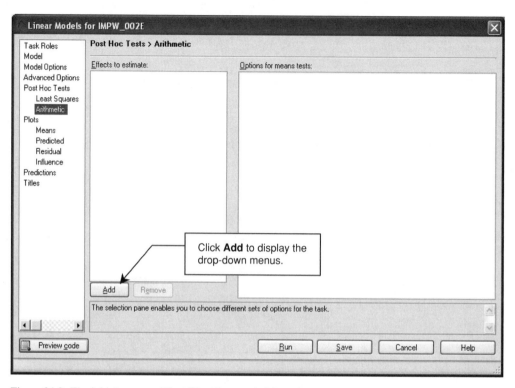

Figure 24.8. The initial screen of **Post Hoc Tests > Arithmetic**.

equal; under this condition, the arithmetically computed means and the least squares means are identical. Because we would obtain identical means from either procedure, we opt to click the **Arithmetic** portion of the **Post Hoc Tests** tab because the descriptive statistics it provides are more complete than those provided by the **Least Squares** procedure. Note that if our group sizes were unequal, it would have been more appropriate to select the **Least Squares** screen directly (Davis, 2007).

Select **Arithmetic** under the **Post Hoc Tests**. The initial screen is blank (see Figure 24.8). Clicking **Add** displays a set of drop-down menus, as shown in Figure 24.9, only a few of which require modifying. For the **Class effects to use** option, select **True** for **therapy type**, **pain level**, and **therapy type*pain level** by clicking on **False** and selecting **True** from the drop-down menu. We will not request a **Homogeneity of variance** test as SAS does not compute this for factorial models. The specifications that we have selected are displayed in Figure 24.10.

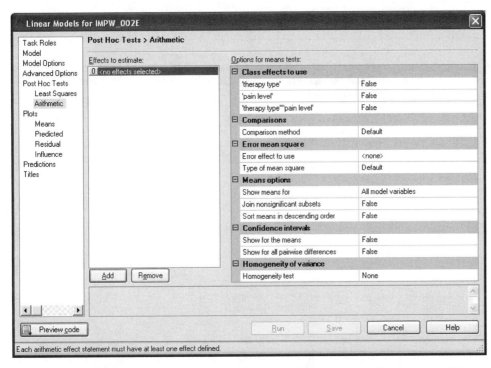

Figure 24.9. After we click **Add**, the **Post Hoc Tests > Arithmetic** screen displays several drop-down menus.

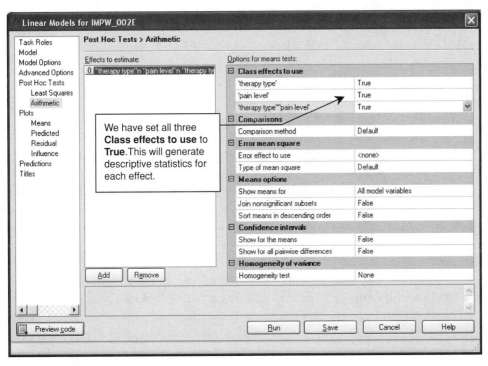

Figure 24.10. The **Post Hoc Tests > Arithmetic** screen is now configured for displaying descriptive statistics on the three effects.

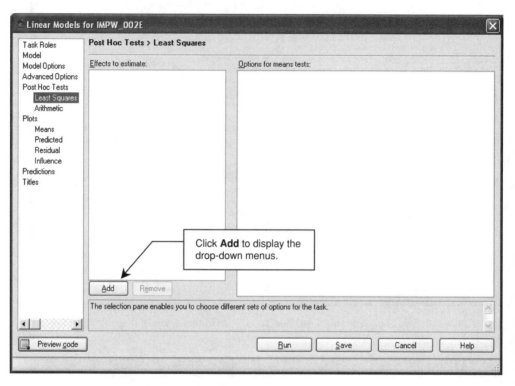

Figure 24.11. The initial screen of **Post Hoc Tests > Least Squares**.

24.4.2 The simple effects analysis

Because there are only two levels of each independent variable, we do not need to do any follow-up tests on the main effects – a significant F ratio automatically informs us that the two means are significantly different. However, even a statistically significant 2×2 interaction effect requires tests of simple effects in order for us to fully describe it. We will configure the setup for the simple effects analyses for the interaction at this point (rather than examine the results of the omnibus analysis and then reanalyze the data to perform the simple effects), because it is very convenient to do so. If the interaction is not statistically significant then we will ignore this portion of the output.

Simple effects analyses to explicate the interaction effect must be specified in the **Least Squares** screen of **Post Hoc Tests**. Select the **Least Squares** portion of the **Post Hoc Tests** tab. This brings you to the blank screen shown in Figure 24.11. Clicking **Add** displays a set of drop-down menus, as shown in Figure 24.12. For the **Class effects to use** option, set **therapy type*pain level** to **True**; this identifies

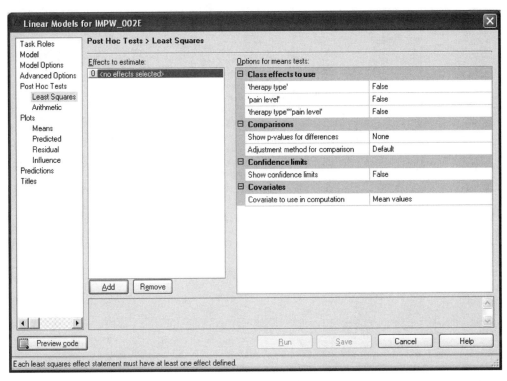

Figure 24.12. After we click **Add**, the **Post Hoc Tests > Least Squares** screen displays several drop-down menus.

the interaction as the focus of the analysis. If we had wished to perform pairwise comparisons for either of the main effects, we would have set one or both of them as appropriate to **True**. For **Comparisons**, set **Show p-values for differences** to **All pairwise differences** and set **Adjustment method for comparison** to **Tukey**. The configured screen is shown in Figure 24.13. Had we wished to perform planned comparisons, we would have to provide the necessary code; this is described in Gamst et al. (2008). Then click **Run** to perform the comparisons.

24.5 The ANOVA output

24.5.1 The omnibus analysis

The descriptive statistics generated by the **Linear Models** procedure are shown in Figure 24.14. The mean, standard deviation, and the number of observations are displayed for the two main effects as well as for the interaction.

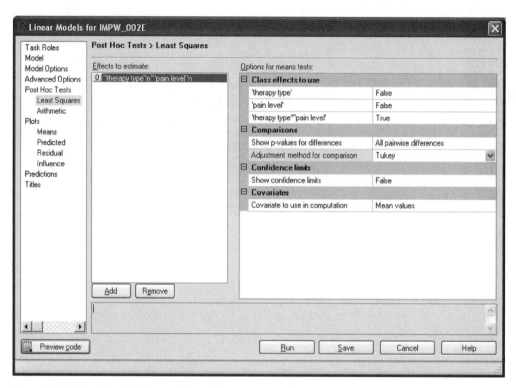

Figure 24.13. The **Post Hoc Tests > Least Squares** screen is now configured to perform the simple effects analysis.

The summary table for the overall model in the omnibus analysis is presented in the top portion of Figure 24.15. The sum of squares associated with **Model** is a compilation of the sums of squares for the three effects (two main effects and the two-way interaction) that comprise the model (each effect is treated as a predictor in the model). The full model is statistically significant, but it is much less interesting than dealing with the effects composing it.

SAS also provides the **Corrected Total** sum of squares; this is based on what is called the reduced or partial model, excluding the y-intercept information from the general linear model computation of ANOVA (see Gamst et al., 2008 for a more complete description of the reduced model).

The bottom table in Figure 24.15 shows the partitioning of the effects comprising the full model. Statistical significance of the F ratio associated with each effect can be gleaned from the last row, labeled **Pr > F**. Using an alpha level of $\alpha = .05$, we see that all three of the effects are statistically significant.

The middle portion of Figure 24.15 presents **R-Square**, which is computed based on the full model with all three effects combined (added) together. In the context of

Level of therapy type	N	function level	
		Mean	Std Dev
1	14	14.7142857	6.5566006
2	14	29.7857143	20.3929798

Level of pain level	N	function level	
		Mean	Std Dev
1	14	9.6428571	2.2738359
2	14	34.8571429	15.2862791

Level of therapy type	Level of pain level	N	function level	
			Mean	Std Dev
1	1	7	8.8571429	2.19306266
1	2	7	20.5714286	2.87849167
2	1	7	10.4285714	2.22539456
2	2	7	49.1428571	4.67006679

Figure 24.14. Descriptive statistics output.

Source	DF	Sum of Squares	Mean Square	F Value	Pr > F
Model	3	7316.107143	2438.702381	244.74	<.0001
Error	24	239.142857	9.964286		
Corrected Total	27	7555.250000			

The **Model** in this top summary table consists of all of the effects of the independent variables. These effects are the two main effects and the two-way interaction which are separated in the bottom summary table.

R-Square	Coeff Var	Root MSE	function level Mean
0.968347	14.18708	3.156626	22.25000

Source	DF	Type III SS	Mean Square	F Value	Pr > F
therapy type	1	1590.035714	1590.035714	159.57	<.0001
pain level	1	4450.321429	4450.321429	446.63	<.0001
therapy t*pain level	1	1275.750000	1275.750000	128.03	<.0001

Figure 24.15. The summary table for the ANOVA.

Least Squares Means
Adjustment for Multiple Comparisons: Tukey

therapy type	pain level	function level LSMEAN	LSMEAN Number
1	1	8.8571429	1
1	2	20.5714286	2
2	1	10.4285714	3
2	2	49.1428571	4

Least Squares Means for effect therapy t*pain level
Pr > |t| for H0: LSMean(i)=LSMean(j)
Dependent Variable: function level

i/j	1	2	3	4
1		<.0001	0.7885	<.0001
2	<.0001		<.0001	<.0001
3	0.7885	<.0001		<.0001
4	<.0001	<.0001	<.0001	

The groups coded 1 and 3 (the two mild pain groups receiving either massage or sham therapy) have the only two means that are not significantly different from each other.

Figure 24.16. The pairwise comparisons comprising the simple effects analysis.

ANOVA, we ordinarily wish to obtain the eta-square value for each separate effect. To do this, we must perform the hand calculation, dividing each sum of squares by the total sum of squares associated with the **Corrected Total**. The resulting eta-square values for therapy type, pain level, and the two-way interaction are thus approximately $\eta^2 = .21$, .59, and .17, respectively. The coefficient of variation, labeled **Coeff Var** (computed by multiplying the ratio of the root mean square error divided by the mean of the dependent variable by 100), the root mean square error (**Root MSE**), and the grand mean of the dependent variable (labeled as **function level Mean**) are also displayed in that middle table.

24.5.2 Simple effects analysis

Figure 24.16 displays the pairwise comparisons of the means of the interaction. The upper table gives code numbers to the groups and the lower table shows the p values associated with the pairwise comparisons. Recall that for **therapy type**, massage therapy was coded as 1 and sham laser treatment was coded as 2. Thus, in the top table, the first two rows contain the means for the groups receiving massage therapy and the second two rows contain the means for the groups receiving the sham treatment. Further recall that for **pain level**, clients experiencing mild pain were coded as 1 and those experiencing moderate pain were coded as 2.

Given the coding that was used, we can interpret the top table of Figure 24.16 as follows:

- The first row represents massage therapy for those with mild pain; their least squares mean is approximately 8.86 and this group is coded in the table below as 1.
- The second row represents massage therapy for those with moderate pain; their least squares mean is approximately 20.57 and this group is coded in the table below as 2.
- The third row represents sham laser treatment for those with mild pain; their least squares mean is approximately 10.43 and this group is coded in the table below as 3.
- The fourth row represents sham laser treatment for those with moderate pain; their least squares mean is approximately 49.14 and this group is coded in the table below as 4.

The results of the paired comparisons procedure using the Tukey procedure to adjust the obtained probabilities for familywise error are displayed in the bottom table in Figure 24.16. The code numbers are used by SAS to represent the groups, and the table is "square," thus containing redundant information in its upper and lower portions (with respect to the diagonal). The coordinates of the table present the probabilities of obtaining that large of a mean difference if the null hypothesis was true, and this is the way we evaluate statistical significance. As an example, for the row (group) labeled as **1** and the column (group) labeled as **3**, we are comparing the two groups with mild pain who received either massage therapy (mean of 10.43) or sham laser treatment (mean of 8.86). The **Pr > |t|** or adjusted probability of .7885 informs us that the two means do not differ. However, for the row labeled as **2** and the column labeled as **4**, we are comparing the two groups with moderate pain who received either massage therapy (mean of 20.57) or sham laser treatment (mean of 49.14). The **Pr > |t|** of < .0001 informs us that the two means are significantly different. We may therefore conclude that massage therapy is more effective than the sham laser treatment control for clients with moderate levels of pain but not for those with mild levels of pain.

25 One-Way Within-Subjects ANOVA

25.1 Overview

In a one-way within-subjects design, sometimes referred to as a repeated-measures design, each case is measured on or contributes a data point to every level of the independent variable. Because of this, subjects function in the design as their own controls; this in turn enhances the power of the statistical design. If the drawbacks to this design can be overcome (e.g., carry-over effects; see Gamst et al., 2008), it often becomes the design of choice for a one-way design.

25.2 Numerical example

The Automobile Manufacturers Association wished to study the effects of alcohol consumption on driving different types of vehicles. This hypothetical study called for drivers to consume the equivalent of three alcoholic drinks and then drive a complex prescribed closed-track course in one of four kinds of vehicles. Because of the considerable individual differences in drinking and driving that were expected, and because it was believed that the carry-over effects from the different conditions could be largely negated by knowledge of the track, this was designed as a within-subjects study. The organization recruited 14 college students from a local university who were 21 years of age and familiarized them with the track layout. Students were then scheduled for 4 days over the next 2 weeks to drive the course. On each test day, each student was to drive a different vehicle (determined randomly for each student) around the course. The vehicles and their coding in the data set are as follows: subcompact car (coded as 1), sport sedan (coded as 2), minivan (coded as 3),

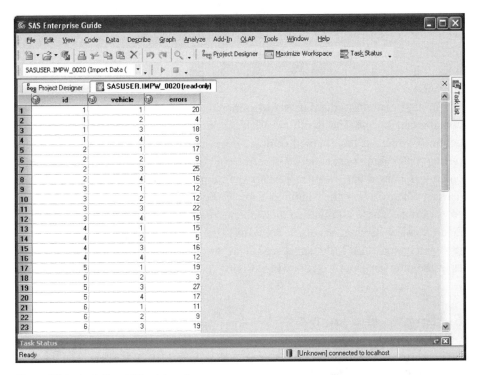

Figure 25.1. A portion of the data set.

and full-sized short-bed pickup truck (coded as 4). The number of driving errors was recorded for each student when driving each vehicle.

25.3 The structure of the data set

SAS Enterprise Guide uses a structure known variously as *univariate, narrow,* or *stacked* form. In univariate or stacked column format, each row is permitted to contain only one score on the dependent variable, and this is the defining feature of univariate format. We have not had to face this issue previously in this book because in all of our examples we have dealt with only one score on each measure. However, in a within-subjects design we measure the cases on the same variable under multiple conditions. Under univariate format, each of those scores must be placed on a different line in the data set.

A portion of the stacked data set is presented in Figure 25.1. Note that the first four lines represent the information for the student identified as **id 1**. This is because each student has four different error scores, one for each level of the within-subjects variable (i.e., one for each vehicle that the student drove). Under the univariate format requirement that only one score on any single variable may appear on any given row, we must use four rows to capture the measurements for each student.

The first column in the data set identifies the particular student whose data are contained in the row. The identifier variable is named **id**. The second variable (second column), which we have named **vehicle**, represents the particular vehicle of concern on that row. Vehicles are coded as described in Section 25.2. The variable in the third column is named **errors**. It represents the number of errors made by the student drivers when driving the signified vehicle. For example, consider the first four rows of data. These all relate to the student whose **id** is **1**. This student committed 20 errors when driving the vehicle coded as 1 (the subcompact), 4 errors when driving the vehicle coded as 2 (the sport sedan), 18 errors when driving the vehicle coded as 3 (the minivan), and 9 errors when driving the vehicle coded as 4 (the pickup).

25.4 Setting up the analysis

From the main menu, select **Analyze → ANOVA → Mixed Models**. The window opens on the **Task Roles** tab as shown in Figure 25.2. Select **errors** and drag it to the icon for **Dependent variable** in the **Task roles** panel. Then select **vehicle** and drag it over to the icon for **Classification variables**. Finally, select **id** and also drag it over to the area under **Classification variables**.

In the navigation panel at the left of the screen, select **Fixed Effect Model**. Click **vehicle** and then select the **Main** push button; **vehicle** will automatically appear in the **Effects** window as shown in Figure 25.3.

In the navigation panel at the left of the screen, select **Fixed Effect Model Options**. Select **Type 3** under **Hypothesis test type**, **Residual maximum likelihood** under **Estimation method** (this is the default), and **Between and within subject portions** under **Degrees of freedom method**. This is illustrated in Figure 25.4.

Selecting the **Random Effects** tab in the navigation tab brings you to the blank initial screen shown in Figure 25.5 (see Gamst et al., 2008 for a discussion of the differences between fixed and random effects). Click the **Add** push button and two displays will be presented. First, the expression <**no effects selected**> will appear in the **Random effects to estimate** panel. Second, several panels in the **Random effects and options** panel will become available. This is shown in Figure 25.6.

Our goal in interacting with this screen is to specify our **id** variable as a random effect and to register with *SAS Enterprise Guide* that this is the way we have

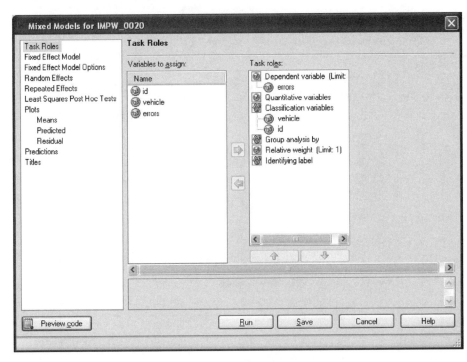

Figure 25.2. The **Task Roles** screen of the **Mixed Models** procedure.

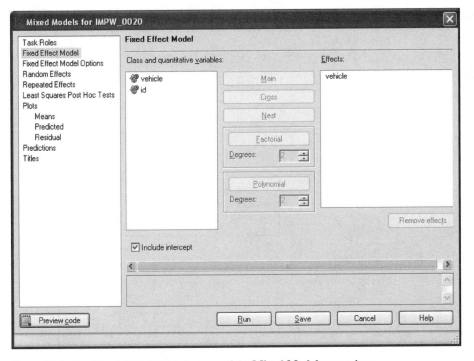

Figure 25.3. The **Fixed Effect Model** screen of the **Mixed Models** procedure.

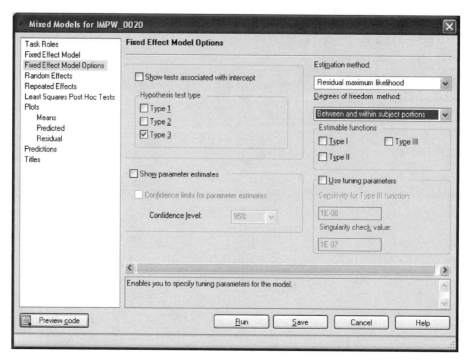

Figure 25.4. The **Fixed Effect Model Options** screen of the **Mixed Models** procedure.

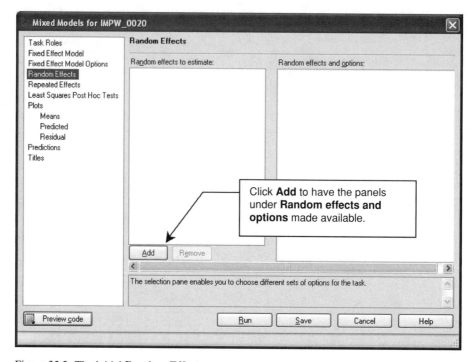

Figure 25.5. The initial **Random Effect**s screen.

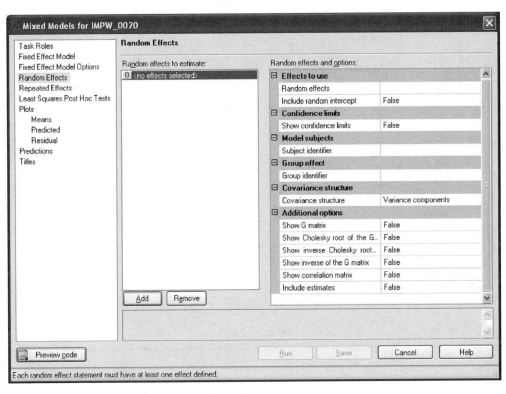

Figure 25.6. The **Random Effects** screen immediately after clicking **Add**.

identified our subjects in the data set. To specify our subject identifier as a random effect, select **Random effects** under the **Effects to use** portion of the **Random effects and options** frame; when it is clicked, a little box with an ellipsis (indicating there is a dialog box available) will appear at the far right end of the menu (see Figure 25.7). Position the cursor over this ellipsis box and click, and a new **Effects Builder – Random effects** screen will appear, as shown in Figure 25.8. Select **id** and then click the **Main** push button; **id** will automatically appear in the **Random effects** pane. Select the **OK** push button. This will return us to the **Random Effects** screen and **id** will now appear in the **Random effects** pane (see Figure 25.9).

With **id** now specified as the random effect, click the **Subject identifier** under the **Model subjects** frame and an ellipsis box will appear at the far right end of that menu (see Figure 25.10). Position the cursor over this ellipsis box and click, and a new **Effects Builder – Subject identifier** screen will appear, as shown in Figure 25.11. Select **id** and then click the **Main** push button; **id** will automatically appear in the **Subject identifier** pane. Select the **OK** push button. This once again returns

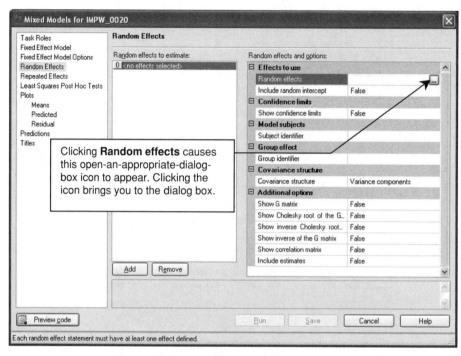

Figure 25.7. Clicking the **Random Effects** pane produces access to a pop-up dialog window.

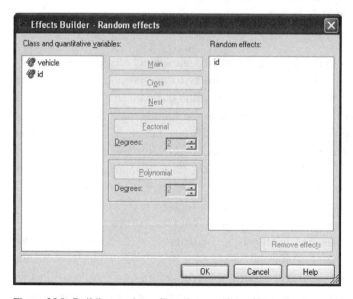

Figure 25.8. Building random effects by specifying **id** as a random effect.

244

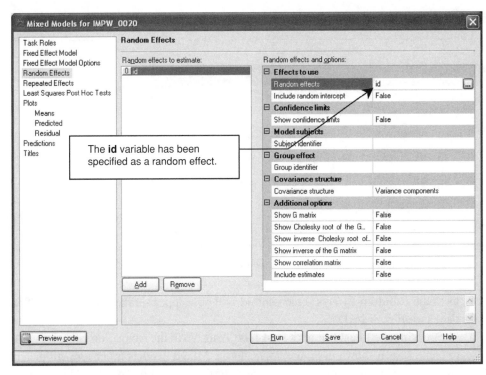

Figure 25.9. The subject identifier **id** is now specified as a random effect.

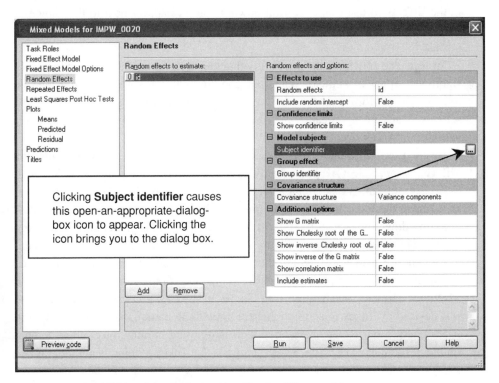

Figure 25.10. Establishing the variable that identifies the different subjects.

Figure 25.11. Specifying **id** as the subject identification variable.

us to the **Random Effects** screen and **id** will now appear in the **Subject identifier** pane (see Figure 25.12).

Selecting the **Least Squares Post Hoc Tests** tab in the navigation tab brings you to blank screen shown in Figure 25.13. In the **Mixed Models** procedure, all means are computed as least squares means (as described in Section 24.4.1). Clicking **Add** displays a set of frames with selection menus (see Figure 25.14). Select **vehicle** in the **Effects to use** frame. A drop-down menu will appear next to the choice of **False** as the default; select **True** as shown in Figure 25.15 to obtain the least squares means.

We can also anticipate the possibility that the ANOVA would yield a statistically significant effect of **vehicle**. With four conditions in the study, it would then be necessary to perform post-ANOVA comparisons to determine which pairs of least squares means are significantly different (we can ignore this portion of the output if **vehicle** is not significant).

In the **Least Squares Post Hoc Tests** window, click on **Show p-values for differences** and select **All pairwise differences** as shown in Figure 25.16. We want to control our familywise alpha level because more than a couple of comparisons are being requested. Clicking **Adjustment method for comparison** gives us access to a drop-down menu next to **Default** that displays various procedures controlling for alpha inflation, as shown in Figure 25.17. We will select **Tukey** from the menu; this will perform an adjustment of the probabilities of our comparisons. The choice of which test to use or whether to perform planned comparisons is a complex one worthy of serious consideration (see Gamst et al., 2008). Our selected procedure was devised by Tukey in an unpublished, limited-circulation manuscript written in 1953 (cited in our Reference section as it is reported in numerous public domain sources). Toothaker (1993, pp. 32–33) suggests that Tukey's "lengthy mimeographed

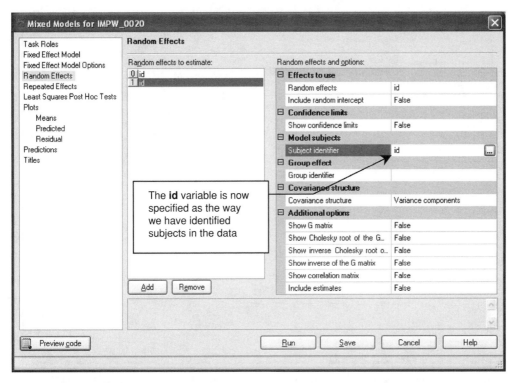

Figure 25.12. The **id** variable is now identified as the **Subject identifier** on the **Random Effects** screen.

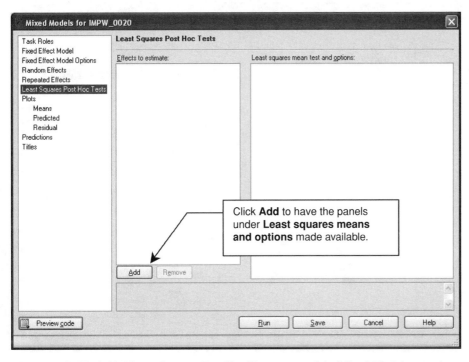

Figure 25.13. The initial **Least Squares Post Hoc Tests** screen of the **Mixed Models** procedure.

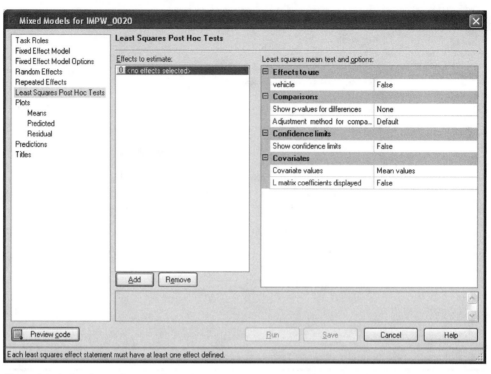

Figure 25.14. The **Least Squares Post Hoc Tests** screen immediately after clicking **Add**.

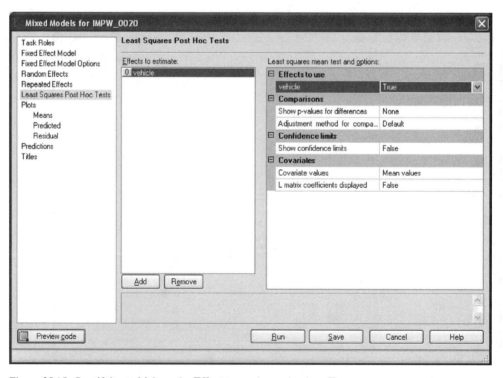

Figure 25.15. Specifying **vehicle** as the **Effect to use** by setting it as **True**.

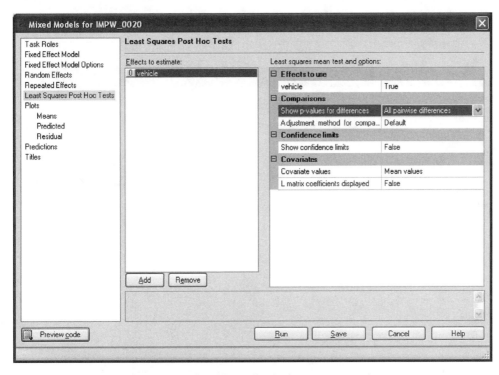

Figure 25.16. Specifying that we want to perform all pairwise mean comparisons.

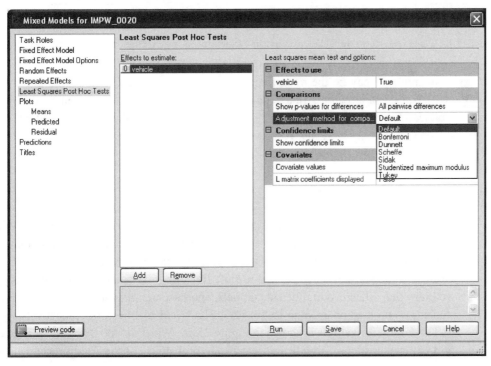

Figure 25.17. The choices available for adjusting our alpha level to control for familywise error (alpha-level inflation).

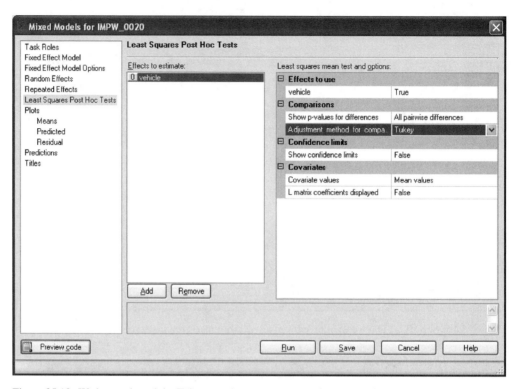

Figure 25.18. We have selected the Tukey post hoc test to control for alpha inflation.

monograph ... may be the most frequently cited unpublished paper in the history of statistics." In any case, Tukey's procedure was elaborated and disseminated by Kramer a few years later (Kramer, 1956, 1957). Selection of the Tukey procedure is shown in Figure 25.18. Click **Run** to perform this analysis.

25.5   Output for the analysis

The mean number of errors for the four types of vehicles is shown in Figure 25.19. These are least squares means – unweighted for sample size when we are combining cells of the design. Because no cells are being combined here, these least squares means are identical to the observed means. Recalling the coding of the vehicles, we know that when driving the subcompact, sport sedan, minivan, and pickup, the students committed on average 15.86, 7.57, 21.14, and 14.14 errors, respectively.

The F ratio for **vehicle** is shown in Figure 25.20. With 3 df and 39 df, the F ratio of 33.22 is statistically significant; that is, the probability of the F ratio occurring

Least Squares Means						
Effect	vehicle	Estimate	Standard Error	DF	t Value	Pr > |t|
vehicle	1	15.8571	0.9796	39	16.19	<.0001
vehicle	2	7.5714	0.9796	39	7.73	<.0001
vehicle	3	21.1429	0.9796	39	21.58	<.0001
vehicle	4	14.1429	0.9796	39	14.44	<.0001

Figure 25.19. The least squares means for the groups.

Type 3 Tests of Fixed Effects				
Effect	Num DF	Den DF	F Value	Pr > F
vehicle	3	39	33.22	<.0001

Figure 25.20. The F ratio for **vehicle**.

Differences of Least Squares Means									
Effect	vehicle	vehicle	Estimate	Standard Error	DF	t Value	Pr > |t|	Adjustment	Adj P
vehicle	1	2	8.2857	1.3733	39	6.03	<.0001	Tukey-Kramer	<.0001
vehicle	1	3	-5.2857	1.3733	39	-3.85	0.0004	Tukey-Kramer	0.0023
vehicle	1	4	1.7143	1.3733	39	1.25	0.2194	Tukey-Kramer	0.6006
vehicle	2	3	-13.5714	1.3733	39	-9.88	<.0001	Tukey-Kramer	<.0001
vehicle	2	4	-6.5714	1.3733	39	-4.79	<.0001	Tukey-Kramer	0.0001
vehicle	3	4	7.0000	1.3733	39	5.10	<.0001	Tukey-Kramer	<.0001

Figure 25.21. Pairwise comparisons of the means.

by chance given the truth of the null hypothesis (**Pr > F**) is < .0001, which is less than our alpha level of $\alpha = .05$. We may therefore conclude that at least one pair of means of the conditions are significantly different.

Results of the post hoc Tukey–Kramer test can be seen in Figure 25.21. The two columns labeled **vehicle** toward the left of the table indicate which two means are being compared. In the first row, for example, we note that vehicles 1 and 2 (the subcompact and the sport sedan) are being compared. The next column (**Estimate**) is the difference between the mean error scores, in the order vehicle 1 errors minus vehicle 2 errors. For the first row, for example, the mean difference is 8.2857 (15.8571 – 7.5714 from the means shown in Figure 25.19).

The pairwise comparisons are evaluated by means of t tests. The column labeled **Pr > |t|** treats each probability level in isolation, that is, as though there were no familywise error inflation to account for. However, the rightmost column labeled **Adj P** uses the Tukey–Kramer procedure to correct for alpha inflation such that all comparisons can be reasonably evaluated against our $\alpha = .05$ alpha level, and this is the evaluation we suggest using. What we find is that all of the pairwise mean differences are statistically significant except those involving vehicles 1 and 4 (the subcompact and the pickup). Noting what the mean errors are from Figure 25.19, we may therefore conclude that while driving under the influence of alcohol, these college students were relatively safer when driving the sport sedan (coded as 2), were relatively moderately dangerous when driving either the subcompact (coded as 1) or the pickup (coded as 4), and were relatively most dangerous behind the wheel of a minivan (coded as 3).

26 Two-Way Mixed ANOVA Design

26.1 Overview

A mixed design is one that contains at least one between-subjects independent variable and at least one within-subjects independent variable. In a simple mixed design, there are only two independent variables, one a between-subjects factor and the other a within-subjects factor; these variables are combined factorially. Because there are two independent variables, there are three effects of interest: the main effect of the between-subjects variable, the main effect of the within-subjects variable, and the two-way interaction.

26.2 The partitioning of the variance in a mixed design

The total variance of the dependent variable is partitioned into between-subjects variance and within-subjects variance. The three effects of interest are as follows.

- *The main effect of the between-subjects variable*: The between-subjects variable is subsumed in the between-subjects portion of the variance. It has its own between-subjects error term that is used in computing its F ratio.
- *The main effect of the within-subjects variable*: The within-subjects variable is subsumed in the within-subjects portion of the variance. It has its own within-subjects error term that is used in computing its F ratio.
- *The two-way interaction*: The interaction effect is subsumed in the within-subjects portion of the variance. We use the within-subjects error term to compute its F ratio for this effect.

26.3   Numerical example

The following hypothetical study illustrates a 2×2 simple mixed design. A popular online social network service decided to introduce a new feature, a chat room dating feature, hoping to increase the time users spent on their Web site. Part of the contract to which users agreed in signing up for the online social network was a stipulation that the Web site managers could monitor the Web site usage of its members. Taking advantage of that stipulation, 24 active users (identified by **id** in the data set) were selected to be studied. Because it was believed that users of different ages might react differently to the new feature, the age of user, named **age** in the data set, was included as a between-subjects variable. Half of the users were 18 years old (coded as 1) and the other half of the users were 25 years old (coded as 2). All individuals were monitored for their time per day on the Web site for 1 week before the feature was introduced (coded as 1) and 1 week after the feature was introduced (coded as 2). The time period, named **time** in the data set, represents a within-subjects variable with two levels (before and after). An average number of hours per day logged on to the Web site, named **hours per day**, comprised the dependent variable.

The data set is shown in Figure 26.1. Note that the data set is in univariate or stacked format because there is a within-subjects variable in the research design (as explained in Section 25.3). We will illustrate how to read the data set by considering the user whose **id** is **1**. The data for this user are in the first two rows. This user is an 18-year-old whose age is coded as **1**. The first row is relevant to **time 1** (before the feature was introduced); **User 1** spent an average of 1.7 hours per day during that week on the Web site. The second row is relevant to **time 2** (after the feature was introduced); **User 1** spent an average of 2.8 hours per day during that week on the Web site.

26.4   Setting up the analysis

26.4.1 The omnibus analysis

From the main menu select **Analyze → ANOVA → Mixed Models**. The window opens on the **Task Roles** tab. From the **Variables to assign** panel, select **hours per day** and drag it to the icon for **Dependent variable**. Then, one at a time, select **age**, **time**, and **id** and drag them over to the area under **Classification variables**. The result of this is shown in Figure 26.2.

In the navigation panel, select **Fixed Effect Model** as shown in Figure 26.3. In the **Class and quantitative variables** panel, select **age** and then select the **Main** push

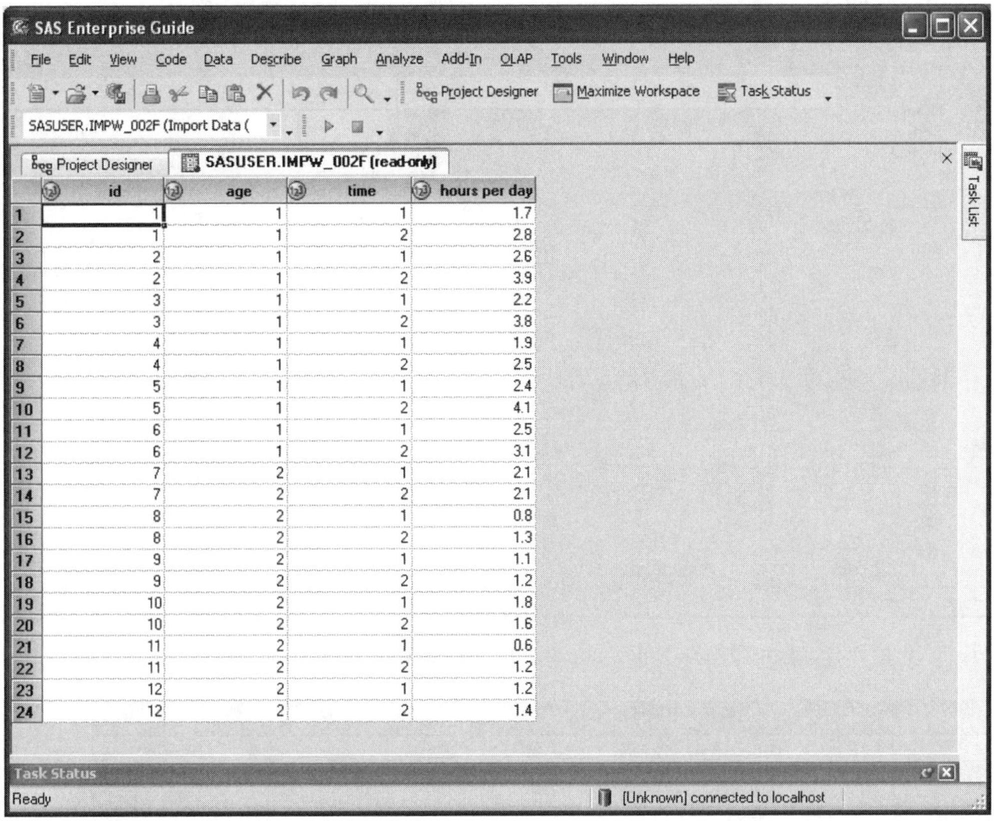

	id	age	time	hours per day
1	1	1	1	1.7
2	1	1	2	2.8
3	2	1	1	2.6
4	2	1	2	3.9
5	3	1	1	2.2
6	3	1	2	3.8
7	4	1	1	1.9
8	4	1	2	2.5
9	5	1	1	2.4
10	5	1	2	4.1
11	6	1	1	2.5
12	6	1	2	3.1
13	7	2	1	2.1
14	7	2	2	2.1
15	8	2	1	0.8
16	8	2	2	1.3
17	9	2	1	1.1
18	9	2	2	1.2
19	10	2	1	1.8
20	10	2	2	1.6
21	11	2	1	0.6
22	11	2	2	1.2
23	12	2	1	1.2
24	12	2	2	1.4

Figure 26.1. The data set.

button; **age** will automatically appear in the **Effects** window. Repeat this procedure for **time**. Then, while holding the Control key down, select both **age** and **time**. With both variables highlighted, click either the **Cross** or **Factorial** push button; **age*time** interaction effect will automatically appear in the **Effects** window.

Select **Fixed Effect Model Options** in the navigation panel as shown in Figure 26.4. Check **Type 3** under **Hypothesis test type.** Then select **Residual maximum likelihood** under **Estimation method,** and **Between and within subject portions** under **Degrees of freedom method.**

Select **Random Effects** in the navigation panel. You will be presented with two empty panels as shown in Figure 26.5. Click **Add** to obtain the menu system in the **Random effects and options** panel to the right. The first tinted menu in the **Random effects and options** panel is the **Effects to use** section. Under it, select **Random effects**. When you do this, an ellipsis box will appear at the far right of

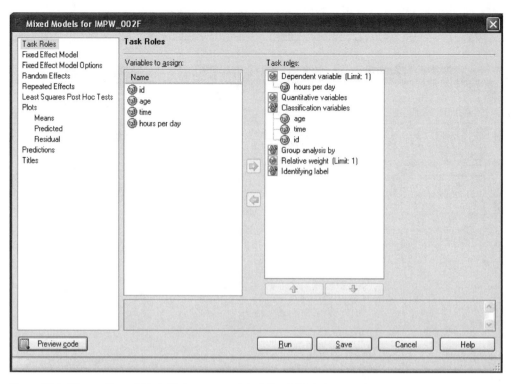

Figure 26.2. The configured **Task Roles** screen of the **Mixed Models** procedure.

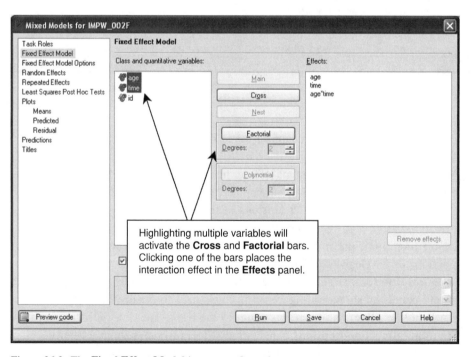

Figure 26.3. The **Fixed Effect Model** is now configured.

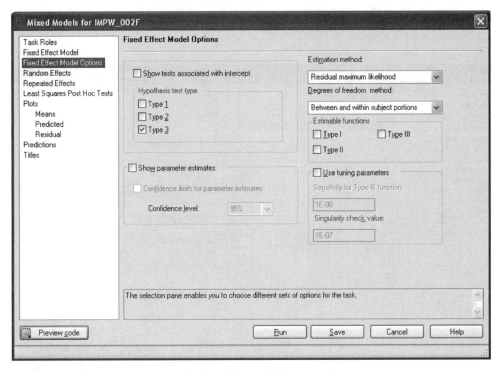

Figure 26.4. The **Fixed Effect Model Options** are specified.

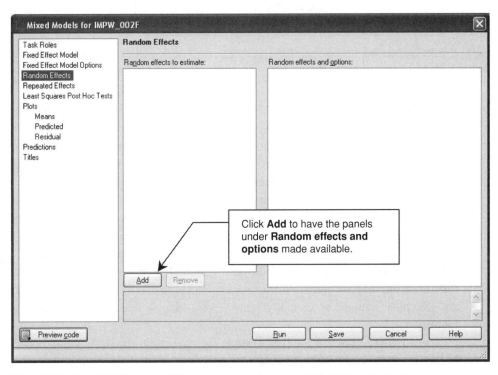

Figure 26.5. The initial **Random Effects** screen requires us to click **Add** to obtain the menu system.

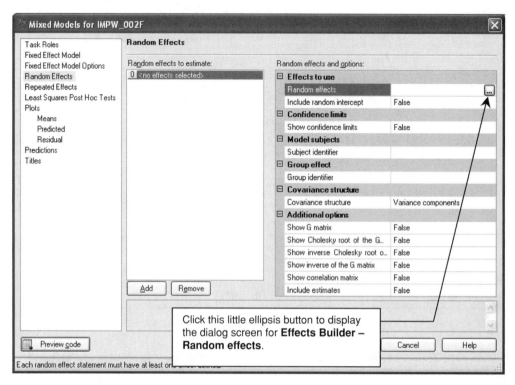

Figure 26.6. Clicking **Random Effects** under **Effects to use** gives rise to the ellipsis box in the upper portion of the panel.

that portion of the panel (see Figure 26.6). Click on that ellipsis box and the **Effects Builder – Random effects** window appears. Select **id** and click the **Main** push button. The **id** variable will automatically appear in the **Random effects** panel as shown in Figure 26.7. Click the **OK** push button to return to the **Random effects** screen and note that **id** is now registered as a random effect (see Figure 26.8).

The third tinted menu in the **Random effects and options** panel is the **Model subjects** section. Under it, select **Subject identifier**. When you do this, an ellipsis box will appear at the far right of that portion of the panel (see Figure 26.9). Click on that ellipsis box and the **Effects Builder – Subject identifier** window appears. Select **id** and click the **Main** push button. The **id** variable will automatically appear in the **Subject identifier** panel. This is shown in Figure 26.10. Select the **OK** push button. As seen in Figure 26.11, **id** now appears as the **Subject identifier**.

Select **Least Squares Post Hoc Tests** in the navigation panel. As we indicated in Section 25.4, in the **Mixed Models** procedure all means are computed as least

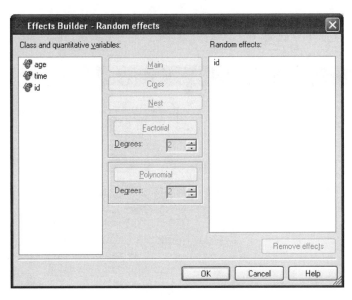

Figure 26.7. We have specified **id** as a random effect.

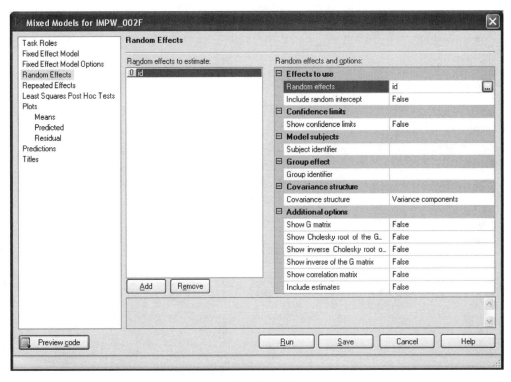

Figure 26.8. The id variable is registered under **Random effects**.

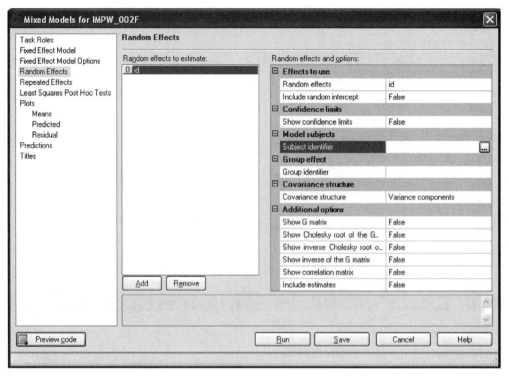

Figure 26.9. The **Subject identifier** portion of the **Random Effects** screen.

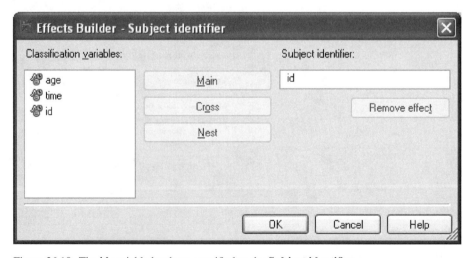

Figure 26.10. The **id** variable has been specified as the **Subject identifier**.

260

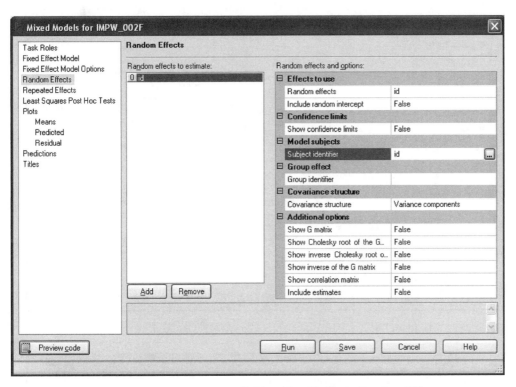

Figure 26.11. The **id** variable now appears as the **Subject identifier** in the **Random Effects** screen.

squares means (least squares means are described in Section 24.4.1). Click the **Add** push button at the bottom of the **Effects to estimate** panel to obtain the menu system shown in Figure 26.12. Highlight each of the three effects in turn under the **Effects to use** menu and select **True** for each; this command will cause the least squares means for each of the effects to be output. Our settings are shown in Figure 26.13.

26.4.2 The simple effects analysis

We will configure this analysis to perform the simple effects tests on the least squares means should the interaction reach statistical significance. Remaining in the **Least Squares Post Hoc Tests** screen, in the **Comparisons** frame set **Show p-values for differences** to **All pairwise differences** and set **Adjustment method for comparison** to **Tukey**. This is shown in Figure 26.14. Click **Run** to perform the analysis.

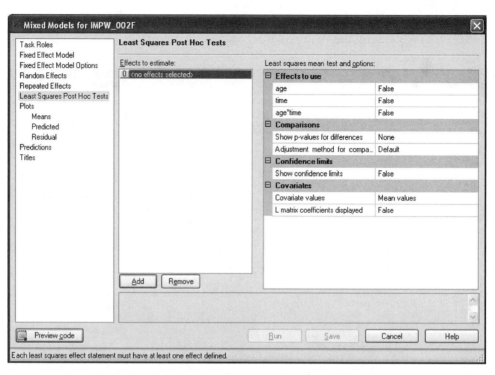

Figure 26.12. The **Least Squares Post Hoc Tests** screen after clicking **Add**.

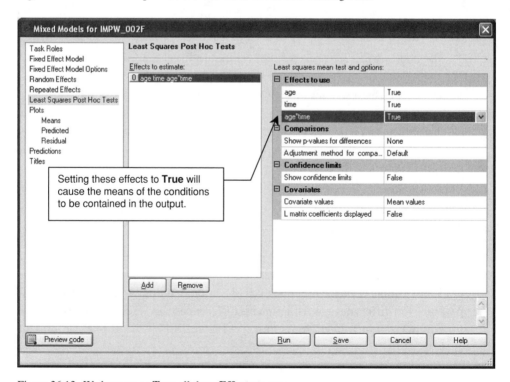

Figure 26.13. We have set to **True** all three **Effects to use**.

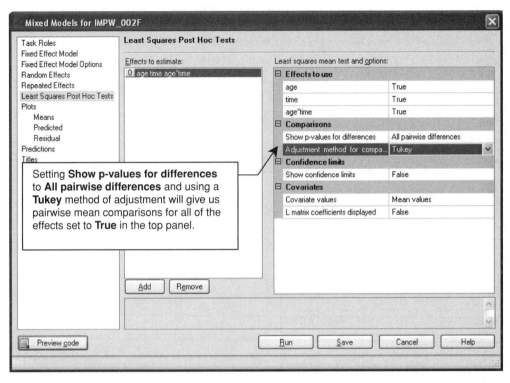

Figure 26.14. The simple effects tests are now specified in the **Comparisons** portion of the **Least squares mean test and options** panel.

26.5   The **ANOVA** output

26.5.1 The omnibus analysis

The least squares means are shown in Figure 26.15 and the results of the omnibus analysis are shown in Figure 26.16 in the form of an abbreviated summary table. As we can see, all of the effects are statistically significant. With the interaction effect being significant, we would have much greater interest under most conditions to focus on it rather than the main effects.

26.5.2 The simple effects analysis

The results of the comparisons of the least squares means for the two main effects are shown in Figure 26.17 in the top two rows. Because each has only two levels, and because both main effects are statistically significant, we know the two means

Least Squares Means							
Effect	age	time	Estimate	Standard Error	DF	t Value	Pr > |t|
age	1		2.7917	0.1882	10	14.83	<.0001
age	2		1.3667	0.1882	10	7.26	<.0001
time		1	1.7417	0.1450	10	12.01	<.0001
time		2	2.4167	0.1450	10	16.66	<.0001
age*time	1	1	2.2167	0.2051	10	10.81	<.0001
age*time	1	2	3.3667	0.2051	10	16.41	<.0001
age*time	2	1	1.2667	0.2051	10	6.18	0.0001
age*time	2	2	1.4667	0.2051	10	7.15	<.0001

Figure 26.15. The least squares means for the conditions.

Type 3 Tests of Fixed Effects				
Effect	Num DF	Den DF	F Value	Pr > F
age	1	10	28.66	0.0003
time	1	10	34.28	0.0002
age*time	1	10	16.97	0.0021

Figure 26.16. The summary table for the ANOVA.

Differences of Least Squares Means											
Effect	age	time	age	time	Estimate	Standard Error	DF	t Value	Pr > |t|	Adjustment	Adj P
age	1		2		1.4250	0.2662	10	5.35	0.0003	Tukey	0.0003
time		1		2	-0.6750	0.1153	10	-5.85	0.0002	Tukey-Kramer	0.0002
age*time	1	1	1	2	-1.1500	0.1630	10	-7.05	<.0001	Tukey-Kramer	0.0002
age*time	1	1	2	1	0.9500	0.2901	10	3.28	0.0084	Tukey-Kramer	0.0355
age*time	1	1	2	2	0.7500	0.2901	10	2.59	0.0272	Tukey-Kramer	0.1053
age*time	1	2	2	1	2.1000	0.2901	10	7.24	<.0001	Tukey-Kramer	0.0001
age*time	1	2	2	2	1.9000	0.2901	10	6.55	<.0001	Tukey-Kramer	0.0003
age*time	2	1	2	2	-0.2000	0.1630	10	-1.23	0.2480	Tukey-Kramer	0.6252

Figure 26.17. The simple effects analysis showing the pairwise comparisons of the cell means.

for each effect are significantly different. The statistical results we see here for these effects are redundant with what we already know from the omnibus analysis, and we can bypass them to examine the interaction.

The simple effects comparisons for the interaction are contained in the remaining rows, as we can see by the row headings in the first column. We can illustrate how to read this table as follows. Consider the first interaction row (the third row in the table). The first age and time combination is 1 and 1, representing the younger users in the week before the feature was introduced. The second age and time combination is 1 and 2, representing the same younger users in the week following the introduction of the feature. It is the means of these conditions that are being compared. Reading across the row we find that the **t Value** for that comparison is −7.05. Its ordinary (unadjusted) probability of occurrence if the null hypothesis is true is listed under the column labeled **Pr > |t|** as < .0001. That probability value is adjusted for alpha-level inflation by means of a Tukey–Kramer procedure (see Section 25.4) to yield an adjusted probability of .0002, which is a value well into our region of statistical significance. Looking at the means, we may then conclude that younger users logged in significantly more time on the Web site during the week after the chat room dating feature was launched than they did the week before it was launched. The last row in the table represents the older users (age code of 2) being compared before (time code 1) and after (time code 2) the launch of the dating feature. The **t Value** for that comparison is −1.23, which is not statistically significant. We may therefore conclude that older users did not significantly change the time they spent logged on to the Web site during the measured time period.

Section IX

Nonparametric Procedures

27 One-Way Chi-Square

27.1 Overview

Chi-square is classified as a nonparametric statistic, a class of statistics described in Section 15.3.2 when we discussed the Spearman rho correlation. The procedure is applied to categorical variables as described in this chapter and the following one. Chi-square was developed in 1900 by Karl Pearson (Pearson, 1900) as the solution to finding a goodness-of-fit test on nonnormal distributions (only quantitative variables can be described by the normal curve).

In the simplest application of chi-square, we apply the chi-square test to the frequency data associated with the categories of a single variable; such a design is known as a one-way chi-square design. The data consist of frequencies of occurrences for each category, and our intent is to determine if those frequencies are distributed as we would expect (expected frequencies for the categories) if only chance influenced the outcome.

The expected frequencies in a chi-square analysis constitute the null hypothesis or the model against which the chi-square statistic is tested. The issue is whether the data fit, that is, conform to, the model or if they significantly diverge from the model; in this sense, the chi-square test can be thought of as a goodness-of-fit test assessing how well the model fits the data.

The crux of the chi-square procedure lies in formulating the expected frequencies to which the observed frequencies are compared. In general, there are three strategies that are commonly employed to generate the expected frequencies of the categories: equal frequencies, preestablished frequencies, and mathematically modeled frequencies.

In the equal frequencies strategy, we might expect that an equal number of cases would be observed for each category if only chance factors were operating.

For example, if we were to poll patrons of a local restaurant about whether they were Democrats or Republicans, and if we hypothesized that chance alone (e.g., flipping an unbiased coin) determined their choices, then we would anticipate that half of the polled patrons would endorse each political party; this would be the null hypothesis against which the chi-square was evaluated. Thus, if 80 patrons were polled, our expected frequencies would be 40 patrons claiming to be Democrats and 40 patrons claiming to be Republicans. A statistically significant chi-square would indicate that the obtained frequencies were distributed differently than our expected frequencies.

In the preestablished frequencies strategy, if we had either empirical or theoretical reasons to expect particular frequencies of cases to be contained within a variable's categories, we could establish these as expected frequencies. For example, we could survey all of the students from a local medical school to determine how many were left handed. Given that approximately 12% of the population is estimated to be left handed, we could establish an expected set of frequencies based on that information. Thus, if the medical school had 100 students enrolled, our expected frequencies would be 12 left-handed and 88 right-handed medical students. A statistically significant chi-square would indicate that the obtained frequencies were distributed differently than our expected frequencies.

In the mathematically modeled frequencies strategy, in some more advanced data-analysis methods such as structural equation modeling (e.g., Meyers et al., 2006), we use a mathematical model to predict the values we would obtain if the assumptions of the model were true. These would represent the expected frequencies, and chi-square is one of the statistics used to determine if the model fit the obtained data.

27.2 Numerical example

Our hypothetical study involves a simple survey of 112 college students enrolled in universities across the country. We asked each of them to select from among three very popular choices the one Gulf Coast destination at which they would elect to spend their spring break (named **destination** in the data set) if they had the funds to do so. The choices were Panama City Beach, located on the Florida panhandle (coded as 1 in the data set); Cancun, Mexico, located at the tip of the Yucatan Peninsula (coded as 2 in the data set); and South Padre Island, located in south Texas near the Mexican border (coded as 3 in the data set). Our interest was in whether or not these destinations were equally preferred by the students in the

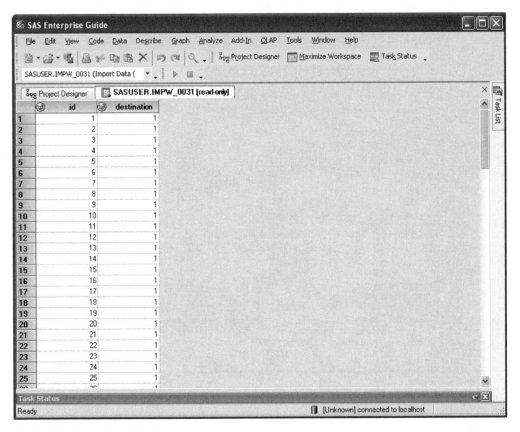

Figure 27.1. A portion of the data set.

sample and, if not, which was most preferred. A portion of the data set (sorted by
destination) is shown in Figure 27.1.

27.3 Setting up the analysis

From the main menu select **Describe → One-Way Frequencies.** The window opens
on the **Task Roles** tab. From the **Variables to assign** panel, select **destination** and
drag it to the icon for **Analysis variables**. The result of this is shown in Figure 27.2.

In the navigation panel, select **Statistics** as shown in Figure 27.3. In the **Frequency table options** panel, check **Frequencies and percentages with cumula-
tives**. In the **Chi-square goodness of fit** panel, check **Asymptotic test** (the choice

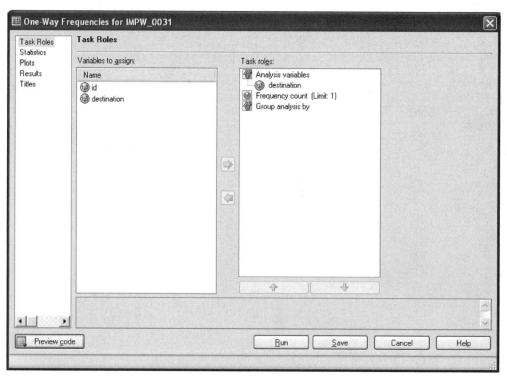

Figure 27.2. The **Task Roles** screen of the **One-Way Frequencies** window.

for **Exact p-values** would yield an exact probability level rather than the extremely good approximation we will obtain with the **Asymptotic test**). Click **Run** to perform the analysis.

27.4   The chi-square output

The output of the chi-square analysis is presented in Figure 27.4. The upper table provides the observed frequencies for each category and their percentages of the total. Given our coding scheme, we can see that Panama City Beach was selected by 61 students comprising 54.46% of the sample, that Cancun was selected by15 students comprising 13.39% of the sample, and that South Padre Island was selected by 36 students comprising 32.14% of the sample.

In the lower table we see the chi-square statistics. Against the null hypothesis of equal cell frequencies, the chi-square value is 28.4107. Degrees of freedom are calculated as $k - 1$ where k is the number of categories. With three categories in the

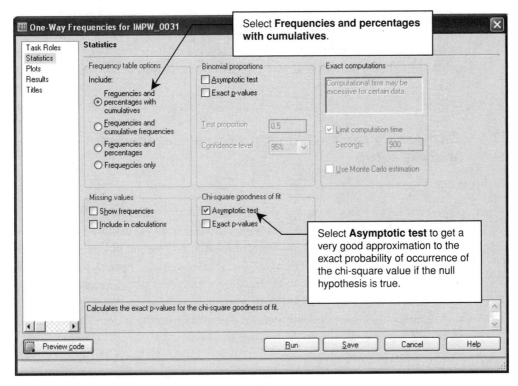

Figure 27.3. The **Statistics** screen of the **One-Way Frequencies** window.

destination				
destination	Frequency	Percent	Cumulative Frequency	Cumulative Percent
1	61	54.46	61	54.46
2	15	13.39	76	67.86
3	36	32.14	112	100.00

Chi-Square Test for Equal Proportions	
Chi-Square	28.4107
DF	2
Pr > ChiSq	<.0001

Figure 27.4. The one-way chi-square output.

present example, there are 2 *df*. With 2 *df*, the chi-square value is likely to occur with a probability (**Pr > ChiSq**) of $< .0001$ if the null hypothesis is true, which is statistically significant against our alpha level of $\alpha = .05$. We can therefore conclude that the three possible spring break destinations were not selected equally often.

27.5   Comparing the two most preferred categories: analysis setup

27.5.1 Overview

The result of the chi-square analysis informed us that there were significant differences between the observed endorsement frequencies for the three spring break destinations. From that result we can deduce that at least the largest difference in frequency between the categories was statistically significant; thus, we can assert that Panama City Beach was more frequently endorsed than Cancun as a spring break destination. What we cannot be certain of is whether Panama City Beach was significantly more frequently endorsed than South Padre Island. To address this latter question, we need to do the following:

- First, we must select only those cases opting for one of those two choices.
- Then we need to perform the same chi-square analysis as we just did but only on the frequencies of the Panama City Beach and South Padre Island categories.

We must also not forget that although only two categories will be compared in this follow-up analysis, these two destinations never went "head to head." Therefore, even if Panama City Beach is endorsed significantly more often than South Padre Island, that preference was in the context of three alternatives having been presented; it is possible that had only these two choices been presented, the results might have turned out differently.

27.5.2 Selecting the two most popular categories

The filtering procedure we engage in to select only those students endorsing either Panama City Beach or South Padre Island was fully discussed in Section 5.3, and we will describe it here in abbreviated form; readers are invited to review Section 5.3 as necessary. With the data set displayed in the active window (if you are viewing the results, click the tab in the **Project Flow** for the data set), select **Data → Filter and Query** to reach the main **Query** screen. The screen opens with the **Select Data**

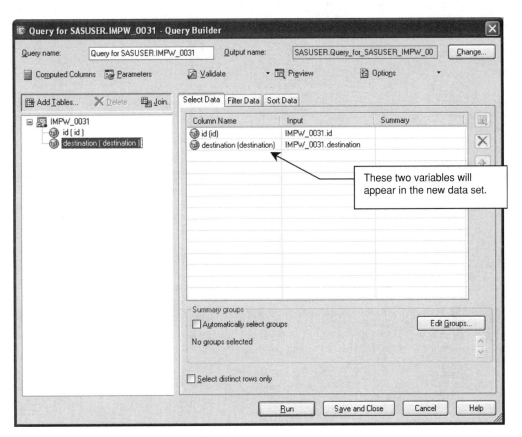

Figure 27.5. The **Select Data** tab of the **Query** screen.

tab currently active. Drag both **id** and **destination** into the **Select Data** panel. This is shown in Figure 27.5.

Click the **Filter Data** tab. Drag **destination**, the variable which we wish to filter, to the **Filter Data** panel. This action automatically opens the **Edit Filter** dialog screen. Set the **Operator** to **Not equal to** and set the **Value** equal to **2** as shown in Figure 27.6. Click **OK** to return to the main **Query** window and click **Run** to execute the procedure.

The resulting data set is shown in Figure 27.7. Our filtered data set, still sorted by **destination**, now contains only Destinations 1 and 3. Although we cannot see the full data set on the screen, we have taken a screenshot of a location toward the middle of the data set. You can see that the **id** code jumps from 61 (the last data point typed into the file representing a student endorsing Category 1) to 77 (the

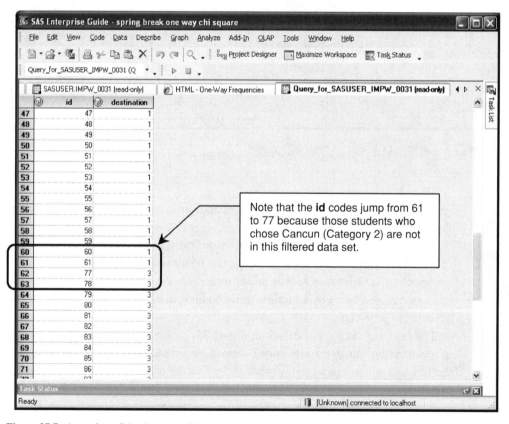

Figure 27.6. We have edited the filter to select the values of **destination** that are not equal to 2.

Figure 27.7. A portion of the data set with those students endorsing Category 2 excluded.

destination				
destination	Frequency	Percent	Cumulative Frequency	Cumulative Percent
1	61	62.89	61	62.89
3	36	37.11	97	100.00

Chi-Square Test for Equal Proportions	
Chi-Square	6.4433
DF	1
Pr > ChiSq	0.0111

Figure 27.8. The output of the two-category chi-square analysis.

first data point typed into the file representing a student endorsing Category 3). We are thus ready to perform the follow-up chi-square analysis on this newly created data set.

27.5.3 Performing the chi-square analysis

We perform this analysis exactly as we described the process in Section 27.3. We will therefore not present any screenshots here, as they are identical to the ones we have shown earlier.

27.6 Comparing the two most preferred categories: chi-square output

The output of the chi-square analysis is presented in Figure 27.8. The upper table provides the observed frequencies for each category and their percentages of the total. Given our coding scheme, we can see that Panama City Beach and South Padre Island were selected by 61 and 36 students, respectively, matching our previous output. Because we have only those cases in the data set, their respective percentages are now 62.89% and 37.11%.

In the lower table we see the chi-square statistics. Against the null hypothesis of equal cell frequencies, the chi-square value is 6.4433. With 1 *df* (two categories have

1 *df*), that chi-square value is likely to occur with a probability (**Pr > ChiSq**) of < .0111 if the null hypothesis is true, which is statistically significant. We can therefore conclude that Panama City Beach was a more preferred spring break destination over South Padre Island when the three destinations of Panama City Beach, Cancun, and South Padre Island were offered to students.

28 Two-Way Chi-Square

28.1 Overview

A chi-square test can be applied to two-way designs as well as to the one-way designs we covered in Chapter 27. The simplest two-way design is a 2×2 and we illustrate it in Figure 28.1. Assume we asked business travelers which of two attributes they valued most in a hotel when they were traveling on business. The row and column variables each have two levels, and the uppercase letters in the cells represent the observed frequencies. Each row and column has a total frequency (e.g., $A + B$ is the total number of women in the study), and the total sample size (N) is the sum of all cell frequencies.

Frequency tables such as we have drawn in Figure 28.1 are called *contingency tables*. This is because the observed frequency is contingent on two (or more) conditions. For example, the frequency of selecting location over service may depend (be contingent) on whether the business traveler is a woman or a man. In two-way contingency tables, such as shown in Figure 28.1, the null hypothesis on which the expected frequencies is based can be stated in several different ways:

- Preference for hotel location and service is independent of (unrelated to) the gender of the traveler.
- The variables of hotel attribute and gender are independent (not related).
- Women and men business travelers have comparable preferences for hotel location and service.
- The proportion of women preferring location to service is not statistically different from the proportion of men preferring location to service.

The last bullet in our list of alternative ways to express the null hypothesis captures the general strategy of deriving the expected cell frequencies. Specifically, we would follow these steps to derive the expected frequencies:

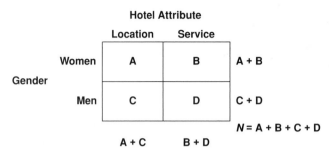

Figure 28.1. A 2×2 contingency table.

- We would determine the proportion of the total sample size that is represented by each column total. For example, we would determine the percentage of the total sample endorsing location $(A + C)$ and the percentage of the total sample endorsing service $(B + D)$.
- We would then apply those percentages separately to the total number of women and to the total number of men to generate their expected frequencies.

A statistically significant chi-square would indicate that the endorsement proportions of the hotel attributes by women were different from that of the men; that is, it would indicate that the two variables were not independent of each other (i.e., how much travelers preferred location or service depended on their gender).

28.2 The issue of small frequency counts

When variables are categorical, that is, when they have relatively few discrete levels or possible values (e.g., gender has two values: male and female), the assumption of continuous measurement cannot be met. However, the chi-square distribution is based on the assumption that the variables are measured on a quantitative scale of measurement. Therefore, as Fisher (1950, p. 96) pointed out, the use of chi-square provides only an approximate rather than an exact way to test the null hypothesis that the expected and observed frequencies are comparable:

> The treatment of frequencies by means of a χ^2 is an approximation, which is useful for the comparative simplicity of the calculations. The exact treatment is somewhat more laborious, though necessary in cases of doubt, and valuable as displaying the true nature of the inferences which the method of χ^2 is designed to draw.

Ever since the days of Fisher, it has been recognized that the chi-square distribution is a close enough approximation for large samples to meet the purposes of most researchers. In other words, chi-square distributions based on large samples can come relatively close to the exact probabilities associated with the observed frequencies to virtually overcome the issue of continuous measurement raised by Fisher. For example, Snedecor (1946) suggested that chi-square was acceptable when the sample size exceeded 200. With decreasingly smaller sample sizes, chi-square may be increasingly too powerful; its use with small sample sizes can lead to an increased chance of committing a Type I error (rejecting the null hypothesis when we should not). To deal with this potential problem, statisticians have suggested that using some alternative or adjustment to chi-square might be in order for small sample sizes. Three such alternatives or adjustments that are commonly cited are the Fisher exact test, the Yates continuity correction to chi-square, and the Freeman and Halton extension of the Fisher test.

28.2.1 Fisher's exact test

R. A. Fisher recognized in the early 1930s that the chi-square approximation could lead researchers to reach some false conclusions (i.e., it could lead to Type I errors). Because of the small sample sizes that agricultural researchers such as Fisher faced regularly, his data analyses and those of his colleagues were particularly at risk. On Tuesday, December 18, 1934, Fisher read a paper before a meeting of the Royal Statistical Society in which he described a procedure for obtaining the exact probability for the configuration of the observed frequencies in a 2×2 contingency table. This paper was published the following year in the Society's journal (Fisher, 1935b). The procedure worked out all of the alternative cell frequencies that were possible given the observed row and column totals. On the basis of that calculation, Fisher showed how to use the procedure to compute the exact probability of obtaining cell frequencies of those configurations that were more extreme than the obtained cell frequencies. Fisher noted that the math was "somewhat more laborious" than that required for performing a chi-square analysis, which is the primary reason that the Fisher test has traditionally been recommended for sample sizes under 20 (e.g., Guilford & Fruchter, 1978; Siegel, 1956). However, even a modestly equipped personal computer can now easily cope with these "laborious" arithmetic calculations, and so the Fisher exact test can be used today with sample sizes well into triple figures.

28.2.2 The Yates correction for continuity

Frank Yates became R. A. Fisher's assistant at Rothamsted Experimental Station in 1931 and inherited the directorship in 1933 (Finney, 1998) when Fisher left to replace Karl Pearson at University College. Aware of the work that his mentor

Fisher was doing to provide an exact test of the null hypothesis for frequencies, Yates (1934) offered his own correction to the chi-square computation: Reduce the absolute differences between the observed and expected frequencies by 0.5 when computing a chi-square with 1 *df*. Some writers (e.g., Guilford & Fruchter, 1978) have suggested using the Yates adjustment when any expected frequency is less than 10, whereas others (e.g., Ferguson & Takane, 1989) have suggested using it when any expected frequency is less than 5. Further, some statisticians (e.g., Hays, 1981) have suggested using the Yates adjustment as a general practice, whereas others (e.g., Jaccard & Becker, 1990) have argued that it should not be used at all because it is too conservative.

28.2.3 Freeman–Halton *R* × *C* exact test

Both the Fisher test and the Yates correction are applied to chi-square analyses with 1 *df*. Freeman and Halton (1951) extended Fisher's exact test to two-way tables exceeding 2 × 2. Their test can be used under circumstances analogous to those for which we would use the Fisher exact test.

28.3   Numerical example

We use as a basis for our hypothetical study the travel illustration with which we began this chapter. Assume that we asked 70 business travelers, 35 women and 35 men, which attribute of the hotel they believed was most important – its location relative to where they needed to conduct their business or the level and quality of service provided by the hotel – when they were traveling on business. In the data set the **gender** variable was coded as follows: women were coded as 1 and men were coded as 2; in the data set the **attribute** variable was coded as follows: location was coded as 1 and service was coded as 2. A portion of the data set is shown in Figure 28.2.

28.4   Setting up the analysis

From the main menu select **Describe → Table Analysis**. The window opens on the **Task Roles** tab. From the **Variables to assign** panel, select **gender** and **attribute** and drag them to the icon for **Table variables.** The result of this process is shown in Figure 28.3.

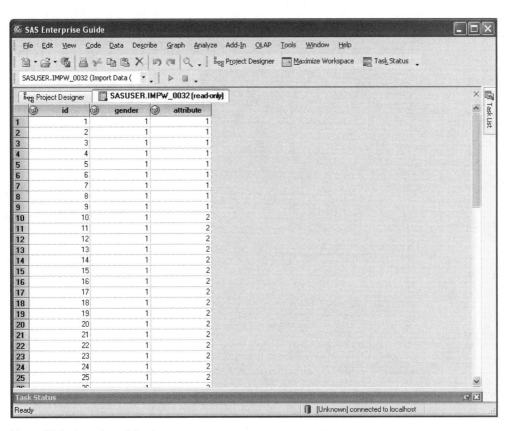

Figure 28.2. A portion of the data set.

In the navigation panel select **Tables**, which brings us to the setup screen shown in Figure 28.4. Dragging the row and column variables to the tinted "mock-up" diagram in the upper right panel will specify the structure of the contingency table. Drag **attribute** to the location directly above the mock-up diagram in the place designated by <**drag variables here**> to have it represent the columns. Your screen will look like what we show in Figure 28.5. Then drag **gender** to the left side of the mock-up diagram to specify it as the variable to be placed on the rows. After you carry out these actions, your screen should resemble Figure 28.6. Note that the bottom panel, labeled **Tables to be generated**, has now registered **gender by attribute** (by convention, we speak of row × column, or $R \times C$, tables).

Selecting **Cell Statistics** from the navigation panel brings us to a screen allowing us to indicate what statistics will appear in the output. Under **Available statistics**, check **Row percentages**, **Cell frequencies**, **Cell percentages**, and **Expected cell frequency**. This is shown in Figure 28.7.

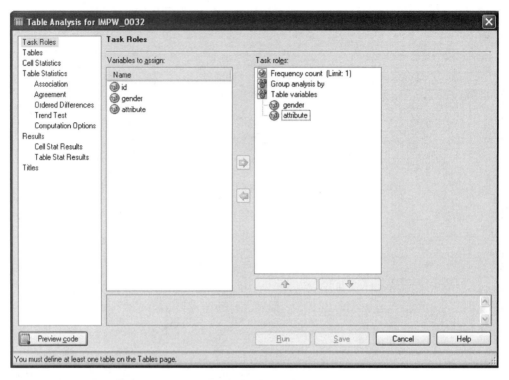

Figure 28.3. The **Task Roles** screen of the **Table Analysis** window.

Selecting **Table Statistics** from the navigation panel opens the **Association** screen shown in Figure 28.8. In the upper left portion of the screen is the panel for **Tests of association**. Check **Chi-square tests**. This will give us, among other statistics, the Pearson chi-square, the Yates-corrected chi-square, and Fisher's exact test. If we had a table larger than 2×2, checking **Fisher's exact test for r x c tables** would produce the Freeman–Halton test. Click **Run** to perform the analysis.

28.5 The chi-square output

28.5.1 Cell statistics

The cell statistics output of the chi-square analysis is presented in Figure 28.9. Each cell contains the following four lines of information, the key to which is found in the little box to the left of the main table: cell frequency, expected frequency, percent of total, and percent of row. For example, the **gender 1**, **attribute 1** cell refers to women travelers preferring location; it has nine endorsements with an

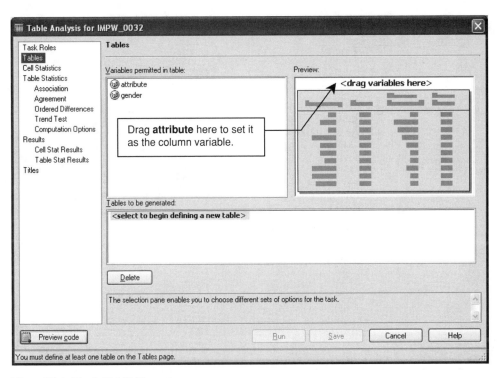

Figure 28.4. The initial **Tables** setup screen.

expected frequency of 15.5. The nine endorsements comprise 12.86% of the total sample and 25.71% of all sampled women travelers.

28.5.2 Chi-Square Statistics

The table statistics output is presented in Figure 28.10. The upper table shows the Pearson chi-square result in the first row. With 1 df, the chi-square value of 9.7849 has a probability of occurrence if the null hypothesis was true of .0018. Given an alpha level of $\alpha = .05$, this result is statistically significant and informs us that the preferred hotel attribute is related to the gender of the business traveler. Examining the observed frequencies, it appears that female business travelers are more concerned about service than location whereas male business travelers, although somewhat less polarized, seem to value location over services.

The **Likelihood Ratio Chi-Square** in the second row of the upper table represents an alternative computational procedure for chi-square using maximum likelihood estimation (see Meyers et al., 2006 for a description of this estimation procedure).

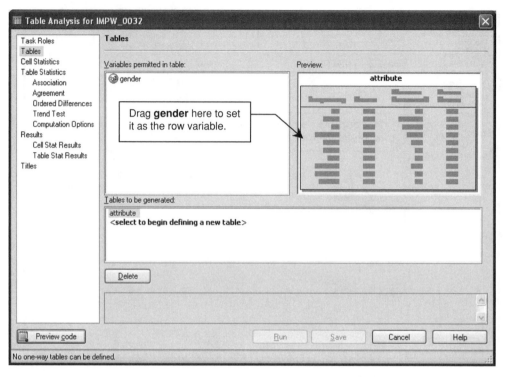

Figure 28.5. The variable **attribute** is represented on the columns.

The **Likelihood Ratio Chi-Square** usually produces an outcome similar to that of the Pearson chi-square.

The third row of the upper table shows the results for what SAS calls the **Continuity Adj. Chi-Square**. This is the Yates-corrected chi-square value. Its value is 8.3375 and its probability of occurrence if the null hypothesis was true is .0039. Comparing this probability to that of the probability associated with the Pearson chi- square illustrates the more conservative nature of Yates' adjustment.

The **Mantel–Haenszel Chi-Square** in the fourth row of the table assesses the association between two ranked (ordinal) variables. It should not be considered when the variables in the analysis were measured on a nominal scale of measurement.

The fifth row of the upper table presents the phi coefficient. Phi is the correlation of two dichotomously (binary) coded variables, and phi square indexes the strength of their relationship in much the same way as r square does in Pearson correlation and as eta square does in ANOVA. Phi square can be computed by dividing chi-square by the sample size. In the present example, phi square is obtained by dividing 9.78 by 70, yielding a value of $\varphi^2 = .14$. However, SAS provides the value of phi directly

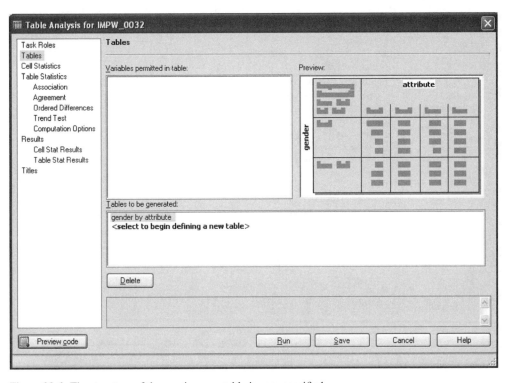

Figure 28.6. The structure of the contingency table is now specified.

in its output (−.3739), and simply squaring that value yields a phi-square value of $\varphi^2 = .14$. Thus, the strength of the relationship between gender and attribute is statistically significant. Based on the criteria we have specified for eta square (see Section 20.6.1), the value of phi squared can be interpreted as representing a moderate strength of relationship.

Cramér's statistic for contingency tables, given as **Cramer's V** in the last row of the table, is a generalized version of phi for tables that are larger than 2×2. Because it reduces to phi for a 2×2 table, the same value (−.3739) is shown for **Cramer's V** as for phi.

28.5.3 Fisher exact test statistics

The lower table presented in Figure 28.10 shows the results of the Fisher exact test. No statistic is associated with this test; rather, the result is simply the exact probability.

The first row of the table is labeled **Cell (1, 1) Frequency (F)** and shows a value of 9. This is the observed frequency associated with the cell for women

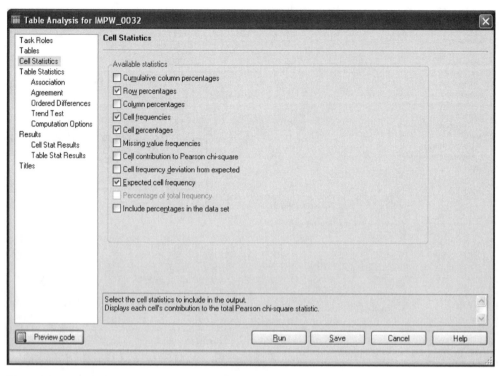

Figure 28.7. The **Cell Statistics** screen of the **Table Analysis** window.

travelers preferring location over service. Because the row and column totals are fixed, knowing the frequency for one cell determines the frequencies of the other three cells (that is why a 2×2 table has only 1 *df*) and why it is unnecessary for *SAS Enterprise Guide* to note the other cell frequencies.

The Fisher exact test can be evaluated in either a one-sided manner or a two-sided manner:

- The *one-sided* probability takes into account all possible tables that are more extreme *in the direction of the observed frequencies*. In the present case, that set would include the possible tables in which the women were even more polarized toward service and men even more polarized toward location.
- The *two-sided* probability takes into account all possible tables that are more extreme *in either direction with respect to the observed frequencies*. In the present case, that set would include the possible tables in which the women were even more polarized toward service and men even more polarized toward location as well as the possible tables in which the women were more polarized toward location and the men were more polarized toward service.

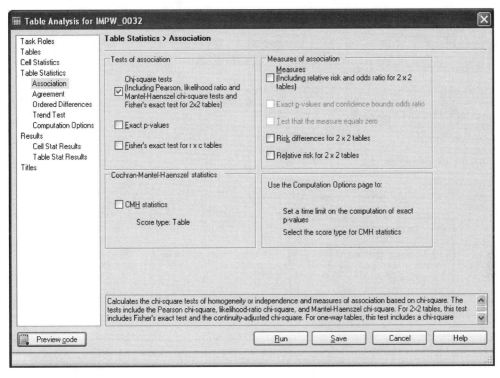

Figure 28.8. The **Table Statistics** > **Association** screen of the **Table Analysis** window.

Frequency	Table of gender by attribute			
Expected		attribute(attribute)		
Percent	gender(gender)			Total
Row Pct		1	2	
	1	9	26	35
		15.5	19.5	
		12.86	37.14	50.00
		25.71	74.29	
	2	22	13	35
		15.5	19.5	
		31.43	18.57	50.00
		62.86	37.14	
	Total	31	39	70
		44.29	55.71	100.00

Figure 28.9. Cell statistics output.

Statistic	DF	Value	Prob
Chi-Square	1	9.7849	0.0018
Likelihood Ratio Chi-Square	1	10.0412	0.0015
Continuity Adj. Chi-Square	1	8.3375	0.0039
Mantel-Haenszel Chi-Square	1	9.6452	0.0019
Phi Coefficient		-0.3739	
Contingency Coefficient		0.3502	
Cramer's V		-0.3739	

Fisher's Exact Test	
Cell (1,1) Frequency (F)	9
Left-sided Pr <= F	0.0018
Right-sided Pr >= F	0.9997
Table Probability (P)	0.0015
Two-sided Pr <= P	0.0036

Figure 28.10. Table statistics output.

Under the two-sided computation, the set of extreme tables is larger than it is under the one-sided computation, and therefore our obtained table represents a proportionally smaller percentage of all possible tables compared to the one-sided computation. Defined in this way, extreme tables are more likely to occur under the two-sided method than under the one-sided method. This computational difference, in turn, renders the two-sided exact test more conservative than the one-sided test, and it is more in keeping with Fisher's original intent. We recommend using the two-sided strategy if you intend to use Fisher's exact test. In any case, when reporting the results of the Fisher exact test, it is incumbent on the researchers to identify which evaluation method was used.

The one-sided outcome is shown in the row labeled **Table Probability (P)**. Here, the exact probability of obtaining our observed frequencies or a set that was more extreme in the same direction as our observed frequencies was computed to be .0015. The two-sided probability is shown on the row labeled **Two-sided Pr < = P**. The exact probability of obtaining our observed frequencies or a set that was more extreme in either direction is .0036.

29 Nonparametric Between-Subjects One-Way ANOVA

29.1 Overview

We covered one-way between-subjects ANOVA in Chapter 23. Among other assumptions of ANOVA are that the scale of measurement underlying the dependent variable is at least an approximation to interval (i.e., it is meaningful to compute means and standard deviations) and that the dependent variable distributions within the groups are relatively normal. If the distributions departed substantially from the normality assumption and if the researchers did not choose to subject their data to a nonlinear transformation, or if the researchers collected ranked data, then they can opt to use a distribution-free nonparametric analogue to the one-way between-subjects ANOVA.

29.2 The nonparametric analogues to One-Way ANOVA

We briefly treat two of the most commonly used nonparametric analogues to a one-way between-subjects ANOVA: the median test and the Kruskal–Wallis test. In both cases, there are two or more independent groups of cases that have been assessed on a dependent variable that reaches at least ordinal measurement.

29.2.1 The median test

The median test is a relatively imprecise test, in the sense that a good deal of the information in the data is discarded in the computation. Its advantage is that it is relatively simple to compute, a modest advantage indeed in computer-based data analysis. For the purposes of the analysis, the data for all groups are momentarily combined so that a median of the entire set of scores is computed. It is then simply determined how many scores in each group are above and below that common median. The null hypothesis holds that each group should contain the same number of scores above and below the median.

29.2.2 The Kruskal–Wallis test

The Kruskal–Wallis test (Kruskal & Wallis, 1952) is the generalized procedure of the Wilcoxon (1945) rank-sum test (not to be confused with the Wilcoxon signed-rank-order test for paired samples) and the Mann–Whitney U test (Mann & Whitney, 1947). It is applied to three or more groups. The Kruskal–Wallis test retains more information from the data than does the median test. For the purposes of the analysis, the data for all groups are momentarily combined and then rank ordered. The actual scores in each of the groups are then replaced in the analysis by the values of their rank-order position. The null hypothesis holds that the sum of the ranks of each group should be the same.

29.3   Numerical example

We will use the same data set as we used for the one-way between-subjects ANOVA design described in Chapter 23 in which we obtained a statistically significant F ratio in the omnibus analysis.

As you may recall, four different exercise regimes (the independent variable is named **exercise** in the data set) were used as possible ways to improve cardiovascular health: bicycling (coded as 1 in the data set), walking (coded as 2 in the data set), dance (coded as 3 in the data set), and weight lifting (coded as 4 in the data set). The dependent variable (named **health** in the data set) was a composite measure, based on blood pressure, blood cholesterol level, and inflammatory markers from a blood test; higher scores represented better cardiovascular health. A portion of the data set is shown in Figure 29.1.

29.4   Setting up the analysis

From the main menu select **Analyze → ANOVA → Nonparametric One-Way ANOVA**. This brings us to the **Task Roles** screen. Drag **health** to the icon for **Dependent variables**. Then drag **exercise** to the icon for **Independent variable**. This is shown in Figure 29.2.

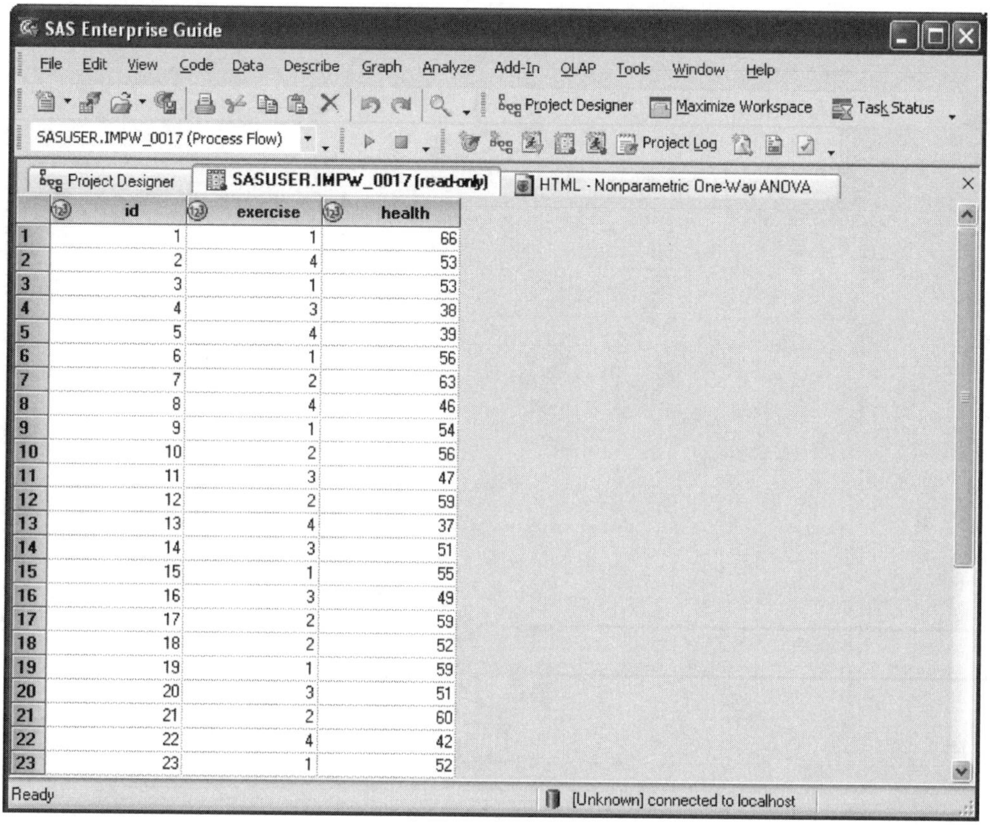

	id	exercise	health
1	1	1	66
2	2	4	53
3	3	1	53
4	4	3	38
5	5	4	39
6	6	1	56
7	7	2	63
8	8	4	46
9	9	1	54
10	10	2	56
11	11	3	47
12	12	2	59
13	13	4	37
14	14	3	51
15	15	1	55
16	16	3	49
17	17	2	59
18	18	2	52
19	19	1	59
20	20	3	51
21	21	2	60
22	22	4	42
23	23	1	52

Figure 29.1. A portion of the data set.

In the navigation panel, select **Analysis**. The left area of the screen presents checkboxes for **Test scores**. As shown in Figure 29.3, check the boxes for **Wilcoxon** and **Median**. Checking the **Wilcoxon** choice will cause SAS to convert the scores of the dependent variable to ranks in order to perform the Kruskal–Wallis test; checking **Median** will cause SAS to derive the common median for the data set and to count the number of cases above and below the median for each group. Click **Run** to perform both analyses.

29.5 Output of the analyses

29.5.1 Median test output

The results of the **Median** procedure appear in Figure 29.4. In the upper table is a column labeled **Sum of Scores**; the values in this column are the numbers of scores

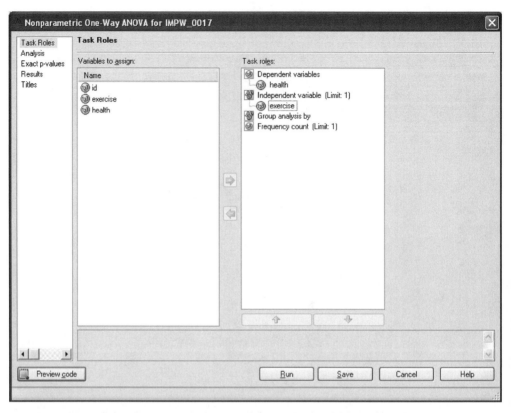

Figure 29.2. The **Task Roles** screen of the **Nonparametric One-Way ANOVA** window.

in each group that were above the common median. In the column next to it, labeled **Expected Under HO**, are the expected numbers of scores that should be above the median based on the null hypothesis.

The median test compares the expected numbers of scores above the median for each group to the obtained number using a chi-square procedure. As we can see in the lower table of Figure 29.4, the chi-square obtained by SAS was 22.6471. With 3 *df* because there are four groups in the study, the likelihood of obtaining that chi-square value if the null hypothesis is true is shown in the row labeled **Pr > Chi-Square**. That probability is < .0001. Against an alpha level of $\alpha = .05$, the chi-square is statistically significant, and we can conclude that different types of exercise have differential health consequences. If we were interested in which groups differed from which, we would need to perform separate median tests on the various pairs of groups.

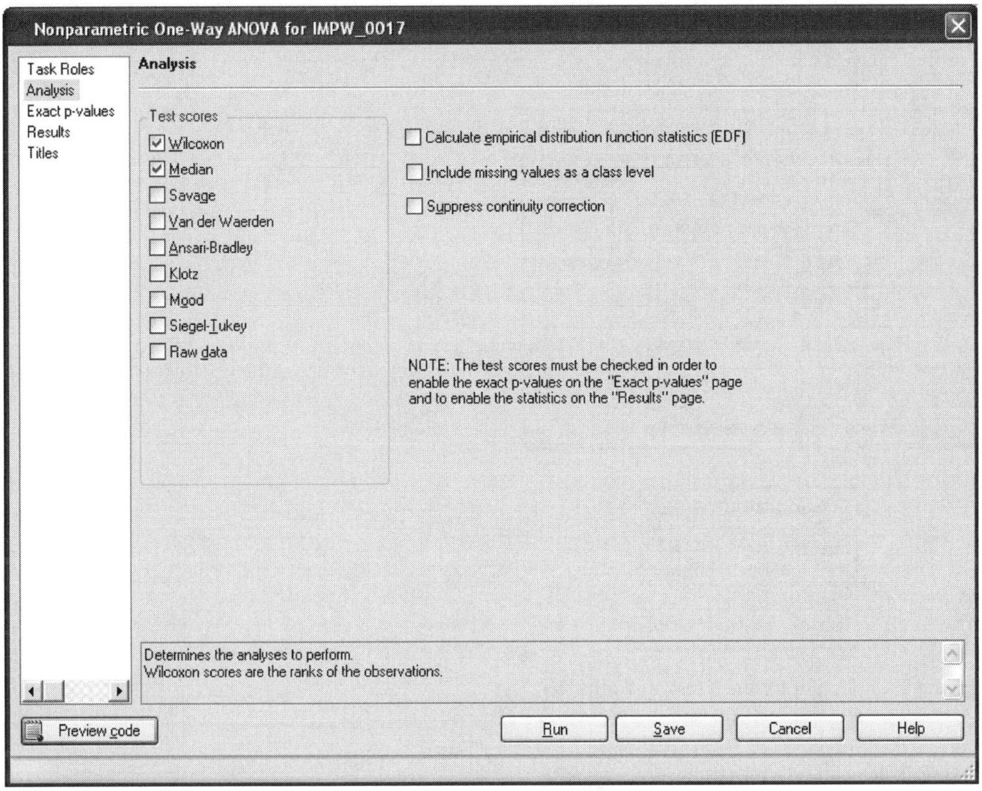

Figure 29.3. The **Analysis** screen is configured.

Median Scores (Number of Points Above Median) for Variable health Classified by Variable exercise					
exercise	N	Sum of Scores	Expected Under H0	Std Dev Under H0	Mean Score
1	9	8.50	4.50	1.280346	0.944444
4	9	1.00	4.50	1.280346	0.111111
3	9	1.00	4.50	1.280346	0.111111
2	9	7.50	4.50	1.280346	0.833333
Average scores were used for ties.					

Median One-Way Analysis	
Chi-Square	22.6471
DF	3
Pr > Chi-Square	<.0001

Figure 29.4. Output for the median test.

Wilcoxon Scores (Rank Sums) for Variable health Classified by Variable exercise					
exercise	N	Sum of Scores	Expected Under H0	Std Dev Under H0	Mean Score
1	9	240.0	166.50	27.342471	26.666667
4	9	64.0	166.50	27.342471	7.111111
3	9	124.0	166.50	27.342471	13.777778
2	9	238.0	166.50	27.342471	26.444444
Average scores were used for ties.					

Kruskal-Wallis Test	
Chi-Square	22.9000
DF	3
Pr > Chi-Square	<.0001

Figure 29.5. Output for the Kruskal–Wallis test.

29.5.2 Kruskal–Wallis test output

The results of the Kruskal–Wallis procedure appear in Figure 29.5. In the upper table is a column labeled **Sum of Scores**; the values in this column are the sums of the ranks of the scores in each group. In the column next to it, labeled **Expected Under H0**, are the expected sums of ranks based on the null hypothesis.

The Kruskal–Wallis test, shown in the lower table of Figure 29.4, compares the expected sum of ranks for each group with the obtained sum of ranks using a chi-square procedure. Chi-square was computed as 22.9000. With four groups in the analysis, there are 3 *df*, and the chi-square statistic is likely to occur with a probability (**Pr > Chi-Square**) of < .0001 if the null hypothesis is true. Against an alpha level of $\alpha = .05$, the chi-square is statistically significant, and we can conclude that different types of exercise have differential health consequences. If we were interested in which groups differed from which, we would need to perform separate Kruskal–Wallis tests on the various pairs of groups.

Section X

Advanced ANOVA
Techniques

30 One-Way Between-Subjects Analysis of Covariance

30.1 Overview

Analysis of covariance (ANCOVA) allows us to statistically control for a variable that potentially exerts an effect on the dependent variable but was not part of or could not readily be incorporated into the experimental design as an independent variable. Using ANCOVA, we bring that variable into the data analysis as a *covariate*. By collecting measures of a variable on the study participants and then treating it as a covariate in the analysis, it is possible to statistically "remove" or "neutralize" its effect on the dependent variable prior to determining the effects of the independent variable on the dependent variable. This allows us to evaluate the effects of the independent variable with the influence of the covariate removed. More complete descriptions of this analysis can be found in Gamst et al. (2008), Kirk (1995), and Maxwell and Delaney (2000).

There are three steps that are involved in performing an ANCOVA.

First, we use the covariate to predict the dependent variable. This is accomplished through a linear regression procedure.

Second, we adjust the values of the dependent variable to remove the effects of the covariate. That is, the regression model uses the scores on the covariate to predict the observed scores on the dependent variable. At the completion of the regression procedure, each case in the data set has a predicted dependent variable score. The predicted values from the linear regression procedure can be viewed as scores on the dependent measures that have used all of the information available from the covariate. These values are referred to as *adjusted values* of the dependent variable in that they no longer contain information related to the covariate – the variance of these predicted or adjusted values is what remains when the effect of the covariate has been accounted for. This means that whatever differences now remain in the predicted (adjusted) values of the dependent measure between the cases, and thus the remaining differences between the groups, are unrelated to the covariate. In this sense, the effect of the covariate has been removed from the scores. It should be noted that the values of the adjusted means of the groups may be quite different from the group means based on the observed dependent variable scores.

Third, we perform an ANOVA on the adjusted dependent variable scores. Therefore, if a statistically significant *F* ratio is obtained for the independent variable in an ANCOVA, it indicates that the groups differ *on the adjusted dependent variable means* (i.e., when the effect of the covariate has been statistically controlled). Another way to think about this is that the adjustment equalizes the groups with respect to the covariate so that we are attempting to determine what group differences on the dependent variable would have been obtained if the participants had been equivalent on the covariate (Maxwell & Delaney, 2000).

30.2 Assumptions of ANCOVA

An ANCOVA is subject to all of the assumptions underlying an ANOVA. Among these assumptions are that the dependent variable is normally distributed and that the variances of the conditions are equal. In addition, there are two other assumptions that are important to meet when one is performing an ANCOVA: linearity of regression and homogeneity of regression.

In *linearity of regression*, it is assumed that the relationship between the covariate and the dependent variable is linear. The most common way to determine if the data meet this linearity assumption is to graph the data in a scatterplot and visually examine it. The *y* axis of such a plot represents the dependent variable and the *x* axis represents the covariate. This analysis can be done conveniently within the **Linear Regression** procedure of *SAS Enterprise Guide*, where we can obtain both the regression model parameters and the scatterplot showing the regression line.

In *homogeneity of regression*, it is assumed that the slope of the regression line in which the covariate is a predictor of the dependent variable is the same for each group. The way in which we test the homogeneity of regression assumption is by setting up an analysis containing the interaction of the independent variable and the covariate. We meet the assumption of homogeneity of regression if the Independent Variable × Covariate interaction effect is not statistically significant.

30.3 Numerical example

In this hypothetical study, a sample of 36 teams (**id** in the data set) of 12-year-old children attending a summer camp participated in a study to determine which one of three different tree-watering techniques worked best to promote tree growth. The techniques are noted in the data set under the variable name **watering technique** and are coded as follows: a code of 1 called for watering the base of the tree for 10 minutes once per day by using a hose; a code of 2 called for watering the ground surrounding the tree for 2 hours each day by using a drip system; a code of 3 called for deep watering for 10 minutes every 3 days through a pipe sunk into the ground by the tree.

From a large set of equally sized and equally healthy fast-growing trees, each team was given a tree to plant at the start of the camp. Teams were responsible for the watering and general care of their trees throughout the summer. At the end of the summer, the height of each tree was measured. The amount of growth in number of inches is the dependent variable, named **tree growth dv** (to help readers remember that this variable is the dependent variable) in the data set.

The camp staff had two related concerns: (a) that some children might have had more gardening experience than others, and (b) that any knowledge gained as a result of that prior experience might affect the way the tree was planted and perhaps even the way in which the children cared for the tree and carried out the watering regime. It was therefore decided that an indicator of such knowledge might be effectively used as a covariate. Thus, the staff rated the amount of gardening experience and knowledge the children had on a 40-point scale. This information is recorded in the data set under the variable **gardening exp cov** (to help readers remember that this variable is the covariate), with higher scores representing more experience, knowledge, or both. By using this variable as a covariate in the study, the staff could evaluate the effects of the watering techniques with the prior gardening experience and knowledge of the children statistically controlled. A portion of the data set is shown in Figure 30.1.

30.4 Evaluating the assumptions of ANCOVA

30.4.1 Linearity of regression

From the main *SAS Enterprise Guide* menu, select **Analyze → Regression → Linear**. This brings us to the **Task Roles** window. Drag **tree growth dv** to the slot under **Dependent variable** in the rightmost panel. Then drag **gardening exp cov** to the slot under **Explanatory variables** in the rightmost panel. This is shown in Figure 30.2.

Click **Statistics** from the navigation panel on the far left. As shown in Figure 30.3, select **Standardized regression coefficients** under **Details on estimates**. Then select under **Correlations** both **Partial correlations** and **Semi-partial correlations**.

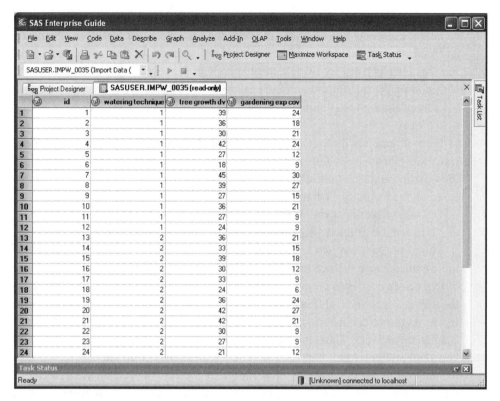

Figure 30.1. A portion of the data set.

Click **Plots** from the navigation panel on the far left and select **Plots > Predicted**. Check **Observed vs independents** (see Figure 30.4) to obtain a scatterplot with the fitted regression line. Then click the **Run** push button to perform the analysis.

The statistical output is shown in Figure 30.5. We note that the Pearson correlation between the dependent variable **tree growth dv** and the covariate **gardening exp cov**, presented under the label **Standardized Estimate** (the beta weight in the simple regression model), is .81150 with an adjusted R-square value of $R^2 = .6485$. Thus, there is clearly a strong linear component to the relationship. This assessment is reinforced by examining the scatterplot shown in Figure 30.6. A visual inspection of the plot with the regression function superimposed on it strongly suggests that tree growth is linearly related to gardening experience. Thus, the linearity of regression assumption appears to be met by the data set.

30.4.2 Homogeneity of regression

To evaluate the assumption of homogeneity of regression in *SAS Enterprise Guide*, select **Analyze → ANOVA → Linear Models.** As shown in the **Task Roles** screen

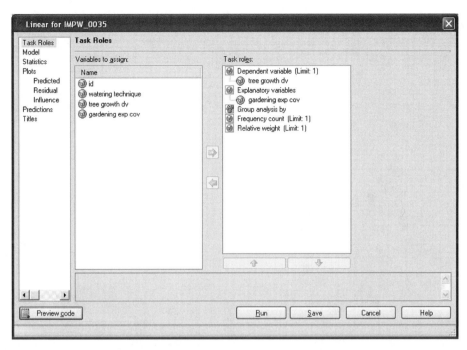

Figure 30.2. The **Task Roles** screen of the **Linear Regression** procedure.

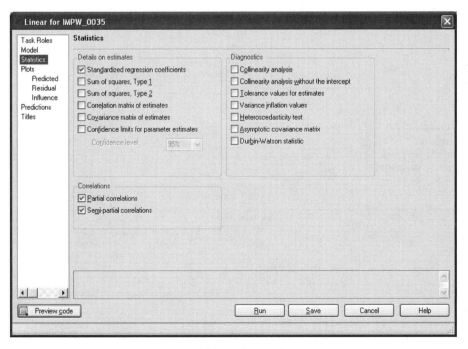

Figure 30.3. The **Statistics** screen for the **Linear Regression** procedure.

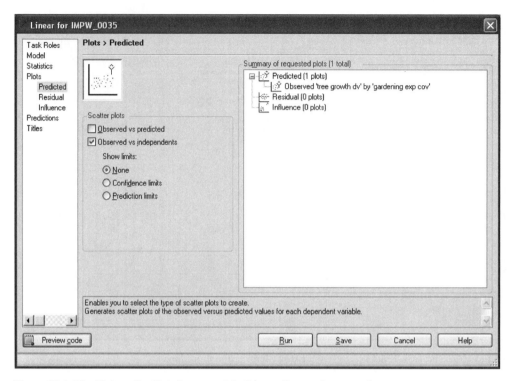

Figure 30.4. The **Plots > Predicted** screen of the **Linear Regression** procedure.

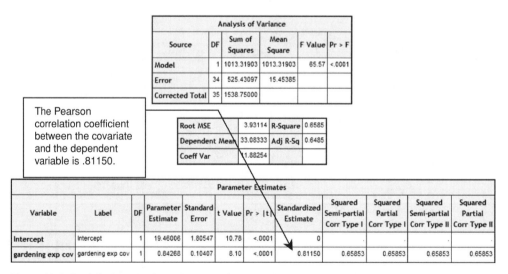

Analysis of Variance					
Source	DF	Sum of Squares	Mean Square	F Value	Pr > F
Model	1	1013.31903	1013.31903	65.57	<.0001
Error	34	525.43097	15.45385		
Corrected Total	35	1538.75000			

The Pearson correlation coefficient between the covariate and the dependent variable is .81150.

Root MSE	3.93114	R-Square	0.6585
Dependent Mean	33.08333	Adj R-Sq	0.6485
Coeff Var	11.88254		

Parameter Estimates											
Variable	Label	DF	Parameter Estimate	Standard Error	t Value	Pr > |t|	Standardized Estimate	Squared Semi-partial Corr Type I	Squared Partial Corr Type I	Squared Semi-partial Corr Type II	Squared Partial Corr Type II
Intercept	Intercept	1	19.46006	1.80547	10.78	<.0001	0				
gardening exp cov	gardening exp cov	1	0.84268	0.10407	8.10	<.0001	0.81150	0.65853	0.65853	0.65853	0.65853

Figure 30.5. Statistical results from the regression analysis.

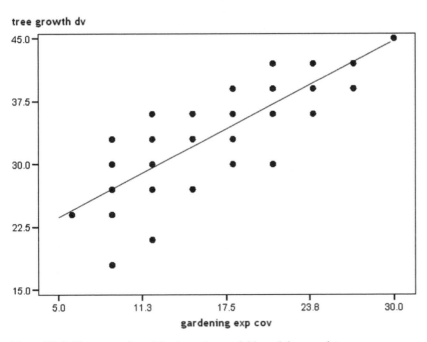

Figure 30.6. The scatterplot of the dependent variable and the covariate.

in Figure 30.7, specify **tree growth dv** under **Dependent variable** and **watering technique** under **Classification variables**. In addition, we also specify **gardening exp cov** under **Quantitative variables** (SAS makes explicit the idea that it treats covariates as quantitative rather than categorical variables).

Select **Model** in the navigation panel on the far left of the screen. Highlight **gardening exp cov** and click the **Main** push button in the middle of the window. This action will place **gardening exp cov** in the **Effects** panel. Do the same for **watering technique**. Next, highlight **gardening exp cov** and, while holding down the Shift key, highlight **watering technique**. Click the **Cross** push button to place the **gardening exp cov*watering technique** interaction in the **Effects** panel. The final configuration of this screen can be seen in Figure 30.8.

Select **Model Options** in the navigation panel. Select only **Type III** as shown in Figure 30.9. Then click **Run** to perform the analysis.

The summary table presenting the results of the analysis is shown in Figure 30.10. We are only interested in the interaction of the independent variable and the covariate, shown in the last row of the bottom table. The *F* ratio is

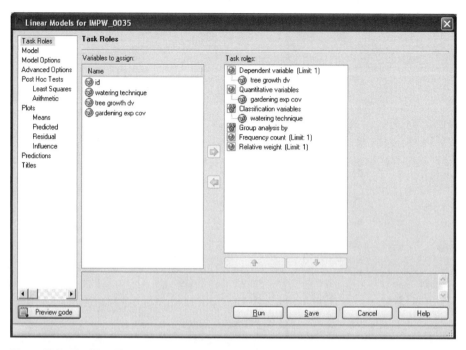

Figure 30.7. The **Task Roles** screen of the **Linear Models** procedure.

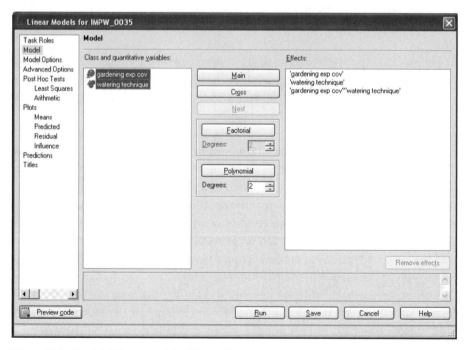

Figure 30.8. The **Model** screen of the **Linear Models** procedure.

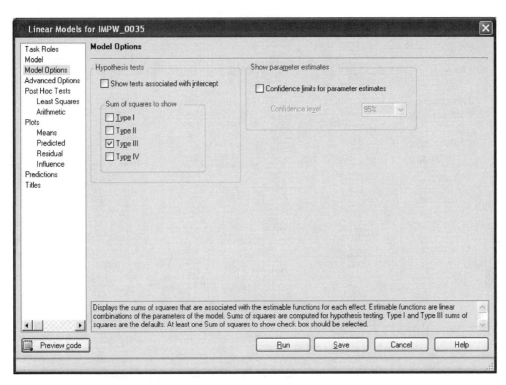

Figure 30.9. The **Model Options** screen of the **Linear Models** procedure.

Source	DF	Sum of Squares	Mean Square	F Value	Pr > F
Model	5	1144.967555	228.993511	17.45	<.0001
Error	30	393.782445	13.126082		
Corrected Total	35	1538.750000			

R-Square	Coeff Var	Root MSE	tree growth dv Mean
0.744089	10.95111	3.622993	33.08333

Source	DF	Type III SS	Mean Square	F Value	Pr > F
gardening exp cov	1	921.2547719	921.2547719	70.19	<.0001
watering technique	2	46.4044824	23.2022412	1.77	0.1881
gardening*watering t	2	14.3848237	7.1924119	0.55	0.5838

The assumption of homogeneity of regression is tested by examining the interaction of the covariate and the independent variable. If it is not statistically significant, as is the case here, then the assumption is met.

Figure 30.10. The summary table for the analysis.

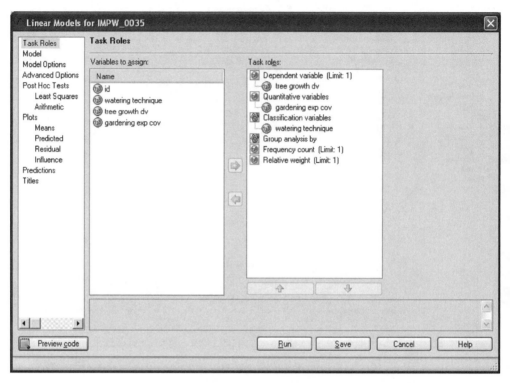

Figure 30.11. The **Task Roles** screen of the **Linear Models** procedure.

0.55 and the probability of such a value occurring by chance if the null hypothesis is true (**Pr > F**) is .5838. It is therefore the case that the interaction of the covariate and the independent variable is not statistically significant. This in turn allows us to conclude that the data do not violate the assumption of homogeneity of regression.

30.5   Setting up the ANCOVA

To perform the omnibus ANCOVA, we configure the analysis in a manner similar to the way in which we ran the test for homogeneity of regression as already described. From the main menu select **Analyze → ANOVA → Linear Models.** As shown in Figure 30.11, specify **tree growth dv** under **Dependent variable**, **watering technique** under **Classification variables**, and **gardening exp cov** under **Quantitative variables.**

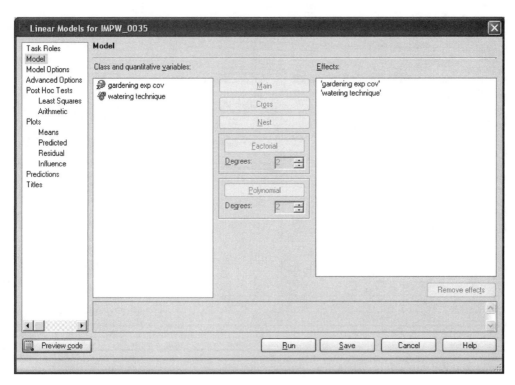

Figure 30.12. The **Model** screen of the **Linear Models** procedure.

In the **Model** window, separately click over **gardening exp cov** and **watering technique**. These will take on the roles of main effects (see Figure 30.12); we do not specify the interaction of these two in the omnibus ANCOVA (as we did in testing the assumption of homogeneity of regression). In the **Model Options** window, specify only **Type III** (not shown).

We also wish to obtain the means for the groups. Because ANCOVA analyzes the adjusted means, it is not appropriate to refer to the observed means as these are not the means that are evaluated. Instead, we need to obtain the adjusted means. SAS calls these means *least squares* means. We can have them displayed in the output by selecting the **Least Squares** portion of the **Post Hoc Tests** window in the navigation panel shown in Figure 30.13. Click **Add** to show the effects in the model and to display the panels under **Options for means tests**. Under **Class effects to use** (the first panel on the right portion of the window), set the **watering technique** effect to **True** (if it is initially set to **False**, double-clicking it displays the **True/False** menu from which you select **True**).

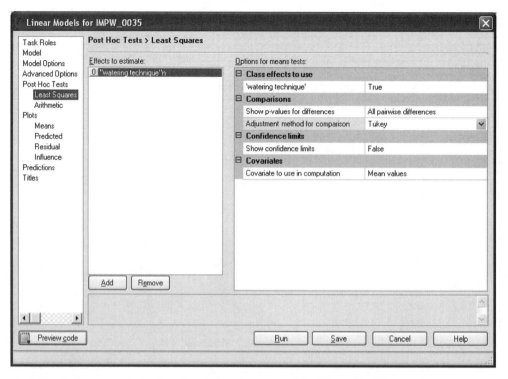

Figure 30.13. The **Post Hoc Tests > Least Squares** screen of the **Linear Models** procedure.

To make the analysis complete, we will specify our pairwise mean comparisons as well because we are already working in this screen (rather than waiting to view the omnibus analysis results and then going back to run our post-ANOVA mean comparisons). Under the **Comparisons** panel, set **Show p-values for differences** to **All pairwise differences** and set **Adjustment method for comparison** to **Tukey**. This configuration is also shown in Figure 30.13. Click **Run** to perform the analysis.

30.6 The ANCOVA output

The output of the omnibus ANCOVA is shown in Figure 30.14. It is structured in the same way as a one-way between-subjects ANOVA. We have discussed the structure of this output in Section 23.6 and will not repeat it. Our interest is in the lower summary table in which the effects of the covariate and the independent variable

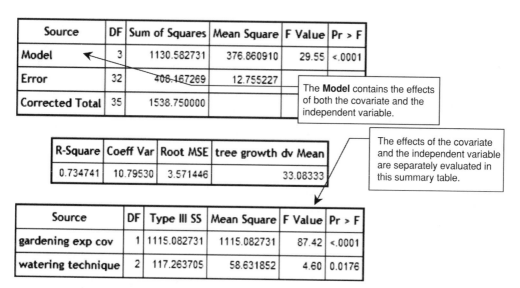

Source	DF	Sum of Squares	Mean Square	F Value	Pr > F
Model	3	1130.582731	376.860910	29.55	<.0001
Error	32	408.167269	12.755227		
Corrected Total	35	1538.750000			

The **Model** contains the effects of both the covariate and the independent variable.

The effects of the covariate and the independent variable are separately evaluated in this summary table.

R-Square	Coeff Var	Root MSE	tree growth dv Mean
0.734741	10.79530	3.571446	33.08333

Source	DF	Type III SS	Mean Square	F Value	Pr > F
gardening exp cov	1	1115.082731	1115.082731	87.42	<.0001
watering technique	2	117.263705	58.631852	4.60	0.0176

Figure 30.14. The results of the omnibus analysis.

are separately evaluated. As we can see, the covariate **gardening exp cov** was statistically significant. Using the corrected total sum of squares shown in the upper table as our base, its eta-square value can be calculated as 1115.082731/1538.75, or $\eta^2 = .725$. We can therefore assert that prior gardening experience and knowledge was quite influential in how well the trees fared under the attention of the young campers.

Of primary interest was the independent variable of **watering technique**. As we can see from the lower summary table, it too was statistically significant. The eta-square value associated with this variable is 408.167269/1538.75, or $\eta^2 = .265$. This suggests that the technique used for watering the trees, *when we statistically control for or equate the gardening experience and knowledge of the children*, was a relatively strong factor in how much growth was seen in the trees.

The results of the pairwise comparisons of the group means are shown in Figure 30.15. The upper table displays the least squares means for the number of inches the trees grew over the summer, adjusted for the gardening experience covariate. Recall that the watering techniques coded 1, 2, and 3 represented hose watering, drip watering, and deep watering, respectively.

The lower table in Figure 30.15 provides the results of the pairwise comparisons after the Tukey–Kramer strategy is used to maintain a familywise error rate at .05. As we can see from the table, the only significant difference was between the means

The GLM Procedure
Least Squares Means
Adjustment for Multiple Comparisons: Tukey-Kramer

watering technique	tree growth dv LSMEAN	LSMEAN Number
1	30.6055339	1
2	33.5835651	2
3	35.0609010	3

Least Squares Means for effect watering technique Pr > |t| for H0: LSMean(i)=LSMean(j) Dependent Variable: tree growth dv			
i/j	1	2	3
1		0.1279	0.0145
2	0.1279		0.5741
3	0.0145	0.5741	

Watering techniques coded as 1 (hose watering) and 3 (deep watering) are the only two groups whose means differ significantly.

Figure 30.15. The results of the Tukey–Kramer adjustment for multiple comparisons.

for the watering techniques coded as 1 and 3. On the basis of the adjusted means, we may therefore conclude that, when we statistically control for gardening experience, deep watering is more effective than hose watering but is not significantly more effective than drip watering.

31 One-Way Between-Subjects Multivariate Analysis of Variance

31.1 Overview

The ANOVA designs discussed in Chapters 23 through 26 examined the effect of one or more independent variables on a *single* dependent variable. Because such designs focus on a single dependent variable, they are labeled as *univariate* ANOVA designs. The present chapter addresses designs in which two or more dependent variables are analyzed simultaneously; such designs are known as *multivariate* analysis of variance (MANOVA) designs. We limit our discussion to the simplest illustration of such a design: a two-group one-way between-subjects design. More information about MANOVA can be found in Meyers et al. (2006), Stevens (2002), and Warner (2008).

31.2 Univariate and multivariate ANOVA

Univariate ANOVA designs are extremely useful but their focus is on a single outcome measure. For example, in evaluating a new curriculum designed to teach children to read more quickly, a natural variable to measure is reading speed. But at the same time that the reading speed of the children was improving (assuming a successful curriculum), there might potentially be other variables changing in synchrony, such as reading comprehension, enhanced levels of self-confidence, and feelings of mastery. Perhaps improvements in other academic subjects might be observed as well. All of these related (correlated) effects could serve as potential dependent variables. To focus only on one of these variables, reading speed for example, narrows the focus of the study perhaps to an unnecessary extent.

Assume that in addition to reading speed we measured several other variables as just noted. The issue then becomes what the best way is to evaluate these related dependent measures. One strategy open to us is to perform a series of univariate ANOVAs, one for each dependent measure. A pitfall associated with this strategy is this: Performing a series of ANOVAs on correlated dependent measures can increase the likelihood that the researchers would obtain a false-positive result on at least one of them. By concluding that the groups are significantly different on that dependent variable when in fact the groups are comparable would lead the researchers to commit a Type I error.

One way to avoid such a pitfall is to postpone performing separate univariate ANOVAs until we have carried out and have obtained a "green light" to proceed from a MANOVA. The steps involved in performing a MANOVA are as follows:

- The dependent variables are first combined together to form a composite dependent variable. We discussed in Section 17.5.1 such a composite in the context of linear multiple regression: The set of predictor variables were weighted so that in combination they would maximally predict a dependent variable. Although we did not use the term then, such a composite variable is known as a *variate*, and it is a weighted linear compilation of the individual independent measures. The value of the variate in MANOVA is known as a *discriminant* score.
- The discriminant scores are treated as a dependent variable in an ANOVA.
- We evaluate group differences on the discriminant scores (variate) by means of a *multivariate* F *ratio*.

If the multivariate F ratio resulting from the MANOVA is statistically significant, we would continue the analysis to then examine the results of the univariate ANOVAs for each separate dependent variable. A common recommendation in performing these univariate evaluations (e.g., Meyers et al., 2006; Stevens, 2002) is to use an adjusted (corrected or modified) alpha level to guard against alpha-level inflation. A Bonferroni-corrected alpha level, for example, is determined by dividing our traditional $\alpha = .05$ value of statistical significance by the number of dependent variables in the analysis.

31.3 Numerical example

The data set, slightly modified for this example, is based on research concerning academic mastery goal orientation conducted by one of our graduate students. Mastery goal orientation refers to preferences for engaging in somewhat challenging academic work in order to achieve greater understanding of the material. A total of 150 undergraduate students (**id** in the data set) were classified as being either

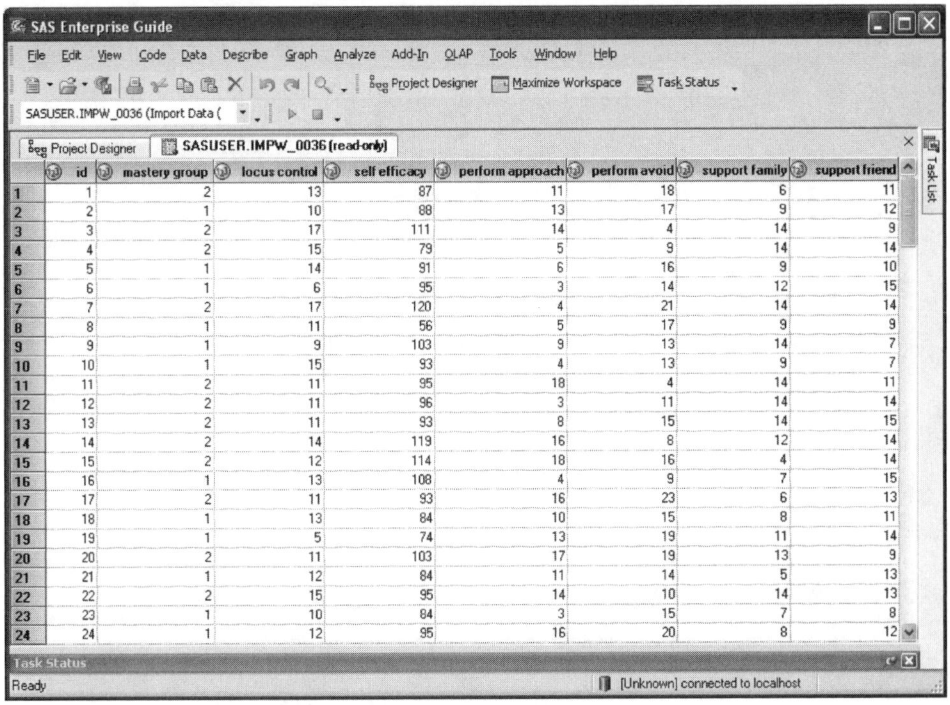

	id	mastery group	locus control	self efficacy	perform approach	perform avoid	support family	support friend
1	1	2	13	87	11	18	6	11
2	2	1	10	88	13	17	9	12
3	3	2	17	111	14	4	14	9
4	4	2	15	79	5	9	14	14
5	5	1	14	91	6	16	9	10
6	6	1	6	95	3	14	12	15
7	7	2	17	120	4	21	14	14
8	8	1	11	56	5	17	9	9
9	9	1	9	103	9	13	14	7
10	10	1	15	93	4	13	9	7
11	11	2	11	95	18	4	14	11
12	12	2	11	96	3	11	14	14
13	13	2	11	93	8	15	14	15
14	14	2	14	119	16	8	12	14
15	15	2	12	114	18	16	4	14
16	16	1	13	108	4	9	7	15
17	17	2	11	93	16	23	6	13
18	18	1	13	84	10	15	8	11
19	19	1	5	74	13	19	11	14
20	20	2	11	103	17	19	13	9
21	21	1	12	84	11	14	5	13
22	22	2	15	95	14	10	14	13
23	23	1	10	84	3	15	7	8
24	24	1	12	95	16	20	8	12

Figure 31.1. A portion of the data set.

relatively high or relatively low on mastery (**mastery group** in the data set with **1** representing relatively low and **2** representing relatively high mastery); this comprised the independent variable in the analysis. The six dependent variables in the study were locus of control (belief as to whether one's life is controlled by oneself or by external forces or events; listed as **locus control** in the data set), self-efficacy (belief about the ability one has to accomplish tasks; listed as **self efficacy** in the data set), performance approach (motivation to show superior performance to others; listed as **perform approach** in the data set), performance avoidance (motivation to avoid negative outcomes; listed as **perform avoid** in the data set), and the level of social support in the pursuit of higher education that the students received separately from family and friends (**support family** and **support friend**, respectively, in the data set). A portion of the data set is shown in Figure 31.1.

31.4 Setting up the MANOVA

From the main menu select **Analyze → Multivariate → Discriminant Analysis.** As shown in the **Task Roles** screen in Figure 31.2, specify **mastery group** as

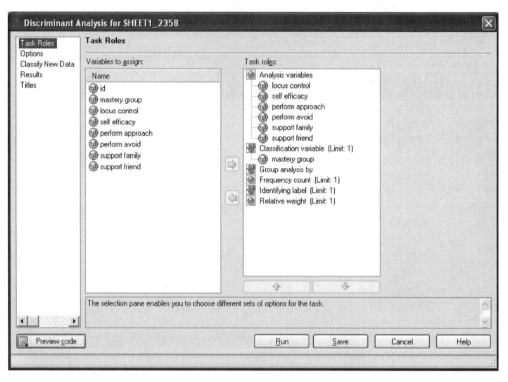

Figure 31.2. The **Task Roles** screen of the **Discriminant Analysis** procedure.

the **Classification variable**, and **locus control**, **self efficacy**, **perform approach**, **perform avoid**, **support family**, and **support friend** as the **Analysis variables**.

In the **Options** window, click the checkboxes corresponding to **Univariate test for equality of class means** and **Multivariate tests for equality of class means** (see Figure 31.3). This will cause *SAS Enterprise Guide* to produce the univariate and multivariate *F* ratios, respectively. Click **Run** to perform the analysis.

31.5   The MANOVA output

The multivariate *F* ratios are shown in Figure 31.4. It is typical for statistical analysis software to produce the results of several different multivariate tests, and researchers should determine in advance which they will use as their criterion. With approximately equal sample sizes and comparable variance for the dependent variables across the groups, the Wilks' lambda statistic is appropriate to use, and we would have selected this at the start of the analysis. Its value in this analysis

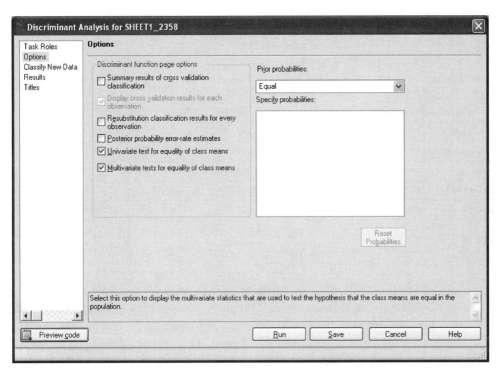

Figure 31.3. The **Options** screen of the **Discriminant Analysis** procedure.

Multivariate Statistics and Exact F Statistics					
S=1 M=2 N=64					
Statistic	Value	F Value	Num DF	Den DF	Pr > F
Wilks' Lambda	0.67534356	10.42	6	130	<.0001
Pillai's Trace	0.32465644	10.42	6	130	<.0001
Hotelling-Lawley Trace	0.48072783	10.42	6	130	<.0001
Roy's Greatest Root	0.48072783	10.42	6	130	<.0001

Of the four different multivariate tests, we will use Wilks' Lambda for our evaluation.

Figure 31.4. Multivariate F tests.

is approximately $\Lambda = .68$ and represents the amount of variance unaccounted for; eta square is equal to the difference between Wilks' lambda and 1.00, which would be approximately $\eta^2 = .32$ in this example. The multivariate F ratio was computed by SAS to be 10.42. With 6 and 130 df, that F ratio has a probability of occurring

Univariate Test Statistics							
F Statistics, Num DF=1, Den DF=135							
Variable	Label	Total Standard Deviation	Pooled Standard Deviation	Between Standard Deviation	R-Square	R-Square / (1-RSq)	F Value	Pr > F
locus control	locus control	3.5406	3.4127	1.3914	0.0778	0.0844	11.39	0.0010
self efficacy	self efficacy	16.5714	14.5985	11.1892	0.2296	0.2981	40.24	<.0001
perform approach	perform approach	5.5203	5.3442	2.0528	0.0697	0.0749	10.11	0.0018
perform avoid	perform avoid	4.8327	4.7576	1.3266	0.0380	0.0395	5.33	0.0225
support family	support family	3.0881	3.0596	0.6958	0.0256	0.0262	3.54	0.0620
support friend	support friend	2.4919	2.3964	1.0053	0.0820	0.0893	12.06	0.0007

Figure 31.5. Univariate F ratios.

(**Pr > F**) of $< .0001$ if the null hypothesis was true. We therefore reject the null hypothesis and conclude that the multivariate F ratio is statistically significant. Given that we now appear to have obtained group difference on the discriminant variate, we will proceed with the examination of the univariate results (the separate F ratios for each dependent variable).

The univariate results are shown in Figure 31.5, where the relevant results for us are shown in the columns labeled **R-Square**, **F value**, and **Pr > F**. These latter two columns present the F ratio and probability of occurrence if the null hypothesis was true for each dependent variable in isolation. With a statistically significant F ratio, the **R-Square** column can be interpreted as an eta-square value for the effect strength associated with that particular dependent variable.

In evaluating the statistical significance of the univariate F ratios, we will use a Bonferroni adjustment. In the present case, we divide .05 by 6 (the number of dependent variables) to derive a Bonferroni-corrected alpha level of $\alpha = .008$ against which we would evaluate the univariate results. Using such a modified alpha level, we find that the dependent variables of **locus control**, **self efficacy**, **perform approach**, and **support friend** yielded statistically significant differences between the groups.

As an example of how to read the output, consider the variable **locus control**. The univariate F ratio associated with this dependent variable is 11.39 with a probability of occurrence if the null hypothesis is true of .001. This probability value meets our modified alpha level of $\alpha = .008$, and we therefore judge the effect of the independent variable to be statistically significant; that is, we judge that the means of the two mastery groups on the measure of locus of control differ significantly. On the basis of the **R-Square** value, we determine that the independent variable of mastery accounted for approximately 8% of the total variance in the locus of control scores.

31.6   Follow-up analyses: setup

There are two desired (useful) aspects of the multivariate analysis that could not be generated in the *SAS Enterprise Guide* **Discriminant Analysis** procedure:

- We did not obtain the means and standard deviations of the groups for each of the dependent variables. That information is needed here to determine which of the two groups yielded higher scores on the statistically significant dependent variables.
- Had the independent variable been composed of three or more groups, we would have been unable to determine which of the pairs of means were significantly different.

To deal with both of these issues (although the second one does not apply here because we have only two groups in our example), we would perform one-way between-subjects analyses as described in Chapter 23 to acquire that desired information. We will very quickly take you through the setup for that process.

From the main menu select **Analyze → ANOVA → One-Way ANOVA**. As indicated in the **Task Roles** screen shown in Figure 31.6, specify **mastery group** as the **Independent variable**, and **locus control**, **self efficacy**, **perform approach**, **perform avoid**, **support family**, and **support friend** as the **Dependent variables**. Because **One-Way ANOVA** is a univariate procedure, one stand-alone analysis will be obtained for each dependent variable.

In the **Tests** screen, select **Welch's variance-weighted ANOVA** and **Levene's test** of homogeneity of variance (see Figure 31.7).

In the **Means > Breakdown** screen, select **Mean, Standard deviation**, and **Number of non-missing observations** (see Figure 31.8).

If we had more than two groups, then we would identify in the **Means > Comparison** screen (see Figure 31.9) a post hoc test that we wished to use to perform the pairwise mean comparisons. In examining the output, we would examine only the post hoc results on those dependent variables that were statistically significant. With only two groups in the present example, we do not make an entry on this screen. Click **Run** to perform the analysis.

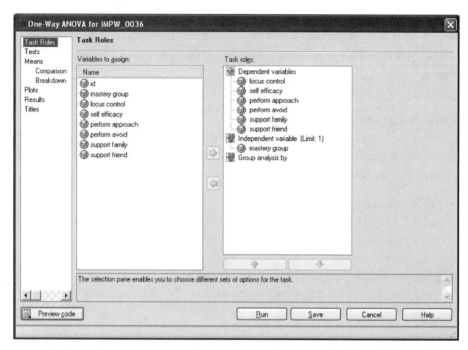

Figure 31.6. The **Task Roles** screen of the **One-Way ANOVA** procedure.

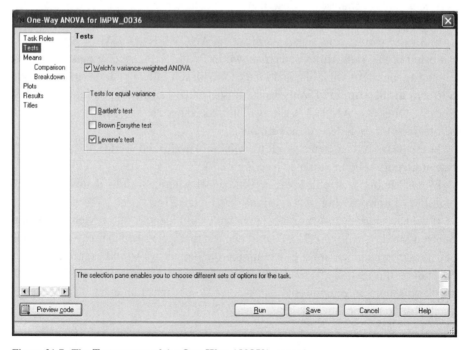

Figure 31.7. The **Tests** screen of the **One-Way ANOVA** procedure.

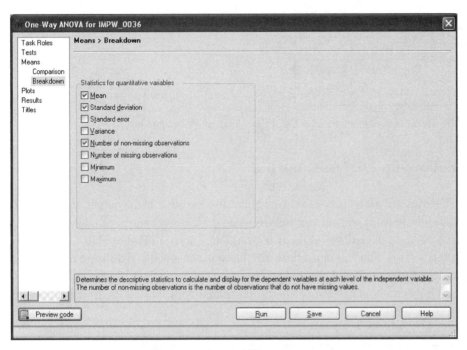

Figure 31.8. The **Means > Breakdown** screen of the **One-Way ANOVA** procedure.

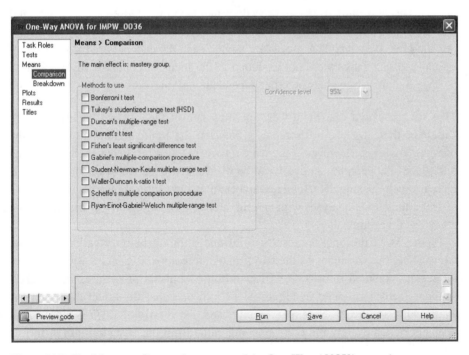

Figure 31.9. The **Means > Comparison** screen of the **One-Way ANOVA** procedure.

Level of mastery group	N	locus control	
		Mean	Std Dev
1	72	11.3055556	3.22681934
2	75	13.3733333	3.75526057

Figure 31.10. Means and standard deviations of the two locus of control groups.

31.7   Follow-up analyses: output

The results of each analysis are listed one after the other in the output. We will illustrate how to work with these results by using the locus of control variable. The means and standard deviations for the two groups are shown in Figure 31.10. Because we already know that this dependent variable was statistically significant in our previous analysis, we would conclude that students with relatively higher mastery levels had a more internal locus of control compared with those with a relatively lower mastery level.

We should note that these descriptive statistics are slightly different from what we would have obtained from the discriminant procedure:

- The **Discriminant Analysis** procedure included only those cases having valid values on *all* of the dependent variables.
- The **One-Way ANOVA** procedure treated each dependent variable on a stand-alone basis. Cases were not excluded in the locus of control analysis because they had missing values on other dependent variables.

Thus, to the extent that there were missing data in the data set values on some variables, there will be a discrepancy between the multivariate analysis and the one-way analyses. However, if there are relatively few missing data points, then the differences between the analyses can be overlooked under most circumstances. If there is much missing data, then researchers may have little choice but to perform a series of univariate analyses with careful attention to conservatively modifying the alpha level they are using.

Figure 31.11 presents the results of Levene's homogeneity of variance test. As we can see, the variances of the two groups are comparable. As a verification of the results obtained through the **Discriminant Analysis** procedure, the ANOVA summary table presented in Figure 31.12 indicates that the effect of mastery is statistically significant. Note that, on one hand, the F ratio of 12.77 is close to but does not match exactly the corresponding value from the **Discriminant Analysis**

Levene's Test for Homogeneity of locus control Variance ANOVA of Squared Deviations from Group Means					
Source	DF	Sum of Squares	Mean Square	F Value	Pr > F
mastery group	1	488.4	488.4	1.61	0.2063
Error	145	43943.8	303.1		

Welch's ANOVA for locus control			
Source	DF	F Value	Pr > F
mastery group	1.0000	12.85	0.0005
Error	143.3		

Figure 31.11. Results of the homogeneity of variance test.

Source	DF	Sum of Squares	Mean Square	F Value	Pr > F
Model	1	157.066712	157.066712	12.77	0.0005
Error	145	1782.824444	12.295341		
Corrected Total	146	1939.891156			

R-Square	Coeff Var	Root MSE	locus control Mean
0.080967	28.36826	3.506471	12.36054

Source	DF	Anova SS	Mean Square	F Value	Pr > F
mastery group	1	157.0667120	157.0667120	12.77	0.0005

Figure 31.12. The ANOVA summary table.

output. Its probability of occurrence based on the null hypothesis is also slightly different, although we are easily led to the same conclusion. On the other hand, the strength of effect estimate (**R-Square**) in the **One-Way ANOVA** procedure still rounds to the same 8% of the locus of control variance accounted for by the independent variable that we obtained in the **Discriminant Analysis** output.

Section XI

Analysis of Structure

32 Factor Analysis

32.1 Overview

Factor analysis refers to a set of procedures whose goal is to organize a relatively large set of variables into a few sets of interrelated variables. One common application of the technique is to identify the subscale structure of a paper-and-pencil inventory. Specifically, we can use factor analysis to organize a set of items on an inventory into relatively homogeneous subsets. Items that are relatively strongly related to a factor may be combined together in the scoring system to yield a subscale score.

32.2 Some history

We generally ascribe the origin of factor analysis to Charles Spearman (1904a), who, according to Harman (1962), developed this statistical tool in the process of constructing his theoretical model of intelligence. Spearman's intent was to determine the conceptual dimensions underlying a series of mostly perceptual and memory testing modules (e.g., sensory discrimination of tones, just noticeable difference measurements for weights, memory span) that he had administered to over 100 English school children that were presumed to measure aspects of intelligence. However, Harman also tells us that one of the bases for Spearman's mathematical treatment of the data was published in an earlier paper by Karl Pearson (1901), who should therefore share a small portion of the credit for the development of the procedure.

The pioneering work of Pearson and Spearman saw considerable development a quarter of century later. First, although Spearman used the term *factor* repeatedly in his 1904 paper, *factor analysis* as a label for the statistical method he had created was actually introduced by Louis Thurstone in 1931 (Carroll, 1993) in the process of describing his more modern approach to the technique (Thurstone, 1931, 1938). Second, *principal components analysis*, a widely used "variation" of factor analysis, the beginnings of which were first discussed in Pearson's (1901) article, was brought to fruition by Harold Hotelling (1933, 1936b) at roughly the same time that Thurstone was publishing his factor analysis work (Jolliffe, 2002). Discussions of principal components analysis and factor analysis can be found in Lattin, Carroll, and Green (1993), Meyers et al. (2006), and Stevens (2002). For more technical and comprehensive treatments of this subject matter, readers should consult Gorsuch (1983), the classic text by Harman (1962), and Thompson (2004).

32.3   The basis of factor analysis

Factor analysis is designed to generate a set of *weighted linear combinations* of the variables in the analysis (e.g., items on an inventory). As we discussed in Section 31.2, weighted linear combinations of variables are known as *variates*. In factor analysis, these variates are the *factors*. Each factor contains all of the variables but the factors differ in that the individual variables are weighted differently in each factor. Ideally, at the end of the process each variable is associated with a relatively strong weight in only one factor and is weighted relatively weakly in the others. Variables weighted relatively strongly in each factor serve as the basis of interpreting the factor.

Factor analysis begins by computing the pairwise correlations of the variables. These correlations are organized in a square correlation matrix with n variables for the rows and the same n variables for the columns, where n is the number of variables in the analysis. The diagonal coordinates of the correlation matrix (upper left to lower right) are the locations where the same variables appear in the row and column and are ascribed values of 1.00. Factor analysis derives the factors based on mathematically processing the correlations in the correlation matrix. The procedure is performed in two phases: extraction and rotation. We very briefly discuss each of these phases here.

32.4   The extraction phase

To *extract* a factor is to fit a straight line through the mathematical space representing the correlations between the variables in a manner analogous to (but much more complex than) the manner in which the line of best fit is determined in ordinary least squares regression. The mathematical space is composed of as many dimensions as there are variables in the analysis; it is therefore labeled as *multidimensional* space. One of the ways the interrelationships between the pairs of correlations in this multidimensional space can be described is in terms of variance. The total amount of variance is numerically equal to the number of variables in the analysis.

The extraction phase of factor analysis is designed to account for this variance. Factors are extracted successively, each accounting for variance not already accounted for by previously extracted factors. Another way to say this is that the factors are independent of or *orthogonal* to each other, and the variance they explain is additive. Each successive factor that is extracted accounts for more variance than those extracted after it. Thus, the first factor extracted accounts for more variance than all the succeeding factors that are extracted; the second factor extracted accounts for more variance than any of its successors but less than the first; and so forth. When all of the factors have been extracted (have been fit into the multidimensional space), all of the variance targeted in the analysis has been explained.

This phase of the analysis is called *extraction* because each factor that fits into the multidimensional space "removes" that increment of variance from what can be potentially accounted for by the remaining factors to be fit. That is, each successive factor must account for whatever variance remains after the earlier-fit factors have done their variance-explaining work. In this sense, variance is being "extracted" (explained or accounted for) successively by the factors as they are fit.

The amount of variance accounted for by a factor is known as an *eigenvalue*. Although as many factors can be extracted as there are variables in the analysis, we usually rapidly reach the point of diminishing returns in terms of accounted for variance; that is, the first few factors typically account for relatively substantial increments of the variance (i.e., they have relatively large eigenvalues) whereas the many factors extracted later account for a relatively small amount of the variance (i.e., they have relatively small eigenvalues).

A pictorial representation of this notion of diminishing returns of explained variance can be seen in the *scree plot*. In a scree plot, the eigenvalues are represented on the y axis and the factors numbered 1 through N (where N is the number of variables in the analysis and also the total number of factors that can be extracted) are represented on the x axis. Drawing a line connecting each point in the scree plot traditionally yields a shape resembling a backward J (negatively decelerating) function. The number of factors researchers will select as the solution is a subjective but educated decision that is based on such criteria as where the scree begins to flatten, the percentage of variance accounted for by the factor structure at that point, the interpretability of the individual (rotated) factors, and the number of variables strongly associated with each (rotated) factor.

We used the term *factor analysis* in Section 32.3 and thus far in Section 32.4 in an informal way that did not distinguish between Pearson's and Hotelling's principal components analysis and Spearman's and Thurstone's factor analysis. However, in discussing the extraction phase of the analysis, we now find it necessary to distinguish between these two techniques; in oversimplified form, they can be summarized as follows.

Principal components analysis: In the correlation matrix, the values of 1.00 on the diagonal are retained. The "factors" of our discussion in Sections 32.3 and 32.4 are properly labeled as *components*, which are fit into the multidimensional space defined by the total variance of the variables in the analysis. Each of these components accounts for a percentage of the *total* variance.

Factor analysis: Factor analysis subsumes a variety of extraction procedures; among the more widely used are *principal factors* (sometimes called *principal axis*), *unweighted least squares*, and *maximum likelihood* factoring. In the correlation matrix, the values of 1.00 on the diagonal are replaced by other values reflecting the *variance each variable has in common* with the other variables. In principal factors analysis, for example, the value for the squared multiple correlation (R^2) between the variable and the other variables is used as a starting value (but is reestimated iteratively). Further, each method uses its own algorithm to generate the weights of the variables on each variate. The resulting variates are here properly labeled as *factors*, which are fit into the multidimensional space defined by the *shared* or *common variance* of the set of variables (the variance that all of the variables have in common). This common variance is different from and less than the total variance of the set of variables addressed in principal components analysis.

32.5   The rotation phase

Rotation of the factor (or component) structure is performed on the first k number of extracted factors, where k is decided upon by using criteria mentioned in Section 32.4. It is the rotated factor or component solution that we interpret. Recall that earlier extracted factors account for more variance than later extracted factors; in fact, it is frequently the case that the first factor is especially dominant in this regard. Rotation attempts to redistribute the accounted for variance more evenly among the factors or components, driving the solution to achieve what Thurstone (1938, 1947, 1954) identified as *simple structure*. In modern practice, we can conceptualize simple structure as a factor structure approximating these general idealized criteria:

- Each variable should correlate close to 1.00 with one factor and close to zero with the other factors.
- Each factor should be associated with some variables correlating near 1.00 with it and many variables correlating near zero with it.

Rotation can be accomplished in several ways but ultimately the various procedures fall into one of two general classes: orthogonal or oblique. Again in oversimplified form, these strategies can be summarized as follows.

The first strategy is known as *orthogonal rotation*. We indicated in Section 32.4 that extraction methods generate factors or components that are independent of or orthogonal to each other. Geometrically, orthogonal factors or components intersect at a 90° angle. An orthogonal rotation strategy requires that the factors or components remain perpendicular (independent) in the rotation process. The most frequently used orthogonal rotation strategy is known as *varimax* rotation.

The second strategy is known as *oblique rotation*. An oblique rotation strategy allows the factors or components to become correlated in the rotation process if that will better fit the data points (come closer to simple structure). It is called *oblique* rotation because the angle at which the factors intersect is allowed to depart from perpendicular alignment; once the lines cross at an angle other than 90°, the factors or components will correlate at least to a certain extent. One frequently used oblique rotation strategy is known as *promax* rotation.

32.6   Numerical example

The numerical example used here represents data collected on 415 professional mental health providers such as psychiatrists, psychologists, marriage and family therapists, and social workers who were delivering services in southern California. These providers completed the California Brief Multicultural Competence Scale (Gamst et al., 2004). This inventory asks respondents to rate on a 4-point scale, from *strongly disagree* to *strongly agree*, the extent to which they believe they have knowledge of multicultural issues or possess an ability to deliver counseling services to individuals of diverse multicultural backgrounds.

The 21 inventory items with the corresponding item names that we used in the data set are shown in Figure 32.1. All items are positively worded, and higher scores indicate greater multicultural competency. We created variable names starting with

The California Brief Multicultural Competence Scale

Item	Name in Data File
1. I am aware that being born a minority in this society brings with it certain challenges that White people do not have to face.	q1challenges
2. I am aware of how my own values might affect my client.	q2values
3. I have an excellent ability to assess, accurately, the mental health needs of persons with disabilities.	q3disabhealth
4. I am aware of institutional barriers that affect the client.	q4barriers
5. I have an excellent ability to assess, accurately, the mental health needs of lesbians.	q5leshealth
6. I have an excellent ability to assess, accurately, the mental health needs of older adults.	q6olderhealth
7. I have an excellent ability to identify the strengths and weaknesses of psychological tests in terms of their use with persons from different cultural, racial and/or ethnic backgrounds.	q7testsculture
8. I am aware that counselors frequently impose their own cultural values upon minority clients.	q8imposevalues
9. My communication skills are appropriate for my clients.	q9commskills
10. I am aware that being born a White person in this society carries with it certain advantages.	q10whiteadvan
11. I am aware of how my cultural background and experiences have influenced my attitudes about psychological processes.	q11backattitude
12. I have an excellent ability to critique multicultural research.	q12cultresearch
13. I have an excellent ability to assess, accurately, the mental health needs of men.	q13menhealth
14. I am aware of institutional barriers that may inhibit minorities from using mental health services.	q14barriersminor
15. I can discuss, within a group, the differences among ethnic groups (e.g. low socioeconomic status (SES), Puerto Rican client vs. high SES Puerto Rican client).	q15talkdiff
16. I can identify my reactions that are based on stereotypical beliefs about different ethnic groups.	q16stereotypes
17. I can discuss research regarding mental health issues and culturally different populations.	q17discussres
18. I have an excellent ability to assess, accurately, the mental health needs of gay men.	q18gayhealth
19. I am knowledgeable of acculturation models for various ethnic minority groups	q19accmodels
20. I have an excellent ability to assess, accurately, the mental health needs of women.	q20womhealth
21. I have an excellent ability to assess, accurately, the mental health needs of persons who come from very poor socioeconomic backgrounds.	q21sociohealth

Figure 32.1. The items of the California Brief Multicultural Competence scale and the corresponding variable names in the data set.

the letter *q* (for *question*), followed by the item number, and finally followed by one or two words briefly characterizing the item. For example, Question 1 on the inventory reads, "I am aware that being born a minority in this society brings with it certain challenges that White people do not have to face." We named this variable **q1challenges** in the data set. A portion of the data set is shown in Figure 32.2.

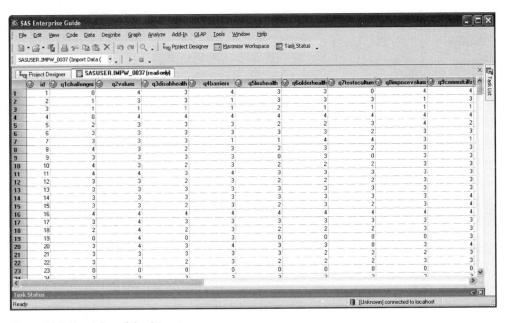

Figure 32.2. A portion of the data set.

32.7   Setting up the factor analysis

From the main menu select **Analyze → Multivariate → Factor Analysis**. As shown in the **Task Roles** screen in Figure 32.3, drag all of the variables except for **id** to the icon for **Analysis variables**.

Select **Factoring Method** in the navigation panel. This brings us to the screen shown in Figure 32.4. If we were exploring different possible solutions, we would perform several analyses by returning to this screen and selecting a different number of factors to rotate for each (based on the percentage of variance accounted for as well as the scree plot as subsequently described). We would also request different extraction methods in a series of analyses to ensure that the factor solution was stable across methods. We will simplify the analysis that we illustrate here. Specifically, assume that we know the following information:

- Different factoring methods yield comparable structures. Thus, the solutions are stable across methods. We will therefore select the simplest of the extraction procedures, principal components analysis, for our illustration.
- Based on the diminishing returns of accounted for variance, the number of factors that are viable appears to range from three to five.

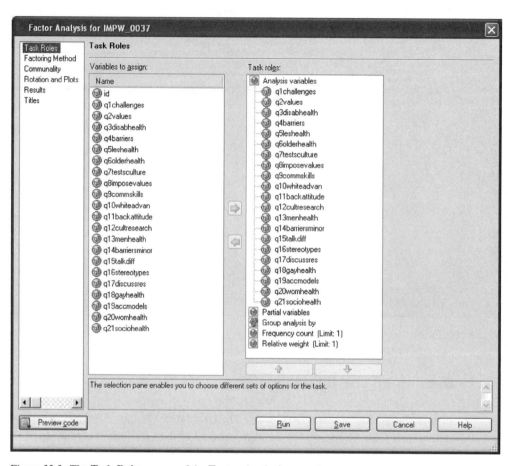

Figure 32.3. The **Task Roles** screen of the **Factor Analysis** procedure.

- The four-factor solution appears to represent the best solution (the most variance we could account for with factors that were interpretable on their own and were consistent with the research literature). We will therefore select this number of factors to rotate.

In the **Factoring method** panel, there are several methods available in the drop-down menu, including **Principal components analysis, Maximum likelihood factor analysis, Iterated principal factor analysis**, and **Unweighted least squares factor analysis**. For illustration purposes, we select **Principal component analysis**, the simplest of the factoring methods. In the panel for **Number of factors**, click the choice for **Number of factors to r . . .** (the "**r . . .**" stands for the word *rotate*) to obtain the drop-down menu. From that drop-down menu, select the value of **4**. This instructs SAS to rotate the first four extracted components.

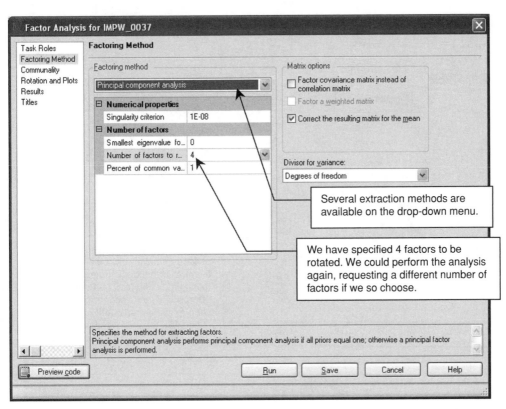

Figure 32.4. The **Factoring Method** screen of the **Factor Analysis** procedure.

The **Rotation and Plots** screen, presented in Figure 32.5, is where we specify the rotation strategy we wish to use and the plot(s) we wish to obtain. If we were performing this analysis for the first time, we would ask for the scree plot but would not perform a rotation. Once we examined the scree plot and the tabular output, we would then ask for an oblique rotation to determine how correlated the factors were: If they were not terribly correlated (correlations below about .20) we would probably switch to an orthogonal rotation strategy; if the correlations were stronger, we would stay with an oblique rotation strategy.

The scree plot is available in the upper right panel labeled **Plots to show**; we have checked the box corresponding to **Show a scree plot of the eigenvalues**. Rotation is addressed in the panel labeled **Rotation method**. We will proceed directly to our preferred solution here to demonstrate the process and to save space. We specify an **Oblique promax** rotation because we know from a preliminary analysis of this data set that the factors are sufficiently correlated to warrant a nonorthogonal rotation strategy. The panel below the place where **Oblique promax** is displayed allows us

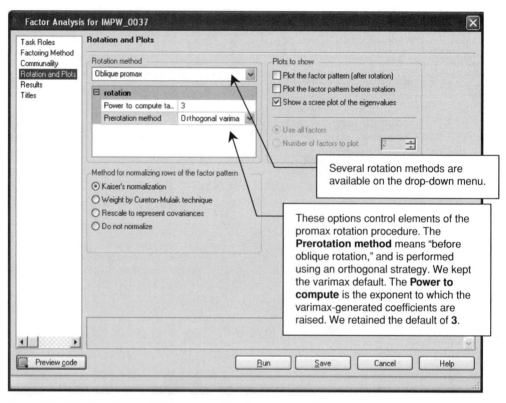

Figure 32.5. The **Rotation and Plots** screen of the **Factor Analysis** procedure.

to specify some details of the promax rotation. Very briefly, a promax rotation is performed in three stages:

- First, the correlation matrix is subjected to an orthogonal rotation. *SAS Enterprise Guide* gives us a choice of rotation strategies, and we keep the default of **Orthogonal varimax**.
- Second, the varimax-generated coefficients are raised to an exponential power, typically between 2 and 4. *SAS Enterprise Guide* uses the power **3** as the default, and we opt to keep it as well.
- Third, an oblique rotation is performed on the new values of the coefficients following our raising them to the specified exponential power.

Under the **Method for normalizing rows of the factor pattern**, we keep the default of **Kaiser's normalization**. The sum of squares of the coefficients (weights) for a factor or component must sum to 1.00 during the rotation, and Kaiser's procedure accomplishes this. Click **Run** to perform the analysis.

	Eigenvalues of the Correlation Matrix: Total = 21 Average = 1			
	Eigenvalue	Difference	Proportion	Cumulative
1	7.38900665	4.95596736	0.3519	0.3519
2	2.43303929	0.65494199	0.1159	0.4677
3	1.77809730	0.22476997	0.0847	0.5524
4	1.55332733	0.49944102	0.0740	0.6264
5	1.05388631	0.22785510	0.0502	0.6765
6	0.82603121	0.14792007	0.0393	0.7159
7	0.67811115	0.03599479	0.0323	0.7482
8	0.64211635	0.07961495	0.0306	0.7787
9	0.56250140	0.05935287	0.0268	0.8055
10	0.50314853	0.01553236	0.0240	0.8295
11	0.48761618	0.03368931	0.0232	0.8527
12	0.45392686	0.05110715	0.0216	0.8743
13	0.40281971	0.03313330	0.0192	0.8935
14	0.36968641	0.01430716	0.0176	0.9111
15	0.35537925	0.00750072	0.0169	0.9280
16	0.34787853	0.04141706	0.0166	0.9446
17	0.30646147	0.03587372	0.0146	0.9592
18	0.27058775	0.01294781	0.0129	0.9721
19	0.25763994	0.03145941	0.0123	0.9843
20	0.22618053	0.12362268	0.0108	0.9951
21	0.10255785		0.0049	1.0000

This is the full principal components extraction, performed as a first step. With 21 variables in the analysis, it is possible to extract 21 components. Note that the eigenvalues for each successive component get smaller. Ultimately, 100% of the total variance is accounted for, but more than half of the variance is accounted for by the first three components.

Figure 32.6. The component extraction table.

32.8   The factor analysis output

32.8.1 Component extraction output

The principal components extraction process is taken to completion by SAS, and the results are shown in Figure 32.6 in the table labeled **Eigenvalues of the Correlation Matrix**. The columns in the table, from left to right, represent the following.

The first column represents the *component number*. The column is not labeled but each row represents a component in the order it was extracted. The numbers down the column thus start at 1 and end at the number of variables in the analysis, in this case 21.

The second column represents the *eigenvalue*. This is the amount of variance accounted for by the component. It is computed as the sum of the squared correlations between the variables and the component. Five components have eigenvalues of 1.00 or greater; it would be unusual for researchers to accept more factors or components in the solution than the number having eigenvalues above 1.00.

The third column represents the *difference*. This is the difference between successive eigenvalues. It gives us a sense of how much more variance is accounted for by the next extracted component. For example, the difference between the 1st and 2nd eigenvalues is 7.38900665 − 2.43303929 or 4.95596736, whereas the difference between the 10th and 11th components is 0.50314853 − 0.48761618 or 0.01553236. *SAS Enterprise Guide* places these difference values in the row corresponding to the earlier extracted component; for this reason, the entry for the difference associated with the 21st component is blank because it is the last component extracted.

The fourth column represents *proportion*. This is the proportion of the total variance accounted for by the component. In principal components analysis, the total variance is equal to the number of variables in the analysis; here, there is a total of 21 units of variance. The first component accounts for approximately 7.39 of those units (that is its eigenvalue), which is approximately 35.19% of the variance (7.39 divided by 21). It is shown as a proportion of **0.3519** in the table.

The fifth column represents *cumulative proportion*. This is the cumulative proportion of the variance accounted for by the first k components. For example, given that the second component has an eigenvalue of approximately 2.43 and itself accounts for about 11.59% of the variance, and given that the accounted for variance is additive, we can determine that the first two components cumulatively account for approximately 46.77% of the total variance (shown as **0.4677** in the table). Note that when we reach the 21st component, we have accounted for 100% of the variance.

You will recall that we asked for the first four factors to be rotated. As we can see in the **Eigenvalues of the Correlation Matrix** table, the first four factors cumulatively accounted for 62.64% or approximately 63% of the variance. All else being equal, a four-factor solution accounting for this much variance would be considered reasonably good.

Figure 32.7 displays the scree plot. The x axis is the component number and corresponds to the first column of the **Eigenvalues of the Correlation Matrix** table. The y axis represents the eigenvalues and corresponds to the values in the second

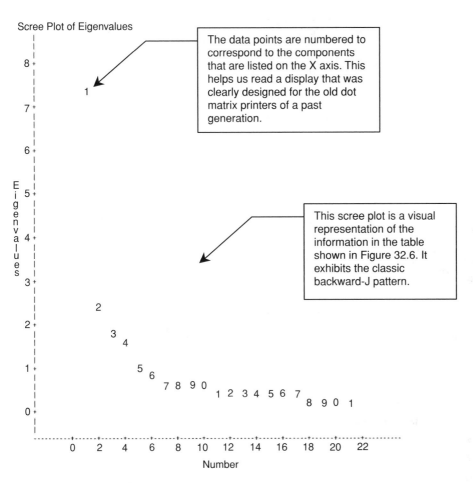

Figure 32.7. The scree plot.

column of the table. For example, the data point identified as **1** is the eigenvalue of 7.39 for the first component, the data point identified as **2** is the eigenvalue of 2.43 for the second component, and so on. The scree plot exhibits the traditional backward-J-shaped function. The function appears to level off with the fifth component; this leveling off location is a general cutoff for the maximum number of factors or components that researchers are likely to accept in their preferred solution.

Figure 32.8 presents the factor or component matrix, named **Factor Pattern**, for the four-component solution. This is the last portion of the extraction process and anticipates the number of factors we will rotate; it is the structure that will be rotated in the next phase of the analysis. The numerical entries in the matrix are the coefficients for the variables on the components.

Factor Pattern					
		Factor1	Factor2	Factor3	Factor4
q1challenges	q1challenges	0.37032	0.62513	0.16466	-0.13930
q2values	q2values	0.44849	0.23115	0.63919	0.28884
q3disabhealth	q3disabhealth	0.69782	-0.42694	0.02723	-0.05282
q4barriers	q4barriers	0.50181	0.33820	0.51893	0.23261
q5leshealth	q5leshealth	0.71932	-0.44525	0.03812	-0.04005
q6olderhealth	q6olderhealth	0.68220	-0.38560	0.06320	-0.16937
q7testsculture	q7testsculture	0.51883	-0.01207	-0.16904	0.50722
q8imposevalues	q8imposevalues	0.54009	0.44506	-0.12619	-0.33895
q9commskills	q9commskills	0.47184	0.04946	0.65936	0.25602
q10whiteadvan	q10whiteadvan	0.41484	0.57478	0.07394	-0.22770
q11backattitude	q11backattitude	0.52631	0.23961	-0.16201	-0.27250
q12cultresearch	q12cultresearch	0.55982	0.02465	-0.27974	0.55821
q13menhealth	q13menhealth	0.74765	-0.32893	0.06364	-0.13941
q14barriersminor	q14barriersminor	0.61705	0.32933	-0.12327	-0.26493
q15talkdiff	q15talkdiff	0.54795	0.21016	-0.33437	0.32948
q16stereotypes	q16stereotypes	0.55289	0.27650	-0.11321	-0.26559
q17discussres	q17discussres	0.52079	0.23582	-0.36403	0.32096
q18gayhealth	q18gayhealth	0.72397	-0.47030	0.01702	-0.02590
q19accmodels	q19accmodels	0.59104	0.15518	-0.44212	0.15775
q20womhealth	q20womhealth	0.69636	-0.21765	0.06807	-0.26393
q21sociohealth	q21sociohealth	0.77966	-0.26579	0.03055	-0.14473

This is the factor (component) matrix at the completion of the extraction phase. Most of the variables have their strongest coefficients on the first component, a statistical artifact of the extraction procedure where the first factor or component is the best-fitting line usually by quite a substantial margin. Our subsequent rotation will distribute these "loadings" more equitably.

Figure 32.8. The component matrix at the completion of the extraction phase.

There are two types of coefficients that are represented in this matrix: *pattern* coefficients and *structure* coefficients. In a factor matrix based on orthogonal factors or components, such as the one we have here, the two different coefficients are numerically identical; SAS therefore provides us with a single value that we can interpret as either a pattern or a structure coefficient. These two types of coefficients represent the following.

For pattern coefficients, each component is a weighted linear combination (a variate) composed of the 21 variables. The pattern coefficients are the standardized

Inter-Factor Correlations			
	Factor1	Factor2	Factor3	Factor4
Factor1	1.00000	0.29985	0.43685	0.25128
Factor2	0.29985	1.00000	0.35744	0.24706
Factor3	0.43685	0.35744	1.00000	0.21358
Factor4	0.25128	0.24706	0.21358	1.00000

> It is always useful to examine the rotated factor or component correlation matrix following an oblique rotation. The correlations here are such that we would stay with this rotation strategy. With very low correlations, we would be inclined to shift to an orthogonal rotation method.

Figure 32.9. The correlations of the components following rotation.

regression weights in this variate (they are akin to beta weights in a linear regression analysis). The different configurations of weights differentiate the components from each other. For example, in the first component (**Factor 1** in the table), the first item is weighted as .37032, the second item is weighted as .44849, and so on. In the second component (**Factor 2** in the table), the first item is weighted as .62513, the second item is weighted as .23115, and so on.

For structure coefficients, each variable is correlated to a certain extent with each component. The structure coefficients are these correlations. The different configurations of correlations differentiate the components from each other. For example, in the first component (**Factor 1** in the table), the first item is correlated .37032 with the component, the second item is correlated .44849 with the component, and so on. In the second component (**Factor 2** in the table), the first item is correlated .62513 with the component, the second item is correlated .23115 with the component, and so on.

Generally, the coefficients under **Factor 1** in the **Factor Pattern** table are larger than those for the other components. This is typical of the extraction results as mentioned in Section 32.4: a dominant first factor and relatively weak remaining factors. It is an artifact of the extraction processes and leaves much to be desired in terms of simple structure.

32.8.2 Component rotation output

The promax rotation strategy allowed the components to be correlated if that would improve the simple structure of the solution, but it does not require them to be correlated. Figure 32.9 displays the correlations of the components following completion of the rotation process. As we can see, the correlations range from the low .20s to the middle .40s. Given such correlations, an oblique rotation is probably preferable to an orthogonal rotation.

Factor Structure (Correlations)		Factor1	Factor2	Factor3	Factor4
q1challenges	q1challenges	0.03692	0.67505	0.18714	0.41735
q2values	q2values	0.25301	0.24996	0.22183	0.86252
q3disabhealth	q3disabhealth	0.81718	0.20057	0.38912	0.21733
q4barriers	q4barriers	0.24989	0.38874	0.29383	0.80386
q5leshealth	q5leshealth	0.84318	0.19655	0.40407	0.23535
q6olderhealth	q6olderhealth	0.80168	0.25953	0.30293	0.20852
q7testsculture	q7testsculture	0.37143	0.14434	0.71512	0.28436
q8imposevalues	q8imposevalues	0.28926	0.78414	0.29841	0.15694
q9commskills	q9commskills	0.36780	0.16072	0.18784	0.82978
q10whiteadvan	q10whiteadvan	0.10932	0.71780	0.20219	0.32473
q11backattitude	q11backattitude	0.36742	0.62204	0.31537	0.09156
q12cultresearch	q12cultresearch	0.37709	0.18622	0.82509	0.24558
q13menhealth	q13menhealth	0.82569	0.32593	0.37209	0.26480
q14barriersminor	q14barriersminor	0.40153	0.73056	0.37706	0.19019
q15talkdiff	q15talkdiff	0.30690	0.39451	0.73708	0.16826
q16stereotypes	q16stereotypes	0.37290	0.65446	0.32101	0.15369
q17discussres	q17discussres	0.27112	0.39992	0.72972	0.13654
q18gayhealth	q18gayhealth	0.85665	0.18035	0.42123	0.21956
q19accmodels	q19accmodels	0.39178	0.46886	0.71164	0.03198
q20womhealth	q20womhealth	0.74520	0.41288	0.27938	0.23070
q21sociohealth	q21sociohealth	0.82169	0.39269	0.41388	0.26917

The rotated factor or component structure matrix is best examined row by row. Entries are correlations of the variables with the factors. For each variable, determine with which factor it is most strongly correlated. If that correlation is sufficiently strong (.3 to .4 is typically a lower limit), then note that in a summary table such as shown in Figure 32.11.

Figure 32.10. The promax rotated component structure matrix.

The key results are contained in the rotated component matrices, one of which is shown in Figure 32.10. The column headings in this **Factor Structure (Correlations)** table have the same headings we saw in the **Factor Pattern** table (the result of the extraction procedure): **Factor 1**, **Factor 2**, **Factor 3**, and **Factor 4**. However, the factor numbers are purely coincidental; these rotated factors have been sufficiently regenerated by the promax rotation that we should not try to match these rotated factor numbers to those factor numbers assigned at the end of extraction.

Because the components are correlated, the pattern coefficients and the structure coefficients are no longer numerically identical as they were at the end of the extraction phase (where the components were independent); thus, the promax output provides a factor matrix for each. It is appropriate to examine both tables, but they almost always paint the same picture, and only one table would ordinarily be presented in a journal article. We present the structure coefficients in the table labeled **Factor Structure (Correlations)** in Figure 32.10. These are the correlations of the variables with the factors, and they are sometimes referred to informally as factor or component *loadings*.

Examining this output, we can quickly see a difference between this and the **Factor Pattern** matrix summarizing the end of the extraction phase: All of the factors now have some variables that are relatively strongly correlated with them (correlations in the .60s and higher) and many variables that are relatively weakly correlated with them. On the basis of these results, we judge that the rotation process did indeed drive the solution toward simple (or at least simpler) structure compared to what we observed in the **Factor Pattern** matrix containing the prerotation coefficients.

These four components still account for the same 63% of the variance that we saw in the extraction phase. In some sense they are still the same four components that we originally extracted but are just differently aligned in the multidimensional space. The key is that this accounted for variance has been redistributed among the four components as a result of the rotation process.

To interpret these results, we examine the matrix row by row, looking for the factor or component with which each variable is most strongly correlated. If that correlation is greater than some preestablished criterion (e.g., .3 or .4), and if that correlation is clearly higher than the others on the row, then we accept that variable as an indicator of that factor or component. The stronger a variable correlates with one component, the weaker it can correlate with any of the others. This is because the sum of the squared correlations for a variable across all components or factors (all 21 in this present case) will equal 1.00. With only four components here, the sum of the squared correlations for each variable (its *communality*) will be less than 1.00; nonetheless, there is only so much of each variable to go around and so high correlations with one component must produce low correlations with the others.

Examining the rotated factor matrix shown in Figure 32.10, we find for example that **q1challenges** correlates ("loads") to an acceptable degree on the second component (**Factor 2** in the matrix with a correlation of .67505). We also note that **q2values** correlates to an acceptable degree on the fourth component (**Factor 4** in the matrix with a correlation of .86252), **q3disabhealth** correlates to an acceptable

Four Component Rotated Solution

Component 1	Component 2	Component 3	Component 4
q18gayhealth (.86)	q8imposevalues (.78)	q12cultresearch (.83)	q2values (.86)
q5leshealth (.84)	q14barriersminor (.73)	q15talkdiff (.74)	q9commskills (.82)
q13menhealth (.83)	q10whiteadvan (.72)	q17discussres (.73)	q4barriers (.80)
q21sociohealth (.82)	q1challenges (.68)	q7testsculture (.72)	
q3disabhealth (.82)	q16sterotypes (.65)	q19accmodels (.71)	
q6olderhealth (.80)	q11backattitude (.62)		
q20womhealth (.75)			
Sociocultural Diversity	**Awareness of Cultural Barriers**	**Multicultural Knowledge**	**Sensitivity and Responsiveness To Consumers**

Figure 32.11. Summary and interpretation of the promax rotated component solution, with the structure coefficients (the correlation of the variable with the factor) shown in parentheses.

degree on the first component (**Factor 1** in the matrix with a correlation of .81718), and so on.

It is most useful to compile this information in order to make sense of it. We have done so in Figure 32.11, and we suggest that you do likewise in your factor analytic work. By examining the variables relatively strongly correlating with a component, it is possible to determine what the variables may have in common. What they have in common is the interpretation of the factor or component. The labels for the components are shown in bold at the bottom of the columns. Given the actual content of the items (and not just the names we used in the data set), the four components were interpreted by Gamst et al. (2004) as representing Sociocultural Diversity, Awareness of Cultural Barriers, Multicultural Knowledge, and Sensitivity and Responsiveness to Consumers. Factor or component names are thus labels put forward by the researchers reflecting their attempt to interpret the factors. These labels aid the researchers in providing conceptual and theoretical clarity to the analysis. At the same time, readers need to examine for themselves the variables identified as indicators of a factor or component so that they can determine how comfortable they are with the interpretations offered by those who performed the data analysis.

33 Canonical Correlation Analysis

33.1 Overview

Canonical correlation analysis is a member of the general linear model family. Introduced by Hotelling (1936a), it is a complex multivariate procedure that tends to be used less frequently than MANOVA and factor analysis. Its purpose is to predict a combination of one set of variables based on a combination of another set of variables. Working with canonical correlation involves conceptually combining elements from both linear regression and factor analysis. Relatively extensive treatments of canonical correlation analysis can be found in Lattin et al. (1993), Stevens (2002), and Thompson (1984).

Although we discuss the details of the procedure, it is worthwhile to note that in recent years researchers have been using canonical correlation analysis less frequently than in the past. One reason for this shift is because the solution optimizes the degree of statistical prediction accomplished by the canonical functions without the benefit of theory within which the relationships can be meaningfully interpreted (e.g., Guarino, 2004; Nunnally, 1978). Such a lack of theoretical framework can sometimes lead to "multivariate fishing expeditions" (Nunnally & Bernstein, 1994). Canonical correlation analysis is becoming increasingly supplanted by the use of structural equation modeling (e.g., Fan, 1997). Such an approach specifies a model that is then able to be tested by determining the degree to which it fits the data. Structural equation modeling is beyond the scope of this book, but readers may consult Byrne (2001), Loehlin (2004), Maruyama (1998), and Meyers et al. (2006) for more complete treatments of the topic.

33.2   Canonical and linear regression

Canonical correlation analysis can be thought of as an extension of the linear multiple regression procedure:

- In ordinary least squares regression (see Chapter 17), we generate a model represented by a weighted linear combination of predictors or independent variables that maximally predicts the values of a single dependent variable; the strength of that predictive relationship is indexed by R-square, the squared multiple correlation.
- In canonical correlation analysis we generate a set of models, each representing a weighted linear combination of predictors or independent variables that maximally predicts the values of a weighted linear combination of dependent variables; the strength of that predictive relationship is indexed by the squared canonical correlation.

As you may recall from our discussion in Section 31.2, a weighted linear combination of variables is known as a variate. In canonical correlation analysis there are two sets of variates or *canonical variables*, one relating to the predictor variables and the other relating to the dependent variables. Thus, we refer to a *predictor variate* or *predictor canonical variable* and to a *dependent variate* or *dependent canonical variable*. Similar to what we saw in linear regression, the weights of the variables in each weighted linear combination are able to be obtained from the canonical analysis in both raw and standard score form.

33.3   Number of canonical functions

Because multiple independent variables are used to predict multiple dependent variables, prediction in canonical correlation analysis can take place along multiple dimensions. For each dimension, there is a prediction model in the following general form:

dependent variate = predictor variate.

Each prediction model is a linear function in which the weights of the variables in each variate are different. These models are known as *canonical functions* or *canonical roots*.

The number of possible canonical functions is limited to the smaller of p and d, where p is the number of variables in the predictor variable set and d is the number of variables in the dependent variable set. As one example, if there are nine variables in the predictor set and four variables in the dependent variable set, then a maximum of four canonical functions can be produced by the analysis. As another example, if there are five variables in the predictor set and eight variables in the dependent variable set, then a maximum of only five canonical functions can be produced by the analysis. In each of these two example situations, and analogous to what we saw in factor analysis in Section 32.3, each canonical function will contain all of the variables; however, the variables will be associated with different weights in each of the functions.

33.4 Canonical and factor analysis

As we have just suggested, canonical correlation analysis also draws on certain aspects of factor analysis. The generation and interpretation of canonical functions corresponds conceptually to the following ways in which factors are generated and interpreted:

- Canonical functions are extracted sequentially and are numbered in the output in the order that they were generated.
- Each canonical function accounts for a certain percentage of the variance as indexed by an eigenvalue.
- The extracted canonical functions are independent of (orthogonal to) each other. Thus, the variance accounted for by the functions is additive.
- The first canonical function accounts for more of the explained variance than any of the others. Typically, this first function is quite dominant in terms of how much variance it accounts for. Each subsequently generated function accounts for decreasingly less of the explained variance.
- Unlike factor analysis, we do not ordinarily rotate the canonical solution. Thus, we accept the extracted canonical functions as representing a description of the predictive information contained in the variables and interpret them directly.
- A set of structure coefficients (the correlations of the variables to the variate) for each variable in each variate for each function is produced in the analysis. These coefficients are used in the same manner to interpret the variate as we described for factor analysis in Section 32.8.2.

33.5 Numerical example

The data for this numerical example were drawn from an unpublished study conducted by one of the authors in collaboration with one of his clinical psychology colleagues in which 426 participants, most of whom were university students, filled out a set of inventories assessing various personality characteristics. Although the study was not designed with canonical analysis in mind, we are using it to illustrate this technique by selecting one set of variables to be included in the predictor set and another to be included in the dependent variable set; we ask the indulgence of the reader when the interpretations we draw appear to be less dramatic than those from the other numerical examples we have used in the earlier chapters.

The variables we use in this example together with a brief partial characterization of them are subsequently presented here; variable names as they appear in the data set are shown in parentheses.

- *Self-esteem* (**selfesteem**): This represents expectations of success and comfort with life.
- *Acceptance of self* (**selfacceptance**): This represents the opinion we have of ourselves in terms of attractiveness, talent, and so on.
- *Trait anxiety* (**traitaxiety**): This represents general feelings of worry and nervousness.
- *Rehearsal* (**rehearsal**): This represents the need to mentally repeat ideas in order to control our thoughts and actions.
- *Emotional inhibition* (**emotioninhibit**): This represents the inhibiting or controlling of our emotions.
- *Neuroticism* (**neuroticism**): This represents the reporting of conditions such as emotional overresponsiveness, somatic complaints, and negative emotional states.
- *Openness to experience* (**openness**): This represents elements such as exploring novel environments, entertaining alternative values, and exhibiting curiosity.
- *Positive affect* (**posaffect**): This represents feelings of positive emotions such as being energetic and alert.
- *Negative affect* (**negaffect**): This represents feelings of unpleasant emotions such as distress, anger, and guilt.
- *Self-control* (**selfcontrol**): This represents the perceived ability to control our emotions and be self-disciplined.
- *Depression* (**depression**): This represents feelings of sadness and hopelessness; it also assesses whether there has been a decreased interest in engaging in usual activities.
- *Self-regard* (**selfregard**): This represents feelings of independence and the perceived ability to cope with life events.

A portion of the data set is presented in Figure 33.1. From what is visible in the screen shot, it can be seen that the values for some variables are whole numbers

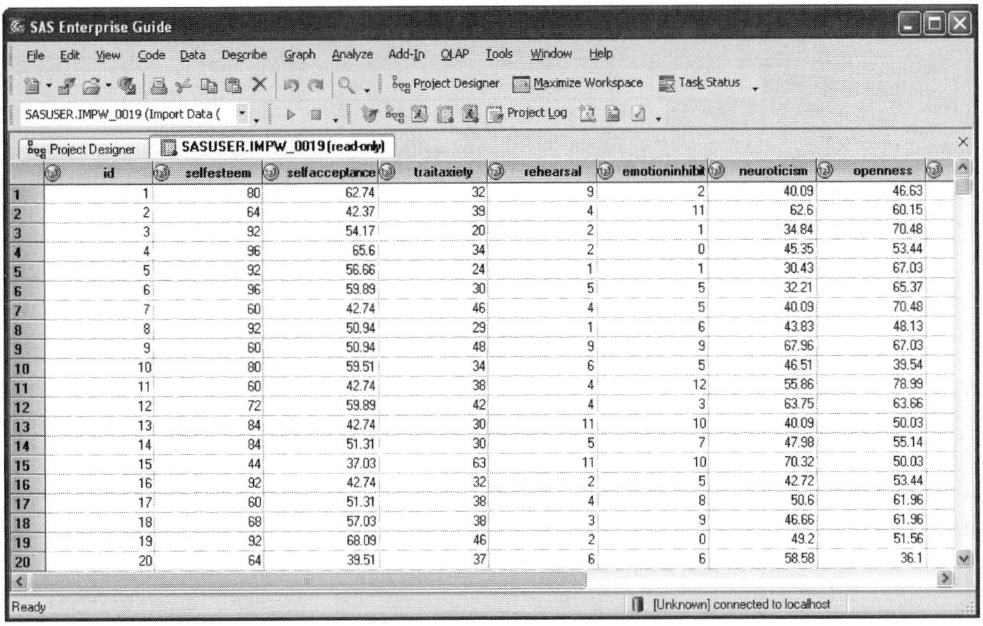

	id	selfesteem	selfacceptance	traitaxiety	rehearsal	emotioninhibit	neuroticism	openness
1	1	80	62.74	32	9	2	40.09	46.63
2	2	64	42.37	39	4	11	62.6	60.15
3	3	92	54.17	20	2	1	34.84	70.48
4	4	96	65.6	34	2	0	45.35	53.44
5	5	92	56.66	24	1	1	30.43	67.03
6	6	96	59.89	30	5	5	32.21	65.37
7	7	60	42.74	46	4	5	40.09	70.48
8	8	92	50.94	29	1	6	43.83	48.13
9	9	60	50.94	48	9	9	67.96	67.03
10	10	80	59.51	34	6	5	46.51	39.54
11	11	60	42.74	38	4	12	55.86	78.99
12	12	72	59.89	42	4	3	63.75	63.66
13	13	84	42.74	30	11	10	40.09	50.03
14	14	84	51.31	30	5	7	47.98	55.14
15	15	44	37.03	63	11	10	70.32	50.03
16	16	92	42.74	32	2	5	42.72	53.44
17	17	60	51.31	38	4	8	50.6	61.96
18	18	68	57.03	38	3	9	46.66	61.96
19	19	92	68.09	46	2	0	49.2	51.56
20	20	64	39.51	37	6	6	58.58	36.1

Figure 33.1. A portion of the data set.

whereas others are in decimal values. The whole numbers usually represent a total raw score on an inventory, whereas the decimal values usually represent linear *T* scores based on existent norms (as described in Chapter 11). In all cases, larger values represent more of the characteristic indicated by the name of the variable. Note that some characteristics are positively oriented (e.g., more self-esteem represents higher levels of mental health) and that others are negatively oriented (e.g., more neuroticism represents lower levels of mental health). This orientation issue will play out when we interpret the results of the canonical analysis because we would expect to see both positive and negative correlations. For example, if we had a canonical variable representing psychological health, we would expect self-esteem to be positively correlated with it (i.e., have a positive structure coefficient) and neuroticism to be negatively correlated with it (i.e., have a negative structure coefficient).

33.6 Setting up the Canonical Correlation Analysis

From the main menu select **Analyze ➔ Multivariate ➔ Canonical Correlation**. As shown in the **Task Roles** screen in Figure 33.2, we have brought **posaffect**,

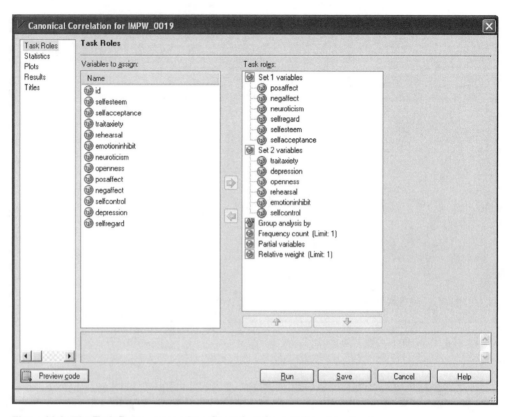

Figure 33.2. The **Task Roles** screen of the **Canonical Correlation** procedure.

negaffect, **neuroticism**, **selfregard**, **selfesteem**, and **selfaccpetance** to the icon for **Set 1 variables**. We will specify in the **Statistics** screen discussed next that these **Set 1 variables** will comprise the dependent variate (the dependent canonical variable) in the analysis. As also shown in Figure 33.2, we have brought **traitanxiety**, **depression**, **openness**, **rehearsal**, **emotioninhibit**, and **selfcontrol** to the icon for **Set 2 variables**. We will specify in the **Statistics** screen that these **Set 2 variables** will comprise the predictor variate (the predictor canonical variable) in the analysis.

Select **Statistics** in the navigation panel. This brings us to the screen shown in Figure 33.3. The top panel labeled **Regression analyses to perform** uses the term *regression* instead of *canonical*, but fundamentally we are using the general linear model and are predicting one canonical variable from another. This is the panel where we identify which set of variables is which. Because we (arbitrarily) placed our dependent variables in **Set 1** and our predictor variables in **Set 2** (we could have done the opposite), we wish to use **Set 2** to predict **Set 1**; thus we

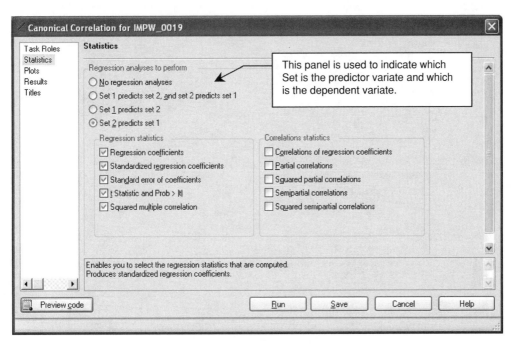

Figure 33.3. The **Statistics** screen of the **Canonical Correlation** procedure.

find the corresponding button (the bottom of the set of four buttons) and select it. The **Regression statistics** panel determines what information will be shown in the output, and we have checked all of the available boxes.

Select **Results** in the navigation panel. This brings us to the screen shown in Figure 33.4. We have checked the box corresponding to **Show results**. Directly under that option is a panel labeled **Number of canonical variables**. This is the number of variables in the smallest variate and the number of canonical functions we will obtain; we have retained the default of **6** (each of our variates contains six variables) so that information relating to all six of the canonical functions will be provided in the output.

SAS Enterprise Guide provides a special type of structural coefficient called a *redundancy coefficient*. Redundancy coefficients are able to be obtained for each variable. They reflect the squared correlation between a given variable and the other canonical variate. For example, the redundancy coefficient for a variable in the dependent variate would be the squared correlation between that variable and the predictor variate. We have not checked the box for **Include canonical redundancy analysis** because it is recommended that we avoid interpreting the redundancy coefficients (Thompson, 2000). Click **Run** to perform the analysis.

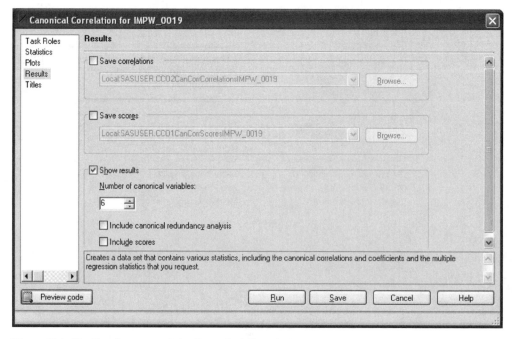

Figure 33.4. The **Results** screen of the **Canonical Correlation** procedure.

Multivariate Statistics and F Approximations					
S=6 M=-0.5 N=202.5					
Statistic	Value	F Value	Num DF	Den DF	Pr > F
Wilks' Lambda	0.14543257	27.41	36	1790	<.0001
Pillai's Trace	1.04512819	14.48	36	2472	<.0001
Hotelling-Lawley Trace	4.64318278	52.32	36	1176.4	<.0001
Roy's Greatest Root	4.38308583	300.97	6	412	<.0001
NOTE: F Statistic for Roy's Greatest Root is an upper bound.					

Figure 33.5. Multivariate tests of significance.

33.7 Output for Canonical Correlation Analysis

33.7.1 The multivariate statistics

Figure 33.5 presents the omnibus multivariate statistics and approximations of the corresponding F ratios. We have seen this same table (with different values in it, of course) in Chapter 31, as MANOVA, discriminant analysis, and canonical correlation analysis are all applications of the general linear model. In canonical correlation analysis, the multivariate statistics we see here are testing the null hypothesis that there is no significant prediction of the dependent variate available from the predictor variate. Specifically, the null hypothesis states that the set of canonical functions taken together (there are six canonical functions in our analysis as the smallest variate contains six variables) are predicting no better than we would expect on the basis of chance.

We ordinarily specify Wilks' lambda as our multivariate significance test. As we can see in the table, the **Wilks' Lambda** value of .14543257 corresponds to an *F* ratio of 27.41. With 36 and 1790 *df*, we note under the **Pr > F** column that the *F* ratio is statistically significant ($p < .0001$). The null hypothesis may therefore be rejected, and we conclude instead that we can predict the values of the dependent set of variables from those of the predictor variable set with better than chance precision.

The **Wilks' Lambda** value of .14543257 is the amount of unaccounted for variance in the dependent variables that remains after we have applied our prediction models (the full set of canonical functions). Subtracting the Wilks' lambda value from 1.00 gives us a value of .8545675, informing us that the amount of total variance accounted for by all of the canonical functions taken together is approximately 85%.

33.7.2 The Canonical Correlation Analysis table

The table labeled **Canonical Correlation Analysis**, shown in Figure 33.6, presents a detailed picture of the results by focusing on subsets of canonical functions. The total number of canonical functions is equal to the number of variables in the predictor or dependent set, whichever is smaller. In our numerical example, each set contains six variables and so the number of canonical functions we obtain in the analysis is six.

Each row in the **Canonical Correlation Analysis** table is focused on a canonical function or a set of canonical functions as indicated by the numbers in the leftmost column. Not counting the first column as a numerical column, and thus starting our count of columns with **Canonical Correlation**, here is what those numbers in the leftmost column represent:

- For the first eight columns, the numbers in the leftmost column represent *individual canonical functions*: 1 is the first canonical function, 2 is the second canonical function, and so on.
- For the last five columns under the heading of **Test of HO: The canonical correlation in the current row and all that follow are zero**, the numbers in the leftmost column represent *hierarchical subsets of canonical functions*: 1 represents Functions 1 through 6, 2 represents Functions 2 through 6, and so on.

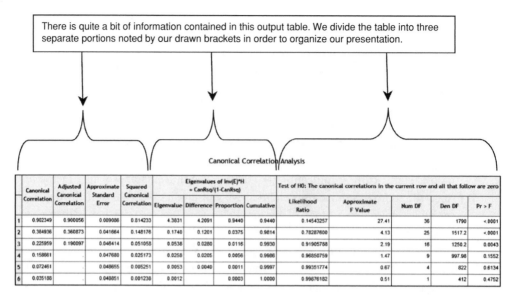

There is quite a bit of information contained in this output table. We divide the table into three separate portions noted by our drawn brackets in order to organize our presentation.

Canonical Correlation Analysis

Canonical Correlation	Adjusted Canonical Correlation	Approximate Standard Error	Squared Canonical Correlation	Eigenvalues of Inv(E)*H = CanRsq/(1-CanRsq)				Test of HO: The canonical correlations in the current row and all that follow are zero				
				Eigenvalue	Difference	Proportion	Cumulative	Likelihood Ratio	Approximate F Value	Num DF	Den DF	Pr > F
0.902349	0.900056	0.009086	0.814233	4.3831	4.2091	0.9440	0.9440	0.14543257	27.41	36	1790	<.0001
0.384936	0.360873	0.041664	0.148176	0.1740	0.1201	0.0375	0.9814	0.78287600	4.13	25	1517.2	<.0001
0.225959	0.190097	0.046414	0.051058	0.0538	0.0280	0.0116	0.9930	0.91905788	2.19	16	1250.2	0.0043
0.158661		0.047680	0.025173	0.0258	0.0205	0.0056	0.9986	0.96850759	1.47	9	997.98	0.1552
0.072461		0.048655	0.005251	0.0053	0.0040	0.0011	0.9997	0.99351774	0.67	4	822	0.6134
0.035188		0.048851	0.001238	0.0012		0.0003	1.0000	0.99676182	0.51	1	412	0.4752

Figure 33.6. The canonical analysis.

To deal with the complex structure of this table, we will separate our discussion by focusing on three sets of columns:

- First, we discuss the last five columns of the table, under the heading of **Test of HO: The canonical correlation in the current row and all that follow are zero**, the most global set of information in the table.
- Second, we discuss the first four columns of the table, which deal with the canonical correlations.
- Third, we discuss the middle columns of the table, which concern eigenvalues.

In the context of these separate discussions, we show individual screen shots for each portion of the table under discussion.

33.7.2.1 The hierarchical portion of the Canonical Correlation Analysis table. The hierarchical portion of the **Canonical Correlation Analysis** table is shown in Figure 33.7. We know from the multivariate tests (e.g., Wilks' lambda) that we can significantly predict the set of dependent variables based on the set of predictor variables by using the six canonical functions that were produced. This rightmost portion of the **Canonical Correlation Analysis** table under the heading **Test of HO: The canonical correlation in the current row and all that follow are zero** tests the statistical significance of subsets of these functions. The **Likelihood Ratio**

Test of H0: The canonical correlations in the current row and all that follow are zero				
Likelihood Ratio	Approximate F Value	Num DF	Den DF	Pr > F
0.14543257	27.41	36	1790	<.0001
0.78287600	4.13	25	1517.2	<.0001
0.91905788	2.19	16	1250.2	0.0043
0.96850759	1.47	9	997.98	0.1552
0.99351774	0.67	4	822	0.6134
0.99876182	0.51	1	412	0.4752

Figure 33.7. The hierarchical portion of the **Canonical Correlation Analysis** table.

is the Wilks' lambda statistic testing the null hypotheses that are specified in each bullet in the subsequent bullet list. This value is converted into an **Approximate F Value**, which is evaluated with degrees of freedom for the numerator (**Num DF**) and denominator (**Den DF**) as shown. The probability of that F ratio occurring if the null hypothesis is true is given under the column labeled **Pr > F**. We now deal with the output of this portion of the table row by row:

- *Row 1*: In the first row, the null hypothesis being tested is that the overall analysis consisting of all six canonical functions as a set offers no statistically significant prediction. This was precisely what was tested by means of the multivariate tests, and the **0.14543257** value of Wilks' lambda under the **Likelihood Ratio** column in Figure 33.7 and the **Approximate F Value** of 27.41 are identical to the ones shown in the multivariate statistics table in Figure 33.5. We can see in the column labeled **Pr > F** that we have achieved statistical significance. Because the functions are numbered such that lower numbered ones (i.e., those closer to Function 1) account for more variance than higher numbered functions, and because the set of six functions as a whole is statistically significant, we can deduce that the first canonical function demonstrates statistically significant prediction.

- *Row 2*: In the second row the null hypothesis being tested is that the second through sixth canonical functions as a set offer no statistically significant prediction. With an approximate F value of 4.13 and with 25 and 1517.2 *df*, that hypothesis is also rejected. Because the functions are numbered such that lower numbered ones (i.e., those closer to Function 1) account for more variance than higher numbered functions, and because the set of five functions as a whole is statistically significant, we can deduce that the second canonical function demonstrates statistically significant prediction.

	Canonical Correlation	Adjusted Canonical Correlation	Approximate Standard Error	Squared Canonical Correlation
1	0.902349	0.900056	0.009086	0.814233
2	0.384936	0.360873	0.041664	0.148176
3	0.225959	0.190097	0.046414	0.051058
4	0.158661	.	0.047680	0.025173
5	0.072461	.	0.048655	0.005251
6	0.035188	.	0.048851	0.001238

Figure 33.8. The canonical correlation portion of the **Canonical Correlation Analysis** table.

- *Row 3*: In the third row the null hypothesis being tested is that the third through sixth canonical functions as a set offer no statistically significant prediction. With an approximate F value of 2.19 and with 16 and 1250.2 *df*, that hypothesis is rejected. Because the functions are numbered such that lower numbered ones (i.e., those closer to Function 1) account for more variance than higher numbered functions, and because the set of four functions as a whole is statistically significant, we can deduce that the third canonical function demonstrates statistically significant prediction.

- *Row 4*: In the fourth row the null hypothesis being tested is that the fourth through sixth canonical functions as a set offer no statistically significant prediction. That null hypothesis is not rejected. Hence, only the first three canonical functions are statistically significant. There is no need to examine the remaining two rows, as the results for those must return outcomes that are not statistically significant as well (given that Function 4 is more potent than either 5 or 6 and given the entire set of Functions 4, 5, and 6 did not reach statistical significance).

33.7.2.2 The Canonical Correlations portion of the Canonical Correlation analysis table. Statistical significance of a canonical function is one thing but the strength of the relationship that it indexes is quite another matter entirely. Analogous to the case for the extraction phase of factor analysis, the first canonical function is almost always dominant, overshadowing the other functions that might be statistically significant. We can determine how potent in terms of prediction the canonical functions are by examining the first four labeled columns in the **Canonical Correlation Analysis** table shown in Figure 33.8. These columns supply information assessing the relationship strength between the predictor and the dependent variable sets.

In this portion of the table, each row corresponds to a single canonical function: Function 1 is the first canonical function, Function 2 is the second canonical function, and so on. In the following paragraphs we briefly discuss the information provided in each of these columns.

The **Canonical Correlation** column represents the correlation between the predictor variate and the dependent variate. It is analogous to a Pearson correlation in which one single variable is correlated with another single variable. With six functions, *SAS Enterprise Guide* displays the canonical correlation for each. For example, **0.902349** is the canonical correlation for Function 1 as shown in the table and **0.384936** is the canonical correlation for Function 2. Given that successively extracted canonical functions account for increasingly smaller amounts of the variance, it is not surprising that the canonical correlation values show a steady decline for successively extracted canonical functions. We also know indirectly from the hierarchical analysis just described in Section 33.7.2.1 that the values of the canonical correlations for Functions 4 through 6 are not statistically different from zero (because there is no viable prediction for Functions 4, 5, and 6, we know that there is no relationship between the two variates in those canonical functions; in other words, the pairs of variates for those canonical functions are not correlated).

The **Adjusted Canonical Correlation** column represents a statistical correction to the canonical correlation to compensate to a certain extent for the effects of chance enhancing the prediction. This is analogous to the adjusted R-square in multiple regression, except that here SAS reports the adjustment of the correlation instead of its squared value. For example, the first function has an adjusted canonical correlation value shown as **0.900056** and the second function has an adjusted canonical correlation value shown as **0.360873**. *SAS Enterprise Guide* reports this adjusted value only for functions that reached statistical significance, and so the table shows no entries for the fourth, fifth, and sixth canonical functions.

The **Approximate Standard Error** column shows the estimated standard error associated with the canonical correlation. Multiplying that value by 1.96 (the z score corresponding to the 95% boundary on the normal curve) and adding and subtracting the multiplication result to and from the canonical correlation can produce a 95% confidence interval around the computed canonical correlation. For example, for the first canonical function, we would multiply 0.009086 by 1.96 to obtain 0.0178. Adding that value to and subtracting that value from the canonical correlation (whose shown value is **0.902349**) yields a 95% confidence interval of 0.8845 to 0.9202; that is, we would expect 95% of the canonical correlations derived from an infinite

Eigenvalues of Inv(E)*H = CanRsq/(1-CanRsq)			
Eigenvalue	**Difference**	**Proportion**	**Cumulative**
4.3831	4.2091	0.9440	0.9440
0.1740	0.1201	0.0375	0.9814
0.0538	0.0280	0.0116	0.9930
0.0258	0.0205	0.0056	0.9986
0.0053	0.0040	0.0011	0.9997
0.0012		0.0003	1.0000

Figure 33.9. The eigenvalue portion of the **Canonical Correlation Analysis** table.

number of new but comparable samples of the same size to fall between 0.8845 and 0.9202.

The **Squared Canonical Correlation** is analogous to R-square in ordinary least squares regression. It is based on the obtained canonical correlation rather than the adjusted value, and it indexes the amount of variance in the dependent variate that is able to be predicted from the predictor variate. Thus, approximately 81.4% of the variance of the dependent variate in the first canonical function is explained by its corresponding predictor variate, whereas only about 14.8% of the variance of the dependent variate in the second canonical function is explained by its corresponding predictor variate.

33.7.2.3 The eigenvalue portion of the Canonical Correlation Analysis table.
The eigenvalue portion of the **Canonical Correlation Analysis** table is shown in Figure 33.9. We discussed eigenvalues in the context of factor analysis in Section 32.4. In canonical analysis, an eigenvalue indexes how much of the total explained variance a given canonical function is able to account for. For example, the first canonical function whose eigenvalue is 4.3831 accounts for 94.40% (seen in the **Proportion** column in decimal value) of the total variance accounted for by all six functions, whereas the second canonical function whose eigenvalue is 0.1740 accounts for only about 3.38% of the accounted for variance.

The **Difference** column indicates the difference between eigenvalues of successive canonical functions. For example, the difference between the eigenvalue of the first function (4.3831) and the second function (0.1740) is 4.2091. This value of **4.2091** appears in the first row.

Note that the cumulative variance accounted for (seen in the **Cumulative** column) adds to 1.0000 in the **Canonical Correlation Analysis** table. However, this 100% of the variance is all of the accounted for variance (all 85% of it as we determined from Wilks' lambda) and is not the total amount of variance in the analysis. Further, from the values of the eigenvalues for each canonical function we would expect most of the predictive information to be contained in the first function. Despite the fact that the second function is statistically significant, we would expect much less information from it. In addition, although the third function is statistically significant, we would not expect to learn much from it at all.

33.7.3 Structural Analysis

Interpretation of the canonical results is ordinarily focused on the sets of canonical coefficients. These are parameters or properties of the model, and they draw on what we covered in both linear regression (Chapters 16 and 17) and factor analysis (Chapter 32). In canonical correlation analysis, the structure coefficients are always provided. We also requested in the **Statistics** dialog window the raw and standardized regression coefficients. Briefly, the coefficients are as follows:

- *Structure coefficients*: These are the correlations of the variables in the canonical analysis with their respective variate. This is precisely the values we used in interpreting the rotated factor matrix in Section 32.8, and we use them in the same way in canonical analysis to interpret the canonical functions. Correlations are provided for each variable in each dependent and predictor variate for each canonical function.
- *Raw coefficients*: These are the weights for the raw scores of the variables in the canonical analysis. These are raw score regression coefficients in the same conceptual sense that we described them in Chapter 17. Weights are provided for each variable in each dependent and predictor variate for each canonical function.
- *Standardized coefficients*: These are the weights for the standardized scores of the variables in the canonical analysis. These are standardized regression coefficients (beta weights) in the same conceptual sense that we described them in Chapter 17. Weights are provided for each variable in each dependent and predictor variate for each canonical function.

The **Canonical Structure** output containing the structure coefficients is shown in Figure 33.10. It consists of two tables. The upper table contains the variables in the dependent variates. The numerical columns are labeled **V1** through **V6**. They are the variates for the dependent variables in Canonical Functions 1 through 6,

Canonical Structure

Correlations Between the Set 1 Variables and Their Canonical Variables		V1	V2	V3	V4	V5	V6
posaffect	posaffect	-0.6245	0.3239	0.1351	0.2809	0.5789	0.2698
negaffect	negaffect	0.8150	0.4766	-0.0110	0.2992	-0.1201	0.0677
neuroticism	neuroticism	0.9190	0.1088	-0.1256	-0.2239	0.2567	0.1089
selfregard	selfregard	-0.7175	0.1541	-0.1946	-0.1948	-0.2676	0.5604
selfesteem	selfesteem	-0.8513	0.3277	-0.3589	-0.0630	0.0535	-0.1797
selfacceptance	selfacceptance	-0.4808	0.6507	0.4283	-0.3844	-0.0879	-0.0805

Correlations Between the Set 2 Variables and Their Canonical Variables		W1	W2	W3	W4	W5	W6
traitaxiety	traitaxiety	0.9604	0.0693	-0.0411	-0.0962	0.2438	0.0496
depression	depression	0.7606	-0.1873	0.5886	-0.0456	0.0616	-0.1848
openness	openness	-0.2893	0.3132	0.4986	-0.2405	0.1498	0.6996
rehearsal	rehearsal	0.6851	0.4100	0.0230	0.4771	-0.3650	0.0325
emotioninhibit	emotioninhibit	0.3285	-0.7330	-0.0909	0.4182	-0.0057	0.4141
selfcontrol	selfcontrol	-0.5994	0.1266	0.1839	0.4498	0.6102	-0.1277

V1 as a set is being predicted by W1 as a set and together represent the first canonical function. Interpret the variates separately using the structure coefficients as we did in factor analysis. Then interpret the canonical function using the variate interpretations. For this first function, for example, we might assert that stress (W1) is predictive of emotional instability (V1).

Figure 33.10. The canonical structure analysis.

respectively. Think of them as factors. The lower table contains the variables in the predictor variates. The numerical columns are labeled **W1** through **W6**. They are the corresponding variates for the predictor variables in Canonical Functions 1 through 6, respectively. Think of them as factors as well.

We interpret the canonical functions one at a time. Based on the amount of variance that the statistically significant functions have accounted for in the present numerical example, we do not wish to interpret beyond the second canonical function.

Interpretation is akin to the way we interpreted the principal components in Section 32.8.2. We start with the dependent canonical variable in the first canonical function. In the present case, the first dependent variate (**V1**) is indicated by higher levels of neuroticism and negative affect (these variables are substantially positively or directly related with the variate, with correlations shown in the table of **0.9190** and **0.8150**, respectively) and lower levels of self-esteem, self-regard, and positive affect (these variables are substantially inversely related to the variate, with correlations of −**0.8513**, −**0.7175**, and −**0.6245**, respectively). One interpretation of this dependent variate is that those respondents with higher scores may be more *emotionally unstable*.

The first predictor canonical variable (**W1**) is indicated by higher levels of trait anxiety, depression, and rehearsal (these variables are positively correlated with the variate, with correlations shown in the table of **0.9604**, **0.7606**, and **0.6851**, respectively), and lower levels of self-control (this variable is negatively correlated with the variate at a value of −**0.5994**). One interpretation of this predictor variate is that those respondents with higher scores may be *experiencing more stress*.

To characterize this first canonical function, we put the interpretations of the dependent and predictor canonical variables together in a single sentence. One way to express this characterization is to assert that *stress is predictive of emotional instability*.

Although the second canonical function contributes relatively little additional accounted for variance, we will attempt to interpret it to illustrate the process. The second dependent variate (**V2**) is indicated by higher levels of self-acceptance and negative affect (correlations shown in the table of **0.6507** and **0.4766**, respectively). One interpretation of this variate is that those individuals with higher scores may be more accepting of themselves while at the same time carrying and exhibiting much negativity; we might think of such individuals toward the higher end of this factor as cynics or naysayers or, to use colloquial expressions, *sourpusses* or *whiners*. The second predictor variate (**W2**) is indicated by lower levels of emotional inhibition (it is correlated −**0.7330** with the variate): this variate thus appears to represent *emotional expression*. Putting these two together, we might suggest that *emotional expression is predictive of whining*. We should note regarding the interpretation of this second canonical function that our model is surely not fully specified in that there are undoubtedly other probably more potent predictors of whining that were not measured in the study.

The raw and standardized canonical coefficients are presented in Figures 33.11 and 33.12, respectively. These weights, as is true for linear regression, are based on the effect (prediction) of each variable when the other variables in the variate are statistically controlled, and they are less frequently used for interpreting each of the variates. As we can see in the figures, the standardized coefficients are quite different from the structure coefficients. We can contrast this to factor analysis in which the structure and pattern coefficients are equal in the case of orthogonal factors or are

Raw Canonical Coefficients for the Set 1 Variables							
		V1	V2	V3	V4	V5	V6
posaffect	posaffect	-0.056781043	0.0484373949	0.1134448572	0.1720715421	0.3182728603	0.1651927249
negaffect	negaffect	0.0741995303	0.2242446544	-0.05416164	0.2603323286	-0.170159397	0.0237331013
neuroticism	neuroticism	0.0370036767	0.0169573003	-0.055292007	-0.10324028	0.0811398327	0.0263866012
selfregard	selfregard	-0.01063903	0.0047857364	-0.029867343	-0.024576537	-0.047980006	0.113130131
selfesteem	selfesteem	-0.010407463	0.0268294029	-0.061896561	-0.004241387	0.0086825794	-0.039524592
selfacceptance	selfacceptance	-0.005144495	0.0508507744	0.0786507096	-0.063959493	-0.011524968	-0.021004763

Raw Canonical Coefficients for the Set 2 Variables							
		W1	W2	W3	W4	W5	W6
traitaxiety	traitaxiety	0.0610456838	0.0327514583	-0.073129343	-0.033316141	0.1057506545	0.0286024657
depression	depression	0.0229754817	-0.060904082	0.1730533778	-0.006093587	-0.029674085	-0.082301996
openness	openness	-0.007119461	0.027016995	0.0410778358	-0.01710063	0.0043295341	0.079820751
rehearsal	rehearsal	0.0592801157	0.1991119264	0.0394270082	0.2693247982	-0.185223828	0.0395135888
emotioninhibit	emotioninhibit	0.0221300346	-0.240962347	-0.031260597	0.1642589219	0.0010162224	0.1955531719
selfcontrol	selfcontrol	-0.283098645	0.3847982174	0.297183516	1.3694943879	1.6750845108	-0.388880011

Figure 33.11. Raw canonical coefficients.

Standardized Canonical Coefficients for the Set 1 Variables							
		V1	V2	V3	V4	V5	V6
posaffect	posaffect	-0.1652	0.1410	0.3301	0.5008	0.9262	0.4807
negaffect	negaffect	0.2770	0.8371	-0.2022	0.9719	-0.6352	0.0886
neuroticism	neuroticism	0.4130	0.1892	-0.6170	-1.1521	0.9055	0.2945
selfregard	selfregard	-0.1117	0.0503	-0.3137	-0.2581	-0.5040	1.1883
selfesteem	selfesteem	-0.2182	0.5625	-1.2976	-0.0889	0.1820	-0.8286
selfacceptance	selfacceptance	-0.0533	0.5267	0.8147	-0.6625	-0.1194	-0.2176

Standardized Canonical Coefficients for the Set 2 Variables							
		W1	W2	W3	W4	W5	W6
traitaxiety	traitaxiety	0.6473	0.3473	-0.7754	-0.3533	1.1213	0.3033
depression	depression	0.1591	-0.4218	1.1985	-0.0422	-0.2055	-0.5700
openness	openness	-0.0777	0.2949	0.4484	-0.1867	0.0473	0.8714
rehearsal	rehearsal	0.1849	0.6211	0.1230	0.8402	-0.5778	0.1233
emotioninhibit	emotioninhibit	0.0658	-0.7162	-0.0929	0.4883	0.0030	0.5813
selfcontrol	selfcontrol	-0.1444	0.1963	0.1516	0.6985	0.8543	-0.1983

Figure 33.12. Standardized canonical coefficients.

usually quite similar in the case of oblique factors. One reason for such differences is as follows. In factor analysis, we are dealing with one variate (one set of weights) for each factor, whereas in canonical correlation analysis we are dealing with two variates (two sets of weights) for each canonical function. Because the weights of both sets of variables are optimized in canonical analysis, the mathematical treatment and the interrelationships of the variables is more complex than in factor analysis.

References

Agresti, A., & Finlay, B. (2009). *Statistical methods for the social sciences* (4th ed.). Upper Saddle River, NJ: Pearson/Prentice-Hall.

Byrne, B. M. (2001). *Structural equation modeling with AMOS: Basic concepts, applications, and programming*. Mahwah, NJ: Erlbaum.

Carroll, J. B. (1993). *Human cognitive abilities: A survey of factor-analytic studies*. New York: Cambridge University Press.

Cody, R. P., & Smith, J. K. (2006). *Applied statistics and the SAS programming language* (5th ed.). Upper Saddle River, NJ: Pearson/Prentice-Hall.

Cohen, J. (1969). *Statistical power analysis for the behavioral sciences*. New York: Academic Press.

Cohen, J. (1977). *Statistical power analysis for the behavioral sciences* (Rev. ed.). New York: Academic Press.

Cohen, J. (1988). *Statistical power analysis for the behavioral sciences* (2nd ed.). Hillsdale, NJ: Erlbaum.

Cohen, J., Cohen, P., West, S. G., & Aiken, L. S. (2003). *Applied multiple regression/ correlation analysis for the behavioral sciences* (3rd ed.). Mahwah, NJ: Erlbaum.

Constable, N. (2007). *SAS programming for Enterprise Guide users*. Cary, NC: SAS Institute.

Costa, P. T., & McCrae, R. R. (1991). *NEO Five-Factor Inventory, Form S*. Odessa, FL: Psychological Assessment Resources.

Costa, P. T., & McCrae, R. R. (1992). *NEO PI-R professional manual*. Odessa, FL: Psychological Assessment Resources.

Curran, P. J., West, S. G., & Finch, J. F. (1997). The robustness of test statistics to nonnormality and specification error in confirmatory factor analysis. *Psychological Methods, 1*, 16–29.

D'Agostino, R. B. (1986). Tests for the normal distribution. In R. B. D'Agostino & R. B. Stephens (Eds.), *Goodness-of-fit techniques* (pp. 367–419). New York: Marcel Dekker.

D'Agostino, R. B., Belanger, A., & D'Agostino, R. B., Jr. (1990). A suggestion for using powerful and informative tests of normality. *American Statistician, 44,* 316–321.

D'Agostino, R. B., & Stephens, R.B. (Eds.). (1986). *Goodness-of-fit techniques.* New York: Marcel Dekker.

Davis, J. B. (2007). *Statistics using SAS Enterprise Guide.* Cary, NC: SAS Institute.

DeCarlo, L. T. (1997). On the meaning and use of kurtosis. *Psychological Methods, 2,* 292–307.

Der, G., & Everitt, B. S. (2007). *Basic statistics using Enterprise Guide: A primer.* Cary, NC: SAS Institute.

Estes, W. K. (1997). On the communication of information by displays of standard errors and confidence intervals. *Psychonomic Bulletin & Review, 4,* 330–341.

Fan, X. (1997). Canonical correlation analysis and structural equation modeling: What do they have in common? *Structural Equation Modeling, 4,* 65–79.

Ferguson, G. A., & Takane, Y. (1989). *Statistical analysis in psychology and education* (6th ed.). New York: McGraw-Hill.

Finney, D. J. (1998). Remember a pioneer: Frank Yates (1902–1994). *Teaching Statistics, 20,* 2–5.

Fisher, R. A. (1921a). Some remarks on the methods formulated in a recent article on the qualitative analysis of plant growth. *Annals of Applied Biology, 7,* 367–372.

Fisher, R. A. (1921b). Studies in crop variation. I. An examination of the yield of dressed grain from Broadbalk. *Journal of Agricultural Science, 11,* 107–135.

Fisher, R. A. (1925). *Statistical methods for research workers.* Edinburgh, England: Oliver & Boyd.

Fisher, R. A. (1935a). *The design of experiments.* Edinburgh, England: Oliver & Boyd.

Fisher, R. A. (1935b). The logic of inductive inference. *Journal of the Royal Statistical Society, 98,* 39–54.

Fisher, R. A. (1950). *Statistical methods for research workers* (11th ed.). New York: Hafner.

Fisher, R. A., & Eden, T. (1927). Studies in crop variation. IV. The experimental determination of the value of top dressings with cereals. *Journal of Agricultural Science, 17,* 548–562.

Fisher, R. A., & Mackenzie, W. A. (1923). Studies in crop variation. II. The manorial responses of different potato varieties. *Journal of Agricultural Science, 13,* 311–320.

Freeman, G. H., & Halton, J. H. (1951). Note on an exact treatment of contingency, goodness of fit and other problems of significance. *Biometrika, 38*, 141–149.

Galton, F. (1886). Heredity stature. *Journal of the Anthropological Institute, 15*, 489–499.

Galton, F. (1888, December 13). Co-relations and their measurement, chiefly from anthropometric data. *Proceedings of the Royal Society, 45*, 135–145.

Gamst, G., Dana, R. H., Der-Karabetian, A., Aragon, M., Arellano, L., Morrow, G., & Martenson, L. (2004). Cultural competency revised: The California Brief Multicultural Competence Scale. *Measurement and Evaluation in Counseling and Development, 37*, 163–183.

Gamst, G., Meyers, L. S., & Guarino, A. J. (2008). *Analysis of variance designs: A conceptual and computational approach with SPSS and SAS*. New York: Cambridge University Press.

Gorsuch, R. L. (1983). *Factor analysis* (2nd ed.). Hillsdale, NJ: Erlbaum.

Guarino, A. J. (2004). A comparison of first and second generation multivariate analysis: Canonical correlation analysis and structural equation modeling. *Florida Journal of Educational Research, 42*, 22–40.

Guilford, J. P., & Fruchter, B. (1978). *Fundamental statistics in psychology and education* (6th ed.). New York: McGraw-Hill.

Harman, H. H. (1962). *Modern factor analysis*. Chicago: University of Chicago Press.

Hatcher, L. (2003). *Step-by-step basic statistics using SAS: Student guide and exercises*. Cary, NC: SAS Institute.

Hatcher, L., & Stepanski, E. J. (1994). *Step-by-step approach to using the SAS system for univariate and multivariate statistics*. Cary, NC: SAS Institute.

Hays, W. L. (1981). *Statistics* (3rd ed.). New York: Holt, Rinehart & Winston.

Hosmer, D. W., Jr., & Lemeshow, S. (2000). *Applied logistic regression* (2nd ed.). New York: Wiley.

Hotelling, H. (1933). Analysis of a complex of statistical variables into principal components. *Journal of Educational Psychology, 24*, 417–441, 498–520.

Hotelling, H. (1936a). Relations between two sets of variates. *Biometrika, 28*, 321–377.

Hotelling, H. (1936b). Simplified calculation of principal components. *Psychometrika, 1*, 27–35.

Howell, D. C. (1997). *Statistical methods for psychology* (4th ed.). Belmont, CA: Duxbury.

Jaccard, J., & Becker, M. A. (1990). *Statistics for the behavioral sciences* (2nd ed.). Belmont, CA: Wadsworth.

Jolliffe, I. T. (2002). *Principal component analysis* (2nd ed.). New York: Springer.

Keppel, G., & Wickens, T. D. (2004). *Design and analysis: A researcher's handbook* (4th ed.). Upper Saddle River, NJ: Pearson/Prentice-Hall.

Kirk, R. E. (1995). *Experimental design: Procedures for the behavioral sciences* (3rd ed.). Pacific Grove, CA: Brooks/Cole.

Kline, R. B. (2005). *Principle and practice of structural equation modeling* (2nd ed.). New York: Guilford Press.

Kramer, C. Y. (1956). Extensions of multiple range tests to group means with unequal numbers of replications. *Biometrics, 12*, 307–310.

Kramer, C. Y. (1957). Extensions of multiple range tests to group correlated adjusted means. *Biometrics, 13*, 13–18.

Kruskal, W. H., & Wallis, W. A. (1952). Use of ranks in one criterion variance analysis. *Journal of the American Statistical Association, 47*, 583–621.

Lattin, J. M., Carroll, J. D., & Green, P. E. (1993). *Analyzing multivariate data.* Pacific Grove, CA: Brooks/Cole.

Loehlin, J. C. (2004). *Latent variable models* (4th ed.). Mahwah, NJ: Erlbaum.

Mann, H. B., & Whitney, D. R. (1947). On a test of whether one of two random variables is stochastically larger than the other. *Annals of Mathematical Statistics, 18*, 50–60.

Marascuilo, L. A., & McSweeney, M. (1977). *Nonparametric and distribution-free methods for the social sciences.* Monterey, CA: Brooks/Cole.

Marasinghe, M. G., & Kennedy, W. J. (2008). *SAS for data analysis: Intermediate statistical methods.* New York: Springer.

Maruyama, G. M. (1998). *Basics of structural equation modeling.* Thousand Oaks, CA: Sage.

Maxwell, S. E., & Delaney, H. D. (2000). *Designing experiments and analyzing data: A model comparison perspective.* Mahwah, NJ: Erlbaum.

McDaniel, S., & Hemedinger, C. (2007). *SAS for dummies.* Hoboken, NJ: Wiley.

Meyers, L. S., Gamst, G., & Guarino, A. J. (2006). *Applied multivariate research: Design and interpretation.* Thousand Oaks, CA: Sage.

Nunnally, J. C. (1978). *Psychometric theory.* New York: McGraw-Hill.

Nunnally, J. C., & Bernstein, I. H. (1994). *Psychometric theory* (3rd ed). New York: McGraw-Hill.

Osborne, J. W. (2002). Notes on the use of data transformations. *Practical Assessment, Research & Evaluation, 8*, 1–7.

Pearson, K. (1896). Mathematical contributions to the mathematical theory of evolution. III. Regression, heredity, and panmixia. *Philosophical Transactions of the Royal Society of London, 187*, 253–318.

Pearson, K. (1900). On the criterion that a given system of deviations from the probable in the case of correlated system of variables is such that it can be reasonably supposed to have arisen from random sampling. *Philosophical Magazine, 50*, 157–175.

Pearson, K. (1901). On lines and planes of closest fit to systems of points in space. *Philosophical Magazine, 6*, 559–572.

Peng, C. Y. J. (2009). *Data analysis using SAS*. Thousand Oaks, CA: Sage.

Rosenthal, R., & Rosnow, R. L. (2008). *Essentials of behavioral research* (3rd ed.). Boston: McGraw-Hill.

Royston, P. (1992). Approximating the Shapiro-Wilk W-Test for non-normality. *Statistics and Computing, 2*, 117–119.

Runyon, R. P., Coleman, K. A., & Pittenger, D. J. (2000). *Fundamentals of behavioral statistics* (9th ed.). Boston: McGraw-Hill.

Salsburg, D. (2001). *The lady tasting tea: How statistics revolutionized science in the twentieth century*. New York: Freeman.

SAS Institute. (1990). *SAS/STAT user's guide* (Vols. 1–2). Cary, NC: Author.

SAS Institute. (2002). *Getting started with SAS Enterprise Guide* (2nd ed.). Cary, NC: Author.

Schlotzhauer, S., & Littell, R. (1997). *SAS system for elementary statistical analysis* (2nd ed.). Cary, NC: SAS Institute.

Shapiro, S. S., & Wilk, M. B. (1965). An analysis of variance test for normality (complete samples). *Biometrika, 52*, 591–611.

Shiffler, R. (1988). Maximum z scores and outliers. *American Statistician, 42*, 79–80.

Siegel, S. (1956). *Nonparametric statistics for the behavioral sciences*. New York: McGraw-Hill.

Slaughter, S. J., & Delwiche, L. D. (2006). *The little SAS book for Enterprise Guide 4.1*. Cary, NC: SAS Institute.

Snedecor, G. W. (1934). *Analysis of variance and covariance*. Ames, IA: Collegiate Press.

Snedecor, G. W. (1946). *Statistical methods applied to experiments in agriculture and biology* (4th ed.). Ames, IA: The Iowa State College Press.

Spearman, C. (1904a). General intelligence, objectively determined and measured. *American Journal of Psychology, 15*, 201–293.

Spearman, C. (1904b). The proof and measurement of association between two things. *The American Journal of Psychology, 15*, 72–101.

Stanton, J. M. (2001). Galton, Pearson, and the peas: A brief history of linear regression for statistics instructors. *Journal of Statistics Education, 9*(3). Retrieved September 2008 from http://www.amstat.org/publications/jse/v9n3/stanton.html.

Stevens, J. P. (1999). *Intermediate statistics: A modern approach* (2nd ed.). Mahwah, NJ: Erlbaum.

Stevens, J. P. (2002). *Applied multivariate statistics for the social sciences* (4th ed.). Mahwah, NJ: Erlbaum.

Thompson, B. (1984). *Canonical correlation analysis: Uses and interpretation.* Thousand Oaks, CA: Sage.

Thompson, B. (2000). Canonical correlation analysis. In L. G. Grimm & P. R. Yarnold (Eds.), *Reading and understanding more multivariate statistics* (pp. 285–316). Washington, DC: American Psychological Association.

Thompson, B. (2004). *Exploratory and confirmatory factor analysis.* Washington, DC: American Psychological Association.

Thurstone, L. L. (1931). Multiple factor analysis. *Psychological Review, 38,* 406–427.

Thurstone, L. L. (1938). A new rotational method in factor analysis. *Psychometrika, 3,* 199–218.

Thurstone, L. L. (1947). *Multiple factor analysis.* Chicago: University of Chicago Press.

Thurstone, L. L. (1954). An analytical method for simple structure. *Psychometrika, 19,* 173–182.

Toothaker, L. E. (1993). *Multiple comparison procedures.* Newbury Park, CA: Sage.

Tukey, J. W. (1953). *The problem of multiple comparisons.* Unpublished manuscript, Princeton University (as cited by numerous public domain sources).

Tukey, J. W. (1977). *Exploratory data analysis.* Reading, MA: Addison-Wesley.

Warner, R. M. (2008). *Applied statistics: From bivariate through multivariate techniques.* Thousand Oaks, CA: Sage.

Wheater, C. P., & Cook, P. A. (2000). *Using statistics to understand the environment.* New York: Routledge.

Wilcoxon, F. (1945). Individual comparisons by ranking methods. *Biometrics Bulletin, 1,* 80–83.

Yates, F. (1934). Contingency tables involving small numbers and the χ^2 test. *Journal of the Royal Statistical Society, 1* (Suppl.), 217–235.

Author Index

Subject Index